Dream Octane

Seven Steps To Discover,

Develop and Deliver Your Niche

By

Clifton C. Manning

D1360492

_____

_____

_____

For information regarding special discounts for bulk purchases, booking the author for webinars, speaking engagements or corporate training, please contact:
client.support@dreamoctane.onmicrosoft.com

Cover design by: Germancreative
Page layout design by: Farhan Iqbal

Paperback and hardcover edition first published February 2022

ISBN 978-1-7953-0847-2 (paperback)
ISBN 979-8-4029-3055-1 (hardcover)

www.dreamoctane.org

This book is brought to you by:

God's grace through his son Jesus Christ
My wife Kebra Manning's sincere prayers and
timely encouragement.
My dad, Clifton K Manning's *time capsule* briefcase.
My mom, Evangelist Audrey Manning's loving admonishment
and wisdom.
My son, Elijah N. Manning's fervor, that makes me proud to be
an onlooker to your pursuit towards your dream(s).
My daughter, Chelsea "Princess Peanut Butter" Manning for
your incredible energy and unrestrained laughter that is never
absent from your greetings to me after a long day of work.
My Little Sis, Doctor Natasha N. Manning-Gibbs and Brother-
in-law Rasheen Gibbs for your unwavering support
My big brother Eric Dixon, although distance separate us, I'm
grateful that we are consistently able to pick up wherever we
leave off in our communications.
My little brother, Michael B. Manning for adding helpful hints
in various aspects of this work along the way.
Dr. David Ireland's vision and leadership
For the members of Christ Church's
*Becoming a Frist Time Author…*Connect Group
Professor Farrokh Langdana and the REMBA class of 2019
Vanetta Hill and Pastor Anthony Franklin for your mentorship
Fredrick A. Mann for being a steadfast confidant and brother

Table of Contents

FOREWORD

Prof. Farrokh Langdana,
Rutgers University, New Jersey, USA

There are a multitude of books on transforming one's career. Books on how to better yourself in life. More books on upgrading your career to finally fulfilling your lifelong goals and ambitions....and on and on. Given this plethora of books in this subject, the casual reader may be forgiven for rightfully wondering:

- How is yet one more book on this well-trodden subject going to be different from the rest?

- After all, are not all these books full of subjective advice?

- Don't these books simply articulate the author's tribulations and his/her eventual triumph *"against all odds?"* Isn't this just a diary of a *"personal victory"* from the author's perspective?

- Some of the books help, some do not; isn't it all *hit* or *miss*? After all, there is no "scientific" or "technical" method to this business of unleashing one's potential, right?

All the above are justifiable concerns. All are indeed true. But then comes *Dream Octane* by Mr. Clifton Manning.

This is truly an exceptional book for the following reasons:

This book is different—very different! In direct response to the fourth bullet above, *Dream Octane* is firmly based on sound and technical theoretical concepts from International Trade Theory. The economic models themselves are impeccable. All the theoretical models deployed by Mr. Manning were expounded by economists whose progress has been littered by Nobel prizes or eternal recognition. Economists such as Stolper, Samuelson, Heckscher and Ohlin, and of course David Ricardo, the "father" of free trade theory, are prominently integrated in *Dream Octane*.

But this is all "just" theory, right? Does this actually work? Short answer: Yes. The global applications of these models have been startling if not truly amazing. Entire countries and entire economies have been transformed from poverty and destitution to emerging economy status and phenomenal growth. The list of examples is impressive: Japan and Germany after WW2, China after Deng Xiaoping famously threw open China's door to global trade in 1979. Perhaps the most spectacular example of the undeniable real-world success of the International Trade theories as deployed by countries is with the economy of Hong Kong. In fact, Milton Friedman—Rutgers University's most famous graduate—often marveled at this example. Before opening its economy to international trade and to Global Trade Theory, Hong Kong's per capital GDP was 1/3 that of the UK. After unleashing international trade theory models, Hong Kong's economy was three times that of the UK! Bottom line: The theories deployed by Mr. Manning work!

Mr. Manning's brilliance lies in his amazing adaptation of Free Trade theory to individuals. In the Rutgers Executive MBA class, the extension was made from the growth of countries to companies and sectors; there was perhaps an in-class exercise where the Rutgers Executive MBAs had to apply some of the concepts to their own careers. Mr. Manning's brilliance lies in his expounding this exercise and expertly synthesizing the well-tested global Trade Theories to apply to individuals. He has then overlaid these personal applications with his own real-world experience to yield a most exceptional and unique book indeed. His work will allow readers to transition to higher and more fulfilling careers and lives.

From International Trade to Clifton Manning's "DDD":

The cleverness of *Dream Octane* is the highly creative way Mr. Manning has adapted the deep theory embedded in the Heckscher Ohlin Theorem (HOT) and the Stolper Samuelson Theorem (SST), to allow the reader to transition to a higher standard of living—both physically and emotionally.

7

Mr. Manning deploys the concept of comparative advantage, long reserved for countries/economies/companies, and he inventively adapts this concept to you, the reader! He connects all the theoretical "dots" so that readers come away with a systematic, time-tested, grounded by theory "play-book" that would make this transition possible.

His ***Seven Steps to Discover, Develop and Deliver your Niche*** (DDD) are firmly grounded in a synthesis of deeply grounded international trade theories discussed above, and his personal real-world experiences.

Let me be clear: *Dream Octane* is not just a clever adaption of economic theories. The deep empathy of the author is prevalent throughout the book. This is a man who has seen plenty of adversity in life. In so many ways, we—his readers—can relate to him well; he writes with profound understanding and great sincerity. And he writes to reach us all.

I am privileged in that I know the author personally. As the Director of the Rutgers Executive MBA Program, I interviewed Mr. Manning and awarded him admission to the program. I have had the distinct pleasure of working with him in two courses: Macroeconomic Policy and International Trade. In both, he was a star student. I was also fortunate in accompanying him on his summer Rutgers EMBA course in China. As he is fond of relating in this book, I pointed out that he had a terrific "comparative advantage" in presentation skills. That observation turned out to be pleasantly prescient! This book, *Dream Octane,* is a validation of Mr. Manning's amazing ability to not just present material, but to re-engineer deeply technical global trade theory to benefit our lives.

I would strongly recommend this superb volume to anyone interested in doing more, in unleashing one's inner potential. This is a step-by-step manual on making dreams come true both personally and professionally. I see parents presenting this book to their kids. I see employers discussing this book with their co-workers. I see this book doing what all authors dream of doing: Making a real change in people's lives.

Farrokh Langdana, PhD.,

Professor, Finance/Economics,

Rutgers Business School, NJ, USA

Director, Rutgers Executive MBA Program, NJ,

& Academic Director of Rutgers EMBA (Asia)

https://www.business.rutgers.edu/faculty/farrokh-langdana

PREFACE

Dear Reader:

The inspiration for writing this book was a result of me feeling unqualified. I spent seventeen of my initial twenty-year career in healthcare leadership with an Associate Degree in Applied Science. I was blessed to have a series of promotional opportunities afforded to me, which challenged me to create solutions that became a part of my leadership rudiments. The greatest part of my journey is that it wasn't all sunshine and rainbows: I had my share of failures and even a lay off. However, once I understood how to *discover, develop,* and *deliver* my niche, I rose to several positions over the years from a per diem X-ray tech to the Executive Director for Radiology in a three-hospital healthcare system. Thankfully, this process of feeling unqualified motivated me to seek strategies to address situations. I sought for answers from scriptures, leadership books, seminars and/or wisdom from mentors along the way. Overtime, I found commonalities in how solutions were being derived, which led to the creation of several predictive models I include within these pages. What I learned from solving these problems was that the success that I began experiencing was reproducible and could be applied by others. This process is described in the book as the *Life Cycle of Excavation*. As I applied these principles, promotions and other opportunities were placed back on my career horizon.

What qualifies me to author this book?

Achieving patient-centric goals for the first seventeen of my twenty-year career while working with physicians and administrative leaders came with its share of challenges. At times, those challenges felt formidable—even insurmountable. On many occasions, I felt unqualified to achieve the success I wanted while seated at the table with these other leaders. However, I refocused on becoming intentional and began reading every leadership book that I could find, as well as attending frequent seminars in areas where I saw opportunities to improve. Over time, by applying these insights I gained from these various sources, I was able to cross the hurdles that confronted me both successfully and efficiently. Eventually, varying degrees of success within my sphere of leadership influence became more evident.

My hope is that the challenges that were triumphed in the past will provide insight for your current leadership struggles and unlock the dream of achieving success in your own career. As you do so, may you also be inspired to move past the barriers that have been blocking you from fulfilling your dreams. By discovering, developing, and delivering your niche you uncover a crude resource. Just as crude oil benefits a country, once your niche is excavated, refined, and distributed it provides opportunities for what is unique to you, to also become useful for others. This is the moment that helps us gain a better understanding of this reality, which has become the mantra for *Dream Octane*: "*If innovative change is an engine, your unique dreams and abilities could be its fuel.*" I wish you continued success and look forward to walking along side you in these pages as you *discover, develop,* and *deliver* your niche.

Why should you read this book?

This book is not the typical step-by-step guide of how to become like someone else. These success stories—with coinciding principles for uncovering the niche(s) in your own life—will help you deliver your unique value, which is the secret to your comparative advantage. Many of the methods are simple but have been successfully used in other industries.

Dream Octane is designed to be a tool in a leader's toolbox. The goal is to create something that you can pull out as needed. If you are looking for helpful tips in the area of pursuing *passion, proficiency, identifying personal patterns, problem-solving or purposefulness,* this book will be of value to you. The art of value excavation came as a result of me pursuing development around how to be a better leader. This led me to becoming intentionally focused on combating my own insecurities with my leadership abilities. As I endeavored to help myself, I experienced success and then found that the techniques that I used were reproducible.

Once reproduced, I saw that many of the coachable individuals who applied these same strategies also received some level of success in their area. I hasten to add that excavation is different from motivation, although motivation does have its place. We will uncover this distinction as we discuss more of this principle in detail in Step # 6 *Organize the Delivery of Your Niche to a Wider Audience.* Over the years, the *How Equation* has been a helpful strategy for revealing solutions that often hide inside of operational opportunities for improvement. Just like an oil drill to an untapped reservoir of crude oil, these opportunities needed the right tool to uncover them. When problem-solving, your *Why (reason), Who (resource),* and *Where (region of interest)* are the first three segments in solving the *How Equation.* More on this later in Step # 5 *Neutralize Barriers Blocking You From Fulfilling Your Dream.*

What value could this book bring to you?

Many of these principles are not original but have been codified to help accelerate application for you. What took me twenty years of experience and several years of learning could be used by you the first day you become acquainted with them. The "If Countries Can Do it, So Why Not You" section is based on economic theories from centuries ago that countries have used to increase their overall well-being. I tailored these economic principles to fit the commodity I believe we all have to display in the work we are here to do. As you read through these chapters, may you keep on the forefront of your mind: Day one is waiting for you.

Why read this now?

Old theoretical principles employed

To help bring this perspective to the forefront, we adapted century old theoretical principles employed by a handful of macroeconomic patriarchs: Eli Heckscher, Bertil Ohlin, David Ricardo, Wolfgang Stolper, and Paul Sameulson. Without going too deep into the interesting world of economics, we link the methods these economists used in the early 1900s to increase the overall welfare of a country, to similar process steps an individual could apply in his/her work environments that could increase his/her overall level of influence and income. I call it: *The Seven Steps to Discover, Develop, and Deliver Your Niche*.

The analogous commodity that we use throughout this book is the oil industry. This is where we uncover the wildcatters of the late 1800s who used instincts and some rudimentary discovery techniques to drill for oil. We take these instincts to drill for value in obscure areas, add the refinement process, and describe how that commodity is incorporated into engines. It is hoped that *Dream Octane* will place a drill on the landscape of your life and help to excavate the value you have to offer in the work you do.

"If innovative change is an engine, your unique dream and ability could be its fuel." Clifton Charles Manning

Introduction

I understand now. I understand that life and the various layers of complexity that make it what it is don't make sense, until they do. Unfortunately, by the time many of us come to this realization, we either start believing that our time for accomplishing our dream has passed or we become preoccupied wishing that we knew what we knew now when we were younger. Let me encourage you from the start of our conversational time together: the God given dream that you have is possible because it has been carefully designed for you. It is a gift, yes, but not because you are in receipt of it. No, this unique treasure that God blessed you with—also known as your *dream*—becomes a gift once *you* decide to *give* it away. However, if you believe that fulfilling your specific dream is still—at this point in your life—impossible, keep this Nelson Mandela quote in mind as you become acquainted with the material: "*It always seems impossible until it's done.*"

My Story

I once worked for a Chief Operating Officer that had oversight of a three-hospital healthcare system who began his career as a registered nurse. Driven by ambition, this aspiring serial entrepreneur had gone to business school and was on his way to establishing twenty-plus businesses by the time I began working for him.

On one occasion, we were discussing some common themes I began noticing while transitioning from managing a single imaging department with forty employees, to having oversight of a three-hospital imaging service line with over one hundred and thirty direct reports. I shared how the people management lessons gained along the way began collectively making sense to me.

He agreed and remarked, "When you take care of patients by applying best practice methods and are fiscally responsible for the institution as you provide that care, after a while all these things start coming together. As a leader, at times you will try different strategies, but you can't be afraid to fail." He went on to say how this eureka moment I was experiencing reminded him of a comparable situation that happened for him on a nursing unit shortly after starting his nursing career.

"One day," he continued, "I found myself doing my normal nursing routine when everything began to click."

It was at that moment that the nursing education, patient care experience, and problem-solving efforts stopped being rote. The nursing practices he went through almost mechanically began feeling natural—more intuitive. From there, he went on to explain that this epiphany led to greater confidents and a more fluid service for the patients that were under his care. I could relate to the growth that happens when application of understanding becomes more than just words on a page. However, my journey of getting to that position was much different. I soon realized that one of the secrets to making a difference began with me first "breaking the jar."

Break the Jar

Jim Rowan was the first person I heard tell the story of a farmer's son and his pumpkin seeds. As the story goes, this little farm boy took a jar with some dirt in it and decided to plant the pumpkin seeds inside of it. Every day he would water the dirt and give it adequate sunlight. Over time, the pumpkin seeds sprouted, and the little boy was fascinated at the progress they were making. That fascination, however, only lasted up to the point where he noticed that the pumpkin had stopped growing. No matter the amount of nourishment he gave it, the pumpkin refused to grow beyond the size of the jar.

The father, seeing his son's dilemma, took the jar outside, found some fertile soil, and broke the jar on it. Over time, sunlight hit the shards of glass, rain also fell on the broken jar, and the pumpkin slowly grew again. I believe that the original point is that the jar symbolizes one's environment.

Now, I would like to paint a different picture for you, that the jar represents our mindset, and I would like to explore with you what would happen if that mental framework is broken.

With that said, let's begin with a breakdown of the basic mindset needed to make progress between discovering and delivering your niche. The fact that you are reading this book is an indication that some aspect of discovering, developing, and/or delivering your niche holds some level of value to you. From the onset, here is a lightening overview of the book to help you navigate through the material with maximum efficiency.

Firstly, there are ten chapters—seven of which coincide with each step in the *Lifecycle of Excavation* process. The purpose of the seven chapters is to provide you with not only information, but principles that can be applied to help you find the niche in you. Following a few exploratory portions that highlight the 5P Framework in Chapter 3, are sections entitled *excavation exercises,* which summarize the key take-aways previously covered in the chapter.

The seven steps are divided into three units: *discover,* *develop,* and *deliver.* The goal of each unit is to help frame where a particular chapter sits in the flow of the excavation system. Lastly—but certainly not least—there are the three must-have behaviors connected to each unit: *discovery* requires *determination*; *development* needs *discipline*; and *delivery* necessitates *diligence.*

Theodore Roosevelt said it best, "Nothing worth having was ever achieved without effort." Most people reading a book with steps often want to solve some sort of problem and are looking for a system to help them do it. However, if you are *not* willing to put the required effort behind each unit, please stop reading, pick up a mirror, and take a good look at the *real* problem. That's right, the problem stopping you from uncovering your niche begins and ends with you.

I have compiled expertise from others, as well as my own tips, for excavating the niches buried within us. In my experience of nearly twenty years in healthcare, these insights were useful in my career. Yet more importantly, I found that these learnings were reproducible for other emerging leaders who found similar success once shared. To be completely honest, the reason you are even reading this book is a testament of God's grace and my own application of being determined, disciplined, and deliberate with getting this material to you against all odds. If you are looking for evidence of being able to put these principles into action, an example is at this very moment in your hands. So, if you are ready—which the fact that you are still reading leads me to believe you are—put the mirror down, pick up that jar, and let's break that thing together.

Discover Section

Keep Drilling….

Chapter 1

Discovering My Broken Jar

I remember when the jar was broken for me. It was a few years ago when my wife and I shared a vehicle. I was waiting outside the Rutgers Law School library where she was studying. My son, Elijah, who was seven at the time, had fallen asleep in the back seat of the car and I had dozed off as well. When my wife came outside and saw how tired I was she offered to drive, and I gladly slid into the passenger seat. I remember seeing a greenlight directly ahead of us right before I dozed off again. Not shortly after, a loud explosion awoke me followed by the sound of screeching tires and the feeling that I was strapped into a seat on a rollercoaster ride. Another car had run full speed into the side of our vehicle. The only thing that stopped his car was ours.

Both cars began to tail-spin into the intersection and somehow ended up facing each other like angry lovers saying goodbye for the last time. When I looked at my wife, she seemed okay. My son was shaken up but was unharmed. I jumped out of the car and the other driver, who was already outside of his vehicle, said that he was alright as well. The scene had the look of steam rising from engines, side impact curtains visible—which are used to prevent shattered glass from coming into the vehicle— and air bags in both vehicles fully deployed.

Before I could embrace the gravity of the situation, help was there. The paramedics, police officers, and firefighters were so quick to arrive that it felt like a drill. Although the wreckage looked far worse than the accident itself, the firefighters still had to cut my wife out of the vehicle. I hope that you never experience something like this, as the jaws of life sound like death when firefighters use them.

Before long we were in the emergency room. My wife lay on a stretcher with a neck brace, my son was in his pajamas, and I was walking around the emergency department wearing dress slacks and bed slippers. Both cars were totaled, but thankfully everyone walked away that night without any major injuries. I learned something that day: difference making is often hidden in mere moments. If we peer into the nanoseconds that develop this sequence, we will find difference makers hard at work throughout the time continuum.

These difference makers are found making a difference in numerous ways. It is found in the behind-the-scenes effort of the 911 dispatcher calling the first responders into action, each of them helping to provide some level of specialized service. Even when we fast-forward to us arriving at the hospital, I observed an emergency department nurse treating a drug addict's condition without stripping him of whatever dignity he had left.

It can also be found in other services such as the speech therapist who understands the frustration of a patient who lacks the patience to relearn how to talk because of a traumatic brain injury. We can label it situational ethics, compassion or caring, this difference making happens every day. The simple truth is this: Even if these individuals do not feel ready for this moment, it doesn't mean that they are not designed for it. These are just a few examples of what happens when a niche meets its moment. However, these moments would not be made possible if that specific individual wasn't positioned beforehand with a vision for obtaining that skillset. It is this skillset that helps them to make a difference when opportunities are presented.

The Secret to Difference Making

What would possess a one-hundred-pound woman in a 4-foot 11-inch frame to give up her position as an educator and immerse herself into the slums of Kolkata (Calcutta) India? Although Mother Teresa donned a white and blue sari like other nuns involved in mission work, she seemed to be cut from a different cloth. How did her difference make a difference? Helping the poorest of the poor was commendable but this didn't speak to *how* Mother Teresa made a difference. Some may even argue that the secret to her popularity was in her name. After all, her humanitarian efforts resulted in noteworthy awards such as the internationally recognized Nobel Prize for Peace in 1979, the Bharat Ratna, which is India's highest civilian award in 1980, and several other acclaims she received during her mission work in India.[1]

However, if we drill deeper into the heart of her recognition, we'll find that her success and popularity were what onlookers saw on the surface. The true secret to her success was in how she *served*. Her popularity, successful efforts in rallying aide to the poor, and countless accolades were what she received, but *how* she *made a difference* was what she **gave**. Her giving was against all odds even when the opposition she was against was herself.

Years after Mother Teresa died, some private letters she wrote to her spiritual confidant, the Rev. Michael Van Der Peet, were revealed. At some point in her life, she asked that these writings be destroyed but the church overruled the request.[2] These letters resurfaced during the petitioning process for her sainthood. They exposed a deep inner turmoil with the humanitarian work she had immersed herself in, as well as internal struggles with fundamental aspects of her faith.

However, despite these conflicts, she continued to do the work she felt she was called to do. Although many of her followers were shocked by this revelation, Mother Teresa's letters revealed that true service takes more than just piety. The secret to how this *difference maker* made a difference was in her ability to persevere despite her own internal resistance. Her service was not natural, it was intentional. If we fast-forward that power of intentionality from vocation to YouTube video views, we will find serving is just as important.

The 8 Intentional Questions That Helped to Create 1 Billion Views on YouTube

I remember seeing Prince Ea's name for the first time as I scrolled though the list of guest speaker's slated to present at the upcoming Two Comma Club Conference, I had signed up for that was being hosted by Russell Brunson from Clickfunnels.com. I soon learned that it was called the Two Comma Club Conference because one million dollars has two commas in it and this event put on display those who made over one million dollars using the Click Funnels' platform.

Prince Ea was one of the conference's guest speakers. I thought to myself, "now that is an interesting stage name, I wonder what this guy is all about?" This event was the first Two Comma Club conference that was being held virtually due to the initial onset of COVID-19 around the globe.

Prince Ea was a tall, slender built African American who, from the time he stepped onto the stage, captivated the audience with insightful delivery that was blended with humility and charisma. He was a guy who had over ten billion subscribers to his YouTube channel, three million subscribers to his Instagram account, and had over one billion views from material he posted on YouTube. To be humble with so many accolades as a thirty-something influencer caught my attention even more.

He was known as a rapper, poet, storyteller, and YouTube extraordinaire.[3] He was making a difference by combining his actions with a niche he had refined over the years. But how did his online success come about? He realized that he needed to serve those he was desiring to reach. Whenever his ego got in the way, he redirected his thoughts so that he could touch the hearts of his viewers. In Brendan Kane's book, *One Million Followers: How I Built a Massive Social Following in 30 Days,* the author outlines the following questions that Prince Ea uses to bring his mind into a better service-oriented state:[4]

1. Why am I here?
2. How can I provide service and value to others?
3. If this were the last video I was ever going to make, what would it say?
4. If this is going to be the best video on this topic, how can I make it the best video ever?
5. What will present the content in the best way it has ever been presented before?
6. Why do I share the content that I share?
7. What do I like about the content I see?
8. How can I make a meaningful impact on the world?

To summarize Prince Ea's eight questions into a single word it would be: ***service***.[5] This is the one common denominator that I have found from interviewing experts who make a difference to examples of known influencers such as Mother Teresa and Prince Ea. They all have different vehicles of delivering that service, but all arrive in the same neighborhood of serving.

Service is the key to discovering that special niche that is inside all of us. Now, some people may see this word *service* and think that it requires some level of altruistic sacrifice, but it isn't that deep. The ones who make a difference *just serve* by adding value to a moment of need. In other words, they use something that is unique to them to meet a need of someone else.

To do this in an effective way, it will take some level of understanding of what makes us uniquely equipped to serve someone other than ourselves. Asking the same or comparable questions as Prince Ea will help place us in the vicinity—or an area of—service. However, that may not uncover what makes you unique.

Prince Ea and Mother Teresa already had an awareness of what they had to offer with different methods of expressing it to those they felt called to serve. The same can be done for you. Once you discover, develop, and are ready to deliver your niche you need to pair it with the audience that has the greatest need that is solved by your niche. Your niche is what makes you unique in the marketplace and if refined properly could position you to become like fuel to help drive change in the lives of others.

However, before we can get to that moment of fueling anything, how do we find our niche?

As I was working on this book, I knew that I did not want to do the traditional self-publishing model where I basically sold the book out of the trunk of my car. *Dream Octane* was the third book in this self-publishing hobby of mine, and I was acutely familiar with those friend and family sales.

However, I wanted it to reach a broader market. So shortly after attending the Two Comma Club event, I signed up for the Click Funnels program and believed in the product so much that I became an affiliate. This platform had training that helped me to see that helping people globally was possible if the right tools were used.

I also participated in the One Funnel Away Challenge, which was a crash course on how to build, launch, and market your product/service online. We will go into detail on this later when I discuss the positive aspect I found in my Funnel launch fiasco.

However, before my exposure to this information, Prince Ea's presentation and countless others only reinforced the principles of serving that I had found to be true from my own research on the topic of how difference makers succeed.

Prince Ea said, "...personal growth must happen before you can have professional success." It is in this order of operation—growing   personally   before   flourishing professionally—that was exactly the point I found being echoed by the founder and CEO of GetFriday and Your Man in India (YMII) Virtual Assistant program.

The Value GetFriday and Your Man in India Uncovered Through Service

"Like the ripples from a stone tossed into the pond from the water's edge, the effects of our choices extend infinitely outward. Even the smallest of acts reverberates in the ears of unwritten histories."—Justin Young

I must be honest that when Sunder P, the founder and CEO of YMII, began the interview with me it felt surreal. At the start of the interview, I thought to myself, how full circle is this moment right now? This feeling was rooted in the fact that I signed up for GetFriday's Virtual Assistant program after plucking the idea out of Tim Ferris' book, *The 4-Hour Workweek.* I read Tim Ferris' book a few times and was a fan of his material, so it was exciting to be sitting across from someone who was connected to his journey. There was also a touch of irony in how this was all playing out. Here I was having a conversation with the CEO of GetFriday because I read Tim Ferris' book and was inspired to contact GetFriday to hire a virtual assistant. Which, coincidentally, was a similar path Tim Ferris chose when starting his virtual assistant journey.

I was in the beginning stages of my online content creation and was intent on helping others to start their own ripple in time by first finding their niche. I was fortunate that the inspiration to start delivering my book's content online had me looking for an influencer for the next episode of my podcast called, The Niche Finder.

As my virtual assistant was setting up time for me to meet with his CEO's GetFriday show, I saw an opportunity for Sunder P to also be a guest on my Niche Finder podcast. I humbly asked him, and he graciously accepted my invitation. It was here where the beginning and end points of my full circle mentioned earlier began to connect.

I was new to this content creation space and with my day job being so consuming, GetFriday was helping me create content I had in mind while I focused on my 9am-5pm duties. It was exciting to connect with Sunder P during the interview.

Before we started, I gave him a brief background of what the purpose of the Niche Finder Framework was all about.

"We want to welcome you to this segment of the Niche Finder Framework," I said as my confidence began feeling fully caffeinated by the energy drink I had quickly ingested between sessions. "This podcast is designed to help individuals by displaying the paths others used to take towards success with the hope that traits shared may help the listeners towards their own goals. We strive to have people on who have carved out their niche and are utilizing it in a way that is effective."

I introduced Sunder P and from the start of his greeting to the listeners he disclosed the importance of service. Jumping into the entrepreneurial field was more than just forming a business, he wanted to use that entity to make a difference.

He continued, "My name is Sunder and I'm calling in from Bangalore, India which is the Silicon Valley capital of India. It is my pleasure to be joining Clifton on this particular podcast where he talks about how to discover your niche." He went on to say that he had been an entrepreneur for the last eighteen plus years.

He continued, "After receiving my MBA I began working a traditional nine-to-five job, but the entrepreneur bug bit me." Around the year 2000, during the *dotcom days* as he put it, he saw friends highly active in Indian's Silicon Valley.[6]

He went on to say, "That's what really attracted me to the spirit and entrepreneurial energy that you see in people. This is what motivated me to launch my first start-up, which was way back in the early 2000s. I was trying to connect Indian have-nots with people in the U.S. who had the internet access.

"At that time, India was just about starting its internet access. There were a good number of parents in India who did not have internet access but their children who were studying in the U.S. had very good internet access. In those days, regular mail travel took almost a month before it reached its destination. It would take one month to [deliver a letter] and another month to receive [one] back.

"So, in sum total, that form of communication would take about two months for these Indian parents to correspond with their children in the United States." I was amazed at how cumbersome this process was for local Indians but his simple solution for that dilemma intrigued me.

Sunder continued, "We discovered that we were helping friends by receiving the email from the Indian children living in the U.S., printing it out, and delivering it by mail to the Indian parents. This shortened the communication time from one month down to roughly a week. The Indian parents then began to write the letter for their children, gave it to us, [and] we would scan it and then email it to their children. It became an interface like Hotmail just before Hotmail became really popular. But with time the needs changed: India started having better internet access. The whole service became redundant within a matter of time, but the entrepreneurial spirit got to us. We then began focusing on helping non-resident Indians—that is ex-pat Indians—who were living in the U.S. to get things done in India."

I then asked, "What do you do that's most meaningful or purposeful in your current job?"

Sunder replied, "I think there are two aspects to it. One is: Am I making a difference to people I'm serving? That is my clients, which is one of the most important things that drives me every day to my work and keeps me going without ever questioning or making it sound like drudgery. I'm continuing to make a difference to my clients in their lives, and that drives me every day. The other aspect is in terms of helping people develop. My own colleagues, my coworkers, and people who work in our organizations, how do I get them to live up to their fullest potential? How do they understand themselves? and I sort of do a lot of mentoring for my staff and my employees having various touch points, and of course we have an open-door culture, so anybody can reach out to me and seek advice or help."

"It's funny," Sunder P said with a grin, "incidentally just as you said that you were inspired by Tim Ferris' book, *The 4-Hour Workweek,* Tim himself was actually inspired by an article written by the Editor of *Esquire* magazine, AJ Jacobs." Sunder went on to say that AJ Jacobs penned this article way back in 2005. It outlined the benefits that virtual assistants afforded Fortune 500 companies and explored why an individual could do the same.

Sunder P continued, "It was a very humorous article that was written in the *Esquire* magazine that became very popular and that is how GetFriday was born. Tim Ferris read that article and was inspired—of course he had other inspirations as well. At times, [inspiration operates like a cycle;] each person gets inspired by the next person and can go on to achieve great things."

If not for the account of history, one could be led to believe the stone that started the ripple of events that reverberated to the shorelines of this book was cast by AJ Jacobs. However, Sunder highlighted that AJ Jacob's actually received his inspiration from Thomas Friedman's book, *The World is Flat,* and desired to try out virtual assistant services in India. So, in short order, Thomas Freedman's book, *The World is Flat*, led to AJ Jacobs writing the *Esquire* article, "My Outsourced Life," which inspired Tim Ferris to excerpt that article in his book, *The 4-Hour Workweek.* The mention of YMII in that book caught my attention, which caused me to sign-up for the service and now the ripple of the original stone is bucking against the part of my journey that is helping others to find their niche.

As Sunder and I spoke it fascinated me how his company in India personified the English proverb: *Necessity is the mother of all invention.* The venture that landed his company on the pages of Tim Ferris' *The 4-Hour Workweek*, was created to not only meet the livelihood needs for expatriated Indians living in America, but was the pivot needed for his company's survival.

"Last question that I have for you," I said towards the close of our interview. There was a wealth of information Sunder P shared but my goal—for the most part—was to ask all my interviewees the same questions. This last question became one of my favorites as it is something that I believe every entrepreneur must confront at some point in his/her journey. I continued, "How do you know when to change course versus staying focused on your goal?" The smile that Sunder P met the question with revealed to me that he too was familiar with this dichotomy.

"That's the trickiest thing," Sunder said. "I think by far, this is the most difficult thing: when to stick and when to say quits—or change course. So, I think this comes only with experience. It's not something that can be taught. Each person has to self-discover with all the mistakes that you make as to when it is time to change course because, many times as entrepreneurs— as people do start-ups—you are so wedded to your idea because it's your own. You created your own baby. So, you don't want to give up, even though it is not going to happen. It's really beyond redemption, but you still want to trudge along because it's your baby. So, that is something that every entrepreneur probably experiences, at least once in his life of having to decide whether to change goals or cling on to their original idea."

This interview was done via Zoom and at that point I noticed that the tenor of the conversation began to change. His face took the countenance of an archer in battle who fully extended his bow—with arrow in tow—right before he releases. It is that look of intensity that pre-framed his response. The initial venture he had in operations during the early years of his company's merger with India's larger conglomerate TTK group had begun to fail, but Sunder P determined to do more than watch it happen.

Sunder stated, "At that point, we were trying to do healthcare for the parents of ex-pat Indians…and it was probably an idea that was too early for its time. It failed miserably after three years of efforts. It was easy to say give up, shut down the whole thing, and go home. There was this conversation that happened with our board saying: 'Should we just shut it down and get out of it?' But, I said, 'give me a chance to change the idea.'

"We brainstormed and came up with the idea of a concierge service for ex-pat Indians, which is what Your Man in India started out to be, and it became hugely successful. That led to virtual assistance with GetFriday for anybody across the world—not just ex-pat Indians. So, anything that you can do virtually we could do it for you."

I felt very fortunate to have Sunder P on as his company found a way to make a difference by becoming a resource that met an inherent need. Simply put, this is the value of uncovering one's niche. This company did it and what I learned in the last semester at business school is that countries in times past used these principles as well to improve their well-being.

Chapter 2

If Countries Can Do It, Why Not You?

"Welcome to the Powerhouse."

—Professor Farrokh Langdana PhD.

Farrokh Langdana's demeanor was a mix of light humor, East Indian Zen, and macroeconomic brilliance. This was our final semester at the Rutgers' Executive Master's in Business Administration (REMBA) program and all fifty-seven of us in class were counting down the days until graduation. It was fitting that as the director of the program, Farrokh was one of the instructors in our final semester as each of us were hand selected by him to be a member of the class. In the REMBA program, twenty percent of the curriculum was given in a compact week of classes—known as week in residence—that started at 9am and ended at 9pm the first week of each semester. Class was held at the Heldrich Hotel & Conference Center in New Brunswick, New Jersey that week and there we were on the second day of activities.

The way Farrokh began class felt like a sensei calling his dojo into order.

"Okay everyone, settle down now," he said as the hotel's manager adjusted the volume of his lapel mic to the appropriate level. Farrokh at times spoke a few decibels above a whisper but was able to still hold the attention of the room. This created some challenges with it being first thing in the morning, but the hotel manager was able to quickly get us back on track.

"I'm going to *power you up* slowly," he said, which we all came to understand meant it was time to focus our attention onto the lesson at hand. Although it was a tough audience, Farrokh was skilled in bringing a room full of fifty-seven high-capacity individuals into alignment. The lesson outlined for this day was the six steps a country could use to improve its well-being through trade. The first three steps involved theoretical principles designed by pioneers who first uncovered what the country had in abundance, recognized where that abundance was used intensely, and identified their comparative advantage. Farrokh had a knack for making complex principles simple and easy to understand. One technique he used was to make the information relatable to us. As he began to describe a country's comparative advantage, he engaged the class by asking us how these steps could be applied by an individual.

"Okay...how about individually?" Farrokh questioned.

It was like watching a Star Wars Grand Master training young Jedi on becoming one with the force.

"Good looks," Rob said from the center of the class. As a reader you may be puzzled by what good looks has to do with someone's abundant factor. It is a bit abstract, yes, but in certain arenas it could be seen as an attribute.

"Good looks?" Farrokh acknowledged. "Well, that could be. So, let's say God's been kind to you—that's your abundant factor. If modeling and movies use that intensively, then you may have a comparative advantage at being in places like Hollywood. If you have a massive math background and analytic skills, then supply chain would be the place."

When it came to teaching, Farrokh was a Jedi master who used the *force* within macroeconomics to help his listeners uncover the potential greatness within themselves. If you were in the lecture room, there was a strong possibility that you were paying attention to the way he wielded his dry erase markers across the white board like a lightsaber. He believed that professors should engage their students by using the whiteboard. It is not that he discouraged using power point presentations, however he thought it best to have a healthy balance between handwritten explanations and digital presentations.

But then, as he described comparative advantage, he threw a curve ball into the lesson when he called my name, "I told Cliff some time ago that he needs to be in front of people. I don't care what he does, he needs to be in front of people. I heard him do a talk once and he's got it. He's got the whole presence—God has been kind—and he's got the presentation skills. So, I told Cliff that—I don't know what you do but your comparative advantage is in the area of presenting. Did I not tell you that, Cliff?"

"Yes sir," I said embarrassingly. How ironic is it that someone pays you a compliment of having an apparent gift for being in front of people only to appear introverted when that recognition is given before others? It's not an easy task to get brown skin to blush from embarrassment, but I'm sure my cheeks during our exchange had the look of mahogany.

"I recognized that long before I even defined comparative advantage," Farrokh continued as he shifted the conversation to the class. "So, when we get back from break, think about your abundant factor; think about what you do now: Are you being unleashed in the right direction? If you are then you are lucky; if you are not, now you know where to go."

Farrokh's words were a watershed moment for me. At this point I was starting a new chapter in my life with a new job in a larger healthcare system, was about to graduate with my MBA, and had over one hundred and twenty pages of *Dream Octane* written. Each of the three had its share of challenges but it was a struggle to get the book to coalesce in a way that would be meaningful for the readers I was desiring to help.

However, the exchange between Farrokh and I was a needed course correction for how these ideas where to come together for the book. As I eased back in my chair, Farrokh's words reverberated in my mind: "So…think about your abundant factor; think about what you do now: Are you being unleashed in the right direction?" Then I thought to myself, if a country with all its complexities could use Heckscher Olin Theorem and a few other economist strategies for improving its overall welfare, then with some tweaking of these theories individuals may apply similar principles for themselves. Let's take a closer look at these theories that countries apply to see how these techniques could help us uncover the niche within ourselves.

What does one need to identify to determine comparative advantage?

It was not until taking this international trade and macroeconomic course with Farrokh Langdana that I became acquainted with this term *comparative advantage*. Up until this point, I only heard of the term *competitive advantage* but there are key distinctions between the two.

If we begin with the latter, *competitive advantage* involves factors that afford a company the ability to produce a good or service of higher quality or less expensive than its rival.[7] Some factors that make up competitive advantage are improved customer service, brand recognition, intellectual property, distribution networks, and product offerings to name a few.[8] *Comparative advantage,* on the other hand, involves factors where a company produces a good or service with lower opportunity costs. In other words, the company can produce this at a lower overall cost than its rivals.[9]

Now, if you have any deep understanding around competitive advantage, please allow the above description to be like a papier-mâché mockup being used to describe a robust machine. However, being that *comparative advantage* is part of the information that we will cover later, I rather *power you up* the way Professor Farrokh Langdana describes it.

Let's take a commercial break on *Comparative Advantage* as described by Professor Farrokh Langdana:

Before we go further, allow me to provide an intuitive explanation of the trade theories that so uniquely underlie Dream Octane.

The cornerstone economic model deployed here is the 2-step Ricardian Trade Model, which Clifton will describe in later chapters. Very simply, David Ricardo (1772-1823) proved that a whole economy would be better off if (i) it specialized only in areas in which it had "comparative advantage" and (ii) it then traded freely by exporting the goods/services in which it had just specialized.

The notion of "comparative advantage" (CA) is truly the DNA of global trade theory. It certainly holds true for Dream Octane *and can be intuitively explained as follows. If there are two countries A and B, and if there are just two products X (microprocessors) and Y (bed sheets and pajamas) then country A should only specialize in the good that it makes more efficiently. If this product is X, then A would have a "comparative advantage" in X.*

Well, what does "efficiently" mean? Ricardo deployed an economic concept known as "opportunity cost;" for us here "efficiency" in making X means that A (the U.S.) makes X really well. It can "afford" to make microprocessors. Note that the U.S. (Country A) can certainly make B. We can make amazing bed sheets and pajamas compared to China, but can we afford to deploy workers—to deploy you, the reader—to make bed sheets in Bridgewater, NJ? Or pajamas in Pennsylvania? And what would be the price of those items? The wages from making Y in the U.S. would not put food on the table for U.S. workers. So, no. Country A cannot "afford" to make Y at home. The wages from making Y at home would not be enough to put food on the table for workers making Y at home in country A.

The second step according to Ricardo is that country A that specializes in X (microprocessors) should now export X, and at the same time import Y. Country A can certainly make bed sheets, but its labor can be better deployed. Best to just buy cheaper—and well made—pajamas and bed sheets from China or Vietnam or India, etc., and best to sell U.S.- made microprocessors to China.

Clifton then goes on to blend the Ricardian 2-step model with two more fundamentally powerful concepts: The Heckscher Ohlin Theorem (HOT) and the Stolper Samuelson Theorem (SST).

HOT quite simply explains "where" the comparative advantage (CA) "comes from." In our example, how did Country A actually have a CA in microprocessors, X? What caused that? How do we know what our CA is? Intuitively the answer is quite simple: According to HOT, "Country A has a Comparative Advantage in X if this country uses its abundant factor intensively, to make X." If A has "high skilled labor" as its abundant factor, and if microprocessors deploy this kind of labor, then A has a CA in microprocessors (in X). By this token, China (Country B) may have medium skilled labor as its abundant factor, and bed sheets will demand this kind of labor, so China/Vietnam/India will have a CA in Y (bed sheets).

Country A will make and export microprocessors, while Country B will make and export bed sheets, pajamas, etc. (Please note that these are very intuitive explanations indeed. Detailed algebra best describes these theorems, but this is not necessary here.)

Finally, the Stolper Samuelson Theorem (SST) proves that after specialization and free trade, each country's abundant factor is actually better off! In other words, if the relatively "abundant" factor in A is higher-skilled labor, then with specialization and trade, the wages of these workers <u>will</u> go up. Similarly, lower-skilled Chinese workers making and exporting the bed sheets will find their wages going up too.

As you can see from Farrokh's explanation above, when a country deploys these macroeconomic principles in efficient ways—through specialization and free trade—it affords both countries the opportunity to be better off. Now, let's get back to answering the question: If countries can do it, why not you? To do so, let's head back into the REMBA classroom to gain an even clearer understanding around this subject.

Back to the program…: Understanding *Comparative Advantage*

"So, what does one need to identify in order to determine ***comparative advantage***?" Farrokh said this as he postured himself alongside the white board to record the responses from the class. He had just finished sharing the mathematical aspects of the Heckscher-Olin theorem (HOT) and was now providing practical applications for us. Farrokh had an uncanny way of interfacing the class with the information by having us relate the lesson to our own situations.

He said, "Tell me how you get to it? What is the first step? Look at the Heckscher-Olin theorem then look inside your state or your own native country. What is the first thing that you need to look at to determine where your comparative advantage will come from?"

The responses were hurled toward Farrokh from various parts of the auditorium style classroom. Farrokh nodded as he received them and replied, "*Abundant factor*. Yes, determine the abundant factor. Call it factor or quality—it could be culture or anything…Good, now what is the second thing?" Farrokh looked around the room. "Look at the Heckscher-Olin theorem. C'mon."

My classmate Christine said something inaudible to me but it was picked up clearly by Farrokh as I noticed the countenance of his face brighten.

"Exactly," Farrokh said as he quickly wrote the answer on the whiteboard. "Thank you. Yes, that is it: Step two is to determine the goods or service that employs this abundant factor intensely. Are you getting this, folks?"

Farrokh made a point during his lessons to do these *pulse checks* as if to ensure we focused in on pivotal points of each lesson.

"Now step three?" he said looking like a seasoned pilot bringing an AWACS aircraft in for a landing. "According to the Heckscher-Olin theorem, this then determines *what* for the country? So, you have determined the abundant factor. You found the good or service that uses it intensely." He pointed at step number one and two summarized on the board. "Therefore, you have a…?" He raised his dry erase marker in the air before the class like a conductor waving a baton before an ensemble. It was fitting because our class looked up from our textbooks and replied in concert, "comparative advantage."

"Yes," Farrokh said with a clinched fist as if the answer of the class hit just the right note. "This is how you get to comparative advantage."

Understanding the six steps a country can take to increase its overall welfare in comparison to the steps an individual can take to find his/her niche

I began thinking of the connections between these first three steps a country takes to increase its overall welfare and how an individual could uncover his/her niche. Where a country would identify its abundant factor, a person would recognize his/her abundant factor.

The second step for a country that identifies where that good or service is used intensely would be just like a person optimizing where his/her niche is utilized. The latter finds the areas they have in abundance that have been valuable to others.

The last step in the HOT theorem would be comparative advantage, which is analogous to an individual summarizing his/her unique comparative advantage. As mentioned, a country's comparative advantage comes from possessing a good or service that they have in abundance with the least amount of opportunity cost to produce. Similarly, an individual summarizes his/her comparative advantage derived from an ability he/she possesses in abundance that has been of value in solving a problem for others but also comes easy to him/her requiring a minimal amount of effort.

Discovering your niche is about uncovering what you have that comes easily to you but has a maximum benefit to your audience. By audience I mean, if you are in business this would be your customers, if you were a salesperson, this would be your clients, and if you are an online influencer, it would be your followers. In short, what are you *drawn* to that *draws* others to you? What *interest* do you have that makes you *interesting*?

After you discover what that is, develop your interest by testing it with a core group that you have influence over. Once refined, deliver it to a wider audience online. If you do that, you will find that uncovering your niche is more than merely *being different*—helping others with your niche also affords you the opportunity to *make a difference.*

Your niche is an answer looking for a problem to solve. Your audience has a problem to solve, and they are looking for a solution you possess that could solve that problem. The question then is, how do the two align? The answer is to *become specific through specialization.* This brings us to the last few steps a country uses to increase its overall welfare and is based on the Ricardian Two-Step Trade Model and the Stolper-Samuelson Theorem.

Ricardian Two-Step Theorem

I became intrigued by the conversation around this topic of how countries can benefit from the Heckscher-Olin theorem of (a) identifying their abundant factor (b) finding the goods/services that uses that factor intensely and (c) defining their comparative advantage. This fascination took me to the pages of Farrokh's *International Trade and Global Macropolicies* textbook that he coauthored. Here, he outlined the next two Ricardian steps that essentially comprised steps four and five of the six step strategy a country could use to improve its wellbeing through trade.

The first step indicates that a country might specialize in the good/service in which they have a comparative advantage. The second step is to ensure that the country trades freely. This increases the access to one country with the other country's resources.

"Okay, let me power you back up," Farrokh said as we settled back into our seats immediately following the session breaks. "Before we look at the Ricardian Two- Step Theorem and the Stolper-Samuelson Theorem, give me another country or one more individual to help us pick up where we left off. To recap, at this point we have defined the abundant factor, found the goods or service that uses it intensely, and determined the comparative advantage. How about another country—let's look at one more?"

I heard my classmate Rich respond from directly behind me, "How about Columbia?"

"Okay, Columbia," Farrokh said in response. "What is the abundant factor?"

"Cocaine?" someone murmured with a giggle. There were brilliant minds within the class but there was an *abundant factor* of sarcasm within the group. However, Farrokh responded like a skilled sailor using the headwind confronting him—that would knock most off course—to steer things into the right direction.

"I was going to go with coffee," Adamo stated.

"You have to remember coffee is not the abundant factor," Farrokh replied. "Think about it. The abundant factor is *not* the product. However, certain type of climate and land are conducive to coffee."

I nodded my head and smiled. This made complete sense: Colombian coffee is only possible because of the ideal climate and fertile land that Columbia possesses.

"So, climate and soil…" Farrokh said as he wrote the answer on the whiteboard. "The good that uses this abundant factor intensely is coffee, therefore Juan Valdez Columbian Coffee has a comparative advantage to other similarly priced coffee manufacturers as a result.

"By the way, as we are doing this course, we want to convert our day-to-day language into trade theory language." Farrokh turned towards the class as he placed the dry erase marker on the lectern and continued, "Like for example—I'm making this up now—my neighbor spends an inordinate amount of time looking out of her window. She spies on me all the time—it's so annoying.

"If a Fed-Ex package arrives on my doorstep, I get an instant text from her that it has arrived. Sometimes, I just want to turn to her and say stop looking out of your window—*get a life*! When you say *get a life* in trade language what exactly does that mean?" Farrokh was a strong leader that our class deeply admired. His business acumen, macroeconomics knowledge, and self-effacing transparency all made him endearing. One weakness he expressed to us was that he had a problem telling students their answers were not correct. Maybe he did not want to stop the flow of ideas or hinder them from expressing themselves.

Therefore, if the answer was correct—or close to being correct—he would say, "Yes: Click on that again." Clicking was his way of getting the person to share more ideas about what was said that was in the vicinity of being correct. This was his lighthearted way of making our in-person classes—as he put it—have a web-based feel to it. If, on the other hand, the answer shared was nowhere close he would sigh, *Yeaah*, and look away, which simply meant that the answer wasn't anywhere close to where he wanted us to be—keep thinking.

"C'mon," Farrokh said as he waved his hands at himself like a transit policeperson directing traffic towards him.

"She needs to find her comparative advantage?" Torey said from the left side of the room.

"Yeaah," Farrokh said in response. "Why is she spending all her waking hours looking out of the blinds?" He turned his attention to the right side of the room.

One of my classmates who was seated right next to where Farrokh was standing, replied with an answer that was inaudible to me from where I was sitting. It must have been way off as we all heard from Farrokh was a double "Yeaah... Yeaah." The respondent, as well as the rest of the class, giggled at his delivery.

Bala then said an answer that caused Farrokh to flip around and turn towards his direction.

"Click on that again Bala," Farrokh said, as he waved his hands towards himself again.

"She doesn't have anything better to do," Bala said.

"She doesn't have anything better to do," Farrokh replied. "I like that actually. By the way, is Bala's response trade language?"

"Her opportunity costs are too low," Regina said as Farrokh turned his attention towards her with his hand pointed palm up in her direction.

"Wooow...louder," Farrokh said.

"Her opportunity costs are too low," Regina replied.

"Yes," Farrokh said. "Her opportunity costs are too low. Her day in comparison to my own is vastly different. When I wake up in the morning I have so many things that I am doing on a Saturday: I get up, go to Costco, run some other errands, come home to get ready for an alumni event—or something—attend the event and come home. When I pull into the driveway, instantly I see the parting of the blinds and her eyes peering at me from behind them. Those are the moments where I want to say: 'Get a life!' Why? I don't have time to spend looking out of the window; I have too much to do. Therefore, my opportunity costs are too high, whereas as Bala said, 'she has nothing better to do' so her opportunity costs are low, or she is deriving maximum utility for doing this."

How one can benefit from having low opportunity cost.

The point that Farrokh was making about this make-believe neighbor began to resonate with me. I want to point out something about this illustration that Farrokh was sharing. Having low opportunity costs is not something negative per say. This is important to note as given the right environment, the neighbor's low opportunity costs could become an asset.

On the flip side, Farrokh has his Doctorate Degree in Economics, is the director for an executive MBA program at Rutgers University, as well as an international EMBA program. He is both well read and well versed. If his neighbor had a bachelor's degree in mathematics and both her and Farrokh were given an opportunity to work as a consultant who would establish an EMBA program that specializes in economics, Farrokh's opportunity costs would be low and hers would be too high. In other words, it would take more effort and energy for her to gain the level of understanding and wealth of experience that Farrokh has in abundance within his cachet over hers.

However, let's say the community in which they both lived had a vacant coveted neighborhood watch committee position. In this situation, Farrokh would have high opportunity costs for taking on that position for all the reasons mentioned before of him being too busy, attending program activities, and not having the time to "peer through the window at his neighborhood." His neighbor, on the other hand, would have low opportunity costs because she has time in abundance.

Understanding our individual opportunity costs is key as the areas within our life that have the lowest opportunity costs are where we want to focus our attention. By focusing our attention, I mean we need to specialize in those things we have in abundance. This is Step #1 for us where we recognize our abundant factor. From there, we optimize where our abundant factor is used intensely. Once we have that established, it is easy for you to do what you do in relationship to this niche that you have uncovered. You have it in abundance, but does it come easily to you or, in other words, do you have low opportunity costs connected to it?

This matters because you want to be able to know what you have in your life or in keeping with the analogy your landscape that you can trade with someone else who has a high opportunity cost of acquiring that skill set that comes very easily to you. This is important because what you will be trading, as Russell Brunson would say, is their money for your offer.[10]

To package this offer, we must develop through specialization and eliminate trade barriers that would prevent someone from exchanging their money with your offer that you have low opportunity costs around. When you find your audience, their need will at least bring them to the table and compel them to hear what you have to offer. Providing there aren't any barriers within yourself or between the two— between you and your audience—then you will be able to increase your abundant factor. Specializing and eliminating barriers helps with developing what you have to offer.

"So here we go," Farrokh said refocusing us back to the lesson. "Stay with me here. We identified the comparative advantage by Heckscher-Olin theorem. So, steps one, two, and three we've identified comparative advantage. Step four?" Farrokh looked around the room.

"Specialize," Suzy said in response.

"Yes, specialization," Farrokh said as he wrote the answer to Step four on the board. "Step five?" Farrokh asked turning his attention back to the class.

"Trade freely," Asish said softly.

"Come on, Ashish" Farrokh said turning to face where he was sitting.

"Trade freely," Ashish said louder.

"Trade freely," Farrokh said as he wrote Asish's answer on the board. At times during class, Farrokh would ask a question and go around the room randomly calling out student names to elicit a response.

"Now what do steps four and five describe?" Farrokh asked again looking around. "C'mon…

"Bala?

"John?

"Teg?

"Chris from the Fed?

 "Ricardian Two-Step Theorem," Chris said.

"Thank you," Farrokh replied "This is Ricardo. Don't lose power on me." He turned to face the class. "Step six is the abundant factor getting better off. Now, what is Step six called?"

"SST," Suzy said.

"Yes, SST: the Stolper-Samuelson Theorem." Farrokh wrote the final part from his textbook entitled: *The 6 Steps to Increase the Overall Welfare of a Country* on the white board.

As I wrote the last step, my notes came full circle. The six steps that a country can use to increase their overall welfare coincided perfectly with how someone can discover, develop, and deliver their niche. I quickly drew a side-by-side diagram that outlined how the two would cross-connect with each other and it clarified the flow.

From there, I understood the framework that I would use to outline the content of *Dream Octane*. At that point, I had the concept of discovering, developing, and delivering an individual's unique niche in a helpful way to an audience interested in that offer. However, these steps provided an added construct for the contextual ideas and commentaries to fall within. It all made sense now.

Thank you Langdana I thought; this seminal moment allowed the book to finally coalesce in a way that could be followed. With that I organized the content for *Dream Octane* within this construct beginning with Step # 1: *Recognize your Abundant Factor*. Little did I know that another watershed moment was on the horizon right in the middle of the world's most challenging time.

The 6 Steps to Increase the Overall Welfare of a Country		The 7 Steps to Discover, Develop, and Deliver Your Niche	
Heckscher-Olin Theorem (HOT)	Step #1: *Identify the abundant factor.*	Discover	Step #1: *Recognize your abundant factor*
	Step #2: *Identify the goods that use this factor intensely*		Step #2: *Optimize where your niche is used intensely*
	Step #3: CA (Comparative Advantage) has been identified		Step #3: *Summarize your comparative advantage*
Ricardian Two- Step Trade Model	Step #4: *Specialize*	Develop	Step #4: *Specialize in offering what is helpful to others but unique to you*
	Step #5: *Trade Freely*		Step #5: *Neutralize the barriers blocking the fulfillment of your dream*
Stolper-Samuelson Theorem (SST)	Step #6: *Abundant factor will benefit; scarce factor will suffer*	Deliver	Step #6: *Organize the delivery of your niche to a wider audience*
			Step #7: *Maximize your abundant factor*

Chapter 3

Step # 1: Recognize Your Abundant Factor

What is a Niche Anyway?

A market niche and an individual's niche are often used interchangeably. However, the two are entirely different vantage points. By definition, a person's niche is often discovered in moments in time. It is a place of comfort, an appropriately suited position or activity that best fits an individual.[11] It can apply to life where it is often referred to as being stumbled upon: "Flowers tend to bloom whenever she cares for them, so gardening must be her niche." This phrase is also found in employment: "After years of working as a lawyer covering mesothelioma cases, he found his niche."

When a business looks to penetrate a market as a niche, it first researches the market and strategizes how it will differentiate itself from its competitors. However, those looking to uncover an individualized niche begin with what they are most familiar: themselves. If you scoured the Internet looking for techniques on finding your niche, many authors often begin their articles with how to discover your individual niche but end up outlining how to obtain a business niche. Competitive advantage market penetration, segmentation, efficiencies, brand, and value are all important. However, if we begin with the successes we have had in times past, we may find that the value we seek to discover in the market may be hidden within us. It is often buried like crude oil that is hidden beneath the surface and to get it out will take faith to find it.

What Does Finding our Niche have to do with Adding Value?

Our niche is our value. Although this value may manifest itself in our dreams and inherent abilities, it may not be apparent to us. I discovered this reality one day in the hospital when I was making green tea. At this location, office space was hard to come by and the Keurig coffee machine was in a room where three other individuals had their desks. One of them was a patient navigator who helped to coordinate various screening programs being offered to the local community. For context, I will refer to her as Miss Charlie. I drink a good amount of green tea throughout the day, and I would visit that room two to three times while at work. Like office mates catching up at the water cooler, as my green tea brewed, Miss Charlie and I would, at times, engage in conversation around the importance of finding our niche. As the water percolated, the questions around the importance of finding one's niche began bubbling to the surface.

Discovering the 5P Framework

"I feel like I have a purpose but I'm just running in circles," Miss Charlie said with a puzzled look on her face. This was not the first time I had this type of conversation with her. However, each time we spoke her questions were always sincere and focused in on trying to find the answers. Without coming across as overly stereotypical, she could easily represent that 30-something year old who has an advanced degree, a career that she is good at, yet—according to her— finds herself not advancing beyond her current position.

"How do you get beyond this point that I find myself in?" she said looking at me from the side of her eye while shrugging her shoulders. "Because no matter how many self- help books I read, praying that I feel I do, and messages I listen to…I still feel stuck."

I appreciated conversations with Miss Charlie because she always asked great questions and she was also an attentive listener.

"First off, that is an excellent question," I said. "There's so much to unpack but let us keep it really simple." I finally felt prepared to answer this question for her. She had asked comparable questions in previous conversations, and I remember walking away from them feeling frustrated that I wasn't able to articulate a clear response. Yes, words left my mouth, but I didn't feel that I was able to fully answer her questions around how to recognize her niche by the end of the conversation.

I had experience helping others in similar situations, but our conversations kept hitting a roadblock. She was ready, at times even had a pen and paper as we spoke to take notes. At that point in my life, I didn't realize the difference between experience and expertise.

Michael Mauboussin clearly expressed this distinction in a paraphrased quote from psychologist Gregory Northcraft "the difference between *experience* and *expertise* is that *expertise* is having a predictive model that works."[12] Yes, that was it. I did not have a predictive model that worked so when I shared past experiences, I did not always come across the way that I hoped I would. Things may have worked for that individual who I referenced in the example, but Miss Charlie would receive it as that was either a special moment in time or that successful person possessed a talent that she lacked. Therefore, that experience was not helpful and not transferable once she felt she did not measure up. After researching and reading various articles on how to find one's niche, I began to have something that I would later circle back on with Miss Charlie. However, it wasn't until a Sunday talk by Doctor David Ireland that the Niche Finder 5P Framework began to take shape.

Understanding the Niche Finder 5P Framework

"I wanna talk to you about a topic I entitled Maximizing Your Income," Dr. David Ireland said as he stood on the platform in front of the congregation. He had a way of making his Sunday talks sound like friendly conversations rather than sermons, which was a talent that I deeply admired. "By a show of hands..." Dr. Ireland continued, "is there anyone here who could stand to make a little bit more money?"

I smiled—in concert with the rest of the congregants—at the question as I sat comfortably in my seat several rows back from where he was standing.

"Then you picked the right Sunday service to attend," he said grinning back at us while tapping the screen to see his sermon notes on his iPad. "This sermon is the final talk from a six weeklong series we call the *13,22 Challenge*, which comes from Proverbs chapter 13 and versus 22: '*A good person leaves an inheritance for their children's children...*'"[13] He looked up from his screen and challenged us as he continued, "So we're called to not just think about ourselves and be consumers of everything we make. We are to serve the generation that follows us regardless if we have children or grandchildren. The Lord sets a goal before us: Impact future generations by how you live today."

Dr. David Ireland always had a wealth of information to share that was both wise and practical, which his bio reflected. As the founder and senior pastor of Christ Church, his 9,500-member North Jersey congregation was multisite and multicultural with members representing over 70 nationalities. He was a former consultant to the National Basketball Association (NBA), conducted chapel services for the National Football League's (NFL) New York Giants and New York Jets, and he held services at the U.S. Pentagon. He has taught culturally relevant messages in over seventy-five nations that help to inspire and empower global audiences. Dr. Ireland authored over twenty books and was a contributing columnist to media outlets such as *Fox News, Huffington Post,* and *Patheos*. Additionally, he has appeared on numerous TV and radio shows including *The Dr. Phil Show, The CBS Evening News, The 700 Club*, and *Focus on the Family*.

Suffice it to say, anytime I heard him deliver a message he never failed to provide information to help bring the listener into a meaningful alignment to Biblical truths.

"That's what God does for you and me," Dr. Ireland said as he turned his palms inward and moved them towards the center of his chest. "Each of us have gifts based on our ability. Each of us have a work ethic. Each of us have a work style. Each of us have been entrusted with resources from God that we ought to manage and be stewards of."

Dr. Ireland shared relevant stories on topics that made his sermons captivating. You could just about feel the resonance in the room as he exacted scriptures in the message like a pharmacist providing patients with doses of lifesaving medication. His lesson was based on The Parable of the Bags of Gold that Jesus spoke of in Matthew chapter 25 verses 14-30. In this parable, three servants were each entrusted with different amounts of their Master's gold. The Master distributed the bags according to each servant's abilities. The first received five bags, the second two bags, and the last one bag of gold.

The Master then left the servants to go on a journey and on his return, he checked to see what sort of investment they made with what he provided. The first servant took his five bags, invested it, and had a return of an additional five more bags. The second with the two bags of gold also invested and received the return of two more bags. However, the third servant who received one bag hid his Master's money when he buried it in the ground.

"If I was the pastor of the servant who received the one bag of gold that was equivalent to $19,000- or twenty-years' wages," Dr. Ireland said continuing with the lesson, "before that servant ran off and buried his Master's gold I wish he would have had an appointment with me. Let's give this servant a made-up name—I don't know: Jimmy." He looked at the congregants as he expressed his point while waving his right hand as if he was trying to swat something out of the air.

"I can hear Jimmy saying to me: 'Pastor I just was given $19,000 and I don't know what to do with it. How do I make this money work and grow?' I would say to him, *do what you enjoy.*"

Dr. Ireland had an abundant factor of insight, however his comparative advantage in my opinion was his ability to take incredibly complex theological information and codify it to simple—easy to follow—nuggets of truth. In this sermon he did just that with *Do What You Enjoy* as the first of three talking points. The other two were, *Do What You Are Good At* and the last was *Do Something To Solve People's Problems.* By the end of the lesson, I began to see the patterns within what he was sharing in relationship to the many articles that I had read on how to discover your niche. The principles of each began coming to me like water flowing through a faucet.

And that's when I saw it—, right in the middle of his teaching was the Niche Finder 5P Framework.

Maximize Your Income and other articles on how to find your Niche	The Dream Octane Niche Finder 5P Framework
Do What You Enjoy	*Passions*
	Purposefulness

Do What You Are Good At	Patterns
	Proficiencies
Do Something To Solve People's Problems	Problem-solving

After I wrote down the outline of **The Dream Octane Niche Finder 5P Framework** I realized just having words on a page were not enough. I then designed a document that would help layout these principles in a way that others could use as an exercise to help uncover the niche they have within them.

I sat in the ninth row toggling my view between watching Dr. Ireland on stage and looking at the closer angles the camera displayed on the monitor hanging to the right of me. Easing into that moment I was comforted by the seat I was in but also one other thing. I felt that these five words—*passions, purposefulness, patterns, proficiency,* and *problem-solving*—were the missing pieces that now connected the *Life Cycle of Excavation.* I could now take these five words—along with subsequent questions—back to Miss Charlie and hopefully help others if given the right vehicle.

Towards the close of his *Maximize Your Income* message, Dr. Ireland paused and unknowingly solidified that moment for me. Many would liken him to a dignitary breaking a bottle of champagne against the bow of a vessel during a ceremonial ship launching, but I saw him differently. This was a man who knew how to drop a drill in areas beaming with potential to get both the drill and ideas spinning.

"Use this teaching," he said smiling from ear to ear. "You can just reference my name. Don't worry, I will not send my intellectual property lawyers after you." I smiled in response to his lighthearted charge while thinking to myself, here is another ripple in time. Dr. Ireland closed that morning message shortly thereafter, but for me my excavation had just begun.

This was another watershed moment that felt like oil shooting 150 feet into the air in front of me. I was ready now. From there I realized that in order to complete Step # 1: *Recognize Your Abundant Factor*, it is important to keep drilling.

Keep Drilling

Don't compare yourself with anyone in this world...if you do so, you are insulting yourself. –Bill Gates

The fact that dreams—whether faded or fulfilled—are ubiquitous doesn't diminish the value of these buried treasures. A man named Pattillo Higgins from Spindletop Texas understood that. In the late 1890s he viewed a plot of land in Spindletop Texas as an ideal site for drilling for oil. [14] Consumer demand for oil at this time increased on the heels of agrarian dependents shifting towards more efficient fuels.[15] 1859 had experienced a boom in the United States like that of the 1990s internet inception.

The late 1800s was a different time though, as the closest thing there was to a significant oil discovery was in Pennsylvania over thirty years earlier. The only other remotely close discovery in Texas was Corsicana, which was a few years earlier but that was over two hundred miles away.[16] So, you could understand when Pattillo brought a few people in to survey the area, they considered his proclamation of oil potential as being farfetched and regarded the area worthless.

Some may argue that a one-armed Sunday school teacher with a fourth-grade education wouldn't possess the wherewithal to discover a site that would warrant the investment of time money or drilling effort. In fact, the experts of Pattillo's time—in no uncertain terms—told him just that. Who could blame them: How could this son of a gunsmith know anything about finding oil? If the subject was gun making maybe he could add something of substance to the conversation as he spent a good amount of time as a teenager under the tutelage of his gun crafting father.

However, Pattillo did not let the opinions of others stop him from maximizing his efforts to try and excavate what he saw as potential. If anything, the pushback seemed to churn a deeper resolve inside of him.

Then, on January 10, 1901, that same plot of land discarded by many erupted and shot black gold over 150 feet into the air.[17] The site became the highest producing oil reserve of its time yielding over 100,000 barrels of oil a day.[18] However, just as Beaumont, Texas hid a reservoir of crude oil beneath the surface, so does a repository of valuable resources reside within you.

The 5P Framework was designed to help to focus our attention in the areas with the greatest potential. Eventually, the goal was to take the Niche Finder Framework and make an app out of it, but at the time of this writing, ***The Dream Octane Niche Finder 5P Framework*** document was what I used as a backdrop for my content creation.

I also started the Niche Finder podcast shortly thereafter where I met with experts who found their niche and were kind enough to share their journey. I used ***The Dream Octane Niche Finder 5P Framework*** along with some questions from Russell Brunson's book, *Expert Secrets: The Underground Playbook For Converting Your Online Visitors Into Lifelong Customers* as a part of the questions we covered in the podcast interview.

One of the first interviews that I was able to conduct was with my little sister, Doctor Natasha Manning-Gibbs who found her niche in the psychology arena where she used cognitive behavioral therapy in the juvenile penal system and within her own private practice. It was in this interview that I learned of the internal barrier of Imposter Syndrome. This barrier can hinder people from achieving Step # 1 *Recognized Your Abundant Factor* on the *Life Cycle of Excavation* because they begin to subscribe to false beliefs. With that said, allow me to encourage you that what you have in abundance is worth sharing and once refined, it can help those who may be struggling with an aspect of your journey that you have already overcome.

Opinion Versus Reality

All of us have something that we are supposed to do...all of us have some goodness within us and that goodness gives us a responsibility to manifest our greatness. —Les Brown

Author and speaker, Les Brown tells a story of when he was classified as educable mentally retarded in high school. He had difficulty learning and was placed in specific classes that were different than the standard ones the other kids took because his classes were designed to help him through his challenges.[19] On one occasion, he was waiting on a friend who was in a standard class when the teacher, Mr. Leroy Washington, walked in. Mr. Washington turned to Les Brown and said, "Young man go to the board and write what I'm about to tell you."

Les Brown responded, " I can't do that, sir."

Mr. Washington asked, "Why not?"

Les said respectfully, "I'm not one of your students."

Mr. Washington commanded, "It doesn't matter, follow my directions now!" The exchange happened again where Les Brown stated that he could not do what was being asked of him but this time when Mr. Washington questioned him, Les Brown's response changed. Like a card player exposing the terrible hand life delt him, he said "[I can't] because I'm educable mentally retarded...."

Before Les Brown could finish articulating the last syllables on the word retarded, Mr. Washington cut him off, came from behind his desk, looked squarely into Les Brown's eyes and said, "Don't ever say that again. *Someone's opinion of you does not have to become your reality!*"

It is important to note that the negative perception of others can distort our perspective if we allow it. Conversely, there is a key distinction between comparing ourselves to others with pursuing our comparative advantage. We will do a deeper dive into the importance of comparative advantage in the sections to come. Understanding what our comparative advantages are will be a key step to eventually delivering what we have to offer to others.

However, comparing our personhood with someone else's can have a negative impact on our perspective. It can reshape how we see what's special in our life. Having a wrong perspective can cause us to be victims of someone else's opinion. Subscribing to these false narratives can be crippling and can hinder the process of us excavating the value we have within our own lives. Worrying about what others will say, trying to undo the words of a gossiper when you become the topic, or subscribing to a false narrative as in the Les Brown example, can all cripple the excavation of your value. Recognizing and uncovering what we have in abundance is like drilling for oil. Buying into these erroneous perspectives would be likened to Pattillo Higgins abandoning the drilling site before the geyser was found. It wasn't until I did the Niche Finder Podcast with Dr. Manning-Gibbs that I understood the impact of subscribing to these false beliefs.

Unpacking The 5P Framework: *Passion*

"Getting into the driver's seat of our lives really consists of us saying to ourselves: I'm in control of my mind."

–Dr. Natasha Manning-Gibbs

Towards the tail-end of working on this book, I started to create content to help my audience by packaging the Dream Octane material into different media. One such media became known as the ***Niche Finder Podcast***. This podcast was designed to help listeners by sharing the journeys of people who became successful after finding their niche. Now, there were those who found what they were good at, became successful at what they did, repeated the process, and then discovered that they stumbled upon a niche.

The *Proficiency* aspect of the 5P Framework is at times extracted that way. However, the journey that brought my little sister into the psychology space had more to do with *Passion, Patterns,* and *Purposefulness.* At this point of the interview, we pick up on where these aspects collided. As a psychologist, she provided juveniles within the penal system—that she worked in full-time—with healthy approaches to becoming productive members of society. She called it, 'getting into the driver seat of our lives.' In her private practice, she specialized in helping people overcome negative emotions, which is right where we will pick up with her interview.

"I just got a phone call from a woman who was referred to me by her OB GYN," Dr. Manning-Gibbs said describing the passion that nudged her in the direction of choosing psychology as a profession.

"She was dealing with a bout of depression that appeared to be postpartum depression. As she was on the phone with me, I could sense the anxiety. I could hear in her voice that she was somewhat nervous. She had never done therapy before, but she trusted her physician's advice who referred her to me. So, she took the leap, decided to call, and made an appointment with me."

It felt different speaking to my little sister this way, even though at the time of the conversation she had been in the field for almost ten years. Our family has always been close and although I knew what she did, we never discussed her field in such detail. I was proud of—and captivated by—her.

"I started," she continued, "giving her a snapshot of the work that I do with clients. Just briefly introducing her to cognitive behavioral therapy and explaining how it works—in sort of bite-sized pieces. And during the midst of this three to four-minute introduction to cognitive behavioral therapy, I began sensing the relief in her voice.

"[Her client said] 'Wow! I just thought this was something that I had to sort of deal with and just try to suck it up. I know I've changed since having my kid. I know I have been dealing with insomnia; I'm feeling down; I've been feeling depressed. I haven't been feeling my normal self, but I just felt like I had to deal with it.'

"I think the beauty of my work," Dr. Manning-Gibbs continued, "[and] what makes me so passionate is: Therapy works. Theoretical orientation is grounded in so much research. Is it a panacea for everything in life? —No, but I've seen it really be impactful, in my work in the prison, and in my work with clients with my private practice."

I recorded my podcast using the squadcast.com platform. It made conversations more natural as the interviews were done with video, but it saved the audio for each person speaking separately. This made it a lot easier to edit once the interview was over and I provided the audio files to the engineer who helped me with that. As a result, I was able to see how my little sister glowed as she shared her abundant factor that she was passionate about.

"So, going back to my passion," she said like a seasoned runner stepping into a rhythmic stride. "My passion is about educating people on how the mind works and that we are in control of it. We have got to *get into the driver's seat of our lives*. Sometimes when we're feeling down, depressed, anxious, and stressed we shouldn't just give into our emotions and let it take over us and say, *I'll deal with this indefinitely*. There are things that we can do. Getting into the driver's seat of our lives really consists of us saying to ourselves: *I'm in control of my mind.* I can switch gears in my mind as far as how I interpret situations that come up. Then, also, there's a big component of my work with all clients too, on the behavioral therapy is twofold. It's not just about looking at your negative thoughts and your beliefs, but it's also about looking at your behaviors.

"So, leading people on the importance of exercising, eating well, socializing, completing different tasks that they probably have been suppressing in their lives like, *Oh, you know, I've been meaning to clean out that garage for ten, fifteen years, and the fact that I haven't done it, you know, every time I open up the garage, I feel down, I feel defeated because I haven't gotten to that.* Putting that on a goal list and working towards accomplishing that task is impactful for clients... it changes their mood. So, going back to the main point, my passion is about educating people. Not just on the effectiveness of therapy, but more specifically about the theoretical orientation of cognitive behavioral therapy. I'm a huge advocate and really believe in the effectiveness of it."

As this interview continued, it is important to note that Dr. Manning-Gibbs was a teenage mother and everything she was explaining to me would not have been possible if she did not keep the proverbial drill bit spinning in her life. The drill represents the determination we place behind finding what we have to offer in abundance that is inherent in our lives. It takes faith to keep it spinning even when the outside voices are urging you to abandon your efforts.

Unpacking The 5P Framework: Purposefulness

You Are not An Imposter.

Going back to the Niche Finder Podcast, I asked Dr. Manning-Gibbs, "What do you do that feels meaningful or purposeful?"

"I think that really takes me into the realm of the work that I do in the prison," Dr. Manning-Gibbs replied. "I really do feel like my purpose is to help people who are underserved, who were counted out to re-evaluating, how they view themselves. It's easy sometimes when you're counted out by society for you to take on that judgment, it's easy sometimes for you to take on that negativity, and there's a term that I found myself dealing with in college, which is imposter syndrome. This is when you feel like you're a fraud, you're a phony—like you don't belong.

"In my situation specifically, I knew I could handle the work academically in college: I graduated obviously from high school; my SAT scores were strong enough for me to get into college; there were these concrete markers and indicators that made me say, 'Oh, okay, I can go onto a higher level of education.' But, when I got into college, there was this nagging sort of internal voice at times that started out as an external voice, which was coming from some of the adults in my life at that time saying, 'You know what, maybe you just want to go get a job.' 'You're a teenage mom. Maybe you don't want to go off to higher education.'

"So, it was an external voice, but then it turned into this internal voice I began hearing: 'Oh, really do I belong here? I'm doing well in college, but I'm still a teenage mom. Should I continue to pursue this?' And so, I think what really gives me meaning is just working from that space of helping my young men, even people in my practice that come in to see me that do have that imposter syndrome, helping them to see that, wow, I was once in your shoes and giving them really good therapeutic tools to help overcome that negative mental chatter."

Pulse Check: Recognizing the Abundant Factor *Dr. Manning-Gibbs*

So, based on the little information we have shared thus far, are you able to recognize Dr. Manning-Gibbs' abundant factor?

"Come on," as Professor Farrokh Langdana would say, "talk trade"—or in this case *excavation*— "language back to me." Well, let's start with the obvious: psychology. She is passionate about what she does in the field of psychology that must be it—right? As Farrokh would say "yeah" or in other words: not exactly. Although she is passionate about psychology that is merely the field that uses her abundant factor intensely. We will get to that in Step #2 on the Life Cycle of Excavation.

However, in order to recognize her abundant factor, we have to go back to Farrokh's example in class about Columbia. Remember when he said that *coffee was not the abundant factor*? The abundant factor that Columbia possesses is the *climate* that makes growing coffee possible. Dr. Manning-Gibbs' efforts along with her schooling produced a psychologist, but that is only because she had an environment within her that was conducive to growth within that field. So, what about *working with juveniles*? Again, that is an area where her abundant factor is expressed. To be completely honest, when I asked you about recognizing Dr. Manning-Gibbs' abundant factor it was a bit of a trick question. Because it wasn't until the next portion of the interview that her abundant factor was revealed.

Unpacking The 5P Framework: *Patterns*
Are You Listening?

"What can you call upon," I said continuing with the interview, "that you can say that people actually come to me because I'm naturally good at this thing?"

She did a quick glance into the air as if being careful to pull in the best thought. "I think it's just that I have this ability to listen very well. And that's a good thing for a psychologist, obviously directly. People are coming in and sometimes I feel very honored in my work, oftentimes because I've had countless people say, I'm telling you this for the first time, I'm sharing something with you that I've never said out loud before.

"So, sometimes just creating that space where somebody is feeling heard for the first time in their life when it comes to certain situations, I think that's definitely something that helps me to do my work very well. I think I, in some ways, well, maybe you as my older brother probably wouldn't agree with this, but I feel like I've always been a good listener. As a professional I hone that skill. But I think that's something that's always come sort of naturally to me, I've always been very inquisitive. I would sit there and look at a situation where you always were in church, and I always was a kid looking around and observing people around me.

"I may not engage them in conversation, but I'm there and I'm in tuned with them. I'm observing them very closely. So, I think that's something that comes naturally to me, and it works to my benefit, especially being a psychologist, because that's a big part of my work, helping people to feel heard and just really zoning in on what they have to say. It's like second nature to me to do that."

Did you recognize it yet? Were you able to see what her abundant factor is? Go back to the beginning of her response and see what she said initially after looking into the air. Go ahead and look. I'll wait here until you get back.

Great, so now you see that the answer to the question of what her abundant factor is appears right in that response, "I think it's just that I have this ability to listen very well." She is also empathetic to those who would feel a sense of judgment, which stems from her experience as a teenage mom and how that shaped her to be sensitive to others in similar positions where they feel judged. She honed that listening skill so much over the years that she became more in tune with her internal voice after she surrounded that voice with a healthy perspective.

"So, we have these patterns," I continued, "that I believe are also important. I see them as the natural tendencies we have. We know that we're naturally good at them, like for example, someone may be naturally good at mathematics, and someone may be good at athletics. What patterns can you recall that you find you've had that when you do X, you have success with it?"

Dr. Manning-Gibbs immediately responded, "When I bring my full-self to my work, and I'm not just drawing from my training [or] from the theoretical orientation that I've been trained in. When I bring my full-self to my work with my clients, or even my work with the young men in the prison, when I'm listening to my intuition, when I'm listening to my gut [and] also drawing from theory and research, I feel like I do my best work, because there are moments [when] you can't really pull from research, or you can't really say, okay this is what's happening specifically here based on my theoretical orientation.

"This isn't making sense diagnostically, but sometimes if you're just still, and just really listen to your internal voice, sometimes it really can be very impactful. It can really guide you. So, say for instance, I had a very powerful experience with a woman in my practice about five, six years ago, where in the middle of session, I felt like we were kind of getting off course. She was all over the place, where I was trying to like rein in what it is we were trying to fully understand, and in the midst of all that confusion that was coming up in the session, I felt like she was going off on tangents. I felt like she was trying to deviate from the question. I just was still in that moment, and something said to me, "Just mention her mom. When I just listened to my intuition and gut, when I mentioned her mom, she just broke down.

"What we were able to unpack in that session was that she was intentionally trying to throw me off course, trying to talk about X, Y, and Z. I would try to bring her back to the main point, and she [would] divert again. There was just something about me bringing up her mom that just broke her open in that moment, and that moment when I reflect on it again, I wasn't drawing from my theoretical orientation per se. It was just me saying, Okay, what's coming up in your spirit right now? What do you feel is the reason behind why she's trying to deviate from what we were supposed to be focused on? When I listen to my gut, my intuition, I feel like I really do my best work with my clients in those moments."

After interviewing my sister, I gained a deeper appreciation for the work she was doing both in the juvenile penal system, as well as her private practice. It was encouraging to see how her abundant factor was exposed with *Patterns* and *Purposefulness* questions from the Niche Finder 5Ps mentioned in the Framework. Though she exposed her abundant factor, my next guest on the *Niche Finder Podcast* helped me to see that our patterns could also become our proficiencies over time as well.

Excavation Exercise #1: Passion, Purposefulness, & Patterns

Let's see how this principle applies to you. Take a moment to complete this exercise, follow the instructions, and include those whom you feel will help to provide honest and supportive feedback. Save your score to reference alongside later sections.

Instructions	Quality Scoring Grid Directions				
• List 1-3 qualities you believe is—or has been—associated with you. These characteristics can be your opinion or statements that others have said about you relative to that particular 5P niche category. The qualities do not have to be written in any particular order.	Place a ranking from 1-5 (1 very weak quality; 5 very strong quality) for each quality you believe you have in you.				
• Complete the "self" segment on the quality scoring grid using the noted criteria.	**Quality Scoring Grid Result Range**				
	Strength Likelihood	Self	Family	Friend/ Mentor	Overall
• Ask a family member, trusted friend and/or mentor to give a score for each quality you have identified. If anyone adds a quality that you missed, you will need to place a score for that on the "self" segment.	Very Strong Quality	4-5	4-5	4-5	**12-15**
• Once complete, add up the totals for each quality. Use the Quality Scoring Grid Result Range to obtain the niche with the greatest quality concentration.	Strong Quality	3-4	3-4	3-4	**9-12**
	Moderate Quality	2-3	2-3	2-3	**6-9**
	Weak Quality	1-2	1-2	1-2	**3-6**
• Note: Your responses may repeat between categories. This may be helpful as it could be a strong quality. Your family, friend or mentor will confirm this for you if the score they provide you is also high.	Very Weak Quality	0-1	0-1	0-1	**0-3**

5P QUALITY CATEGORIES	Quality Scoring (1-5)			
PASSION: What do you love to do that ignites and/or excites you? (i.e.: Skillful at playing music, sports, doing well academically, etc.)	Self	Family	Friend/ Mentor	Total
Qualities 1.				
2.				
3.				
PURPOSEFUL: What do you do that adds value to others and/or a particular environment? (i.e.: Serving others at a food pantry, mentoring, teaching, etc.)	Self	Family	Friend/ Mentor	Total
Qualities 1.				
2.				
3.				
PATTERNS: What practice has been consistently successful for you over the years? (i.e.: Exercise, being calm in stressful situations, humor that puts others at ease, etc.)	Self	Family	Friend/ Mentor	Total
Qualities 1.				
2.				
3.				

Unpacking The 5P Framework: Passion, Pattern, & Proficiency

Introducing Dr. James Smith Jr. AKA: *Dr. Energy*

We first met in business school as he was one of the professors who specialized in how to provide outstanding presentations. His resume included over 20 years' experience of helping hundreds of thousands of people both internationally and nationally. His accolades also included being a personal power expert, educator, speaker, coach, author, blogger, and motivational keynote speaker. Dr. James Smith, Jr. was also known as *Doctor Energy* for the power he conveyed not only in his teaching style but also his inherent ability to hold the attention of his listeners. He referred to that quality as being *JIMPACTed*. After graduation, we stayed in contact, and he was gracious enough to take time out of his busy schedule to be one of my next guests on the *Niche Finder Podcast*. We pick up that interview where the principles of *Passions, Patterns,* and *Proficiency* built off one another on Dr. Smith's Journey.

Little Jimmy With The Big Head

"Now, I would like to drill down on your niche in this section," I said as Dr. James Smith and I continued our interview. "So, by niche, I'll give you a little bit of a background of this. I believe that when we look at successful people, we oftentimes hear them at awards ceremonies, or in some speech, they talk about that small little nugget that they had way back in the very beginning. When it was there in the beginning, a lot of people may have overlooked it. There was that one little thing that they did, but it seemed to be tethered to their success, and so instead of looking back, instead of doing it and kind of overlooking those small nuggets, we want to talk about them.

"So, your passions, things that you do that you feel purposeful; patterns, proficiencies, and problems people come to you to solve. This is what we call the 5P Framework, or the Niche Finder Framework. So, I would love to just get your thoughts on going back to your very beginning. In other words, this is your current self, talking to your younger self. What kind of passions did you have, or strong interests do you see you had in your younger self, that you currently say, 'This is a superpower of mine in my current self?'"

Dr. Smith threw his head back and smiled as if his body was saying to the question, I was made for this moment.

"Phenomenal question," he replied. "This is easy for me. I'll give you two examples of the past and how it plays a role in the now. My teachers in grade school would always say, 'Sit down and be quiet. James, sit down and be quiet.' Now, I would get good grades, citizenship, and get my work done—whatever the subject. But when it came to work habits:

I'm running my mouth. I'm getting up; I'm the class clown; I make people laugh. [My teachers would say:] 'Sit down James!'"

"...There it is. I'm now fifty-nine years old and I'm still running my mouth inspiring people, making it happen. So, that was at ages six, seven, eight, nine I was doing that. I'm still doing it now—although I've cultivated my approach—but there was a degree of getting out there; speaking what's on my mind; lifting people up—elevating them. Modeling a message.

"So, I did that a long time ago and here's another example, Clifton. Long story real short:

"My baseball team was in the championship, and the age for this league was ten to twelve. I was twelve years old at the time, and my nickname was *Little Jimmy with the Big Head*. Yeah. I had a big head on this skinny body. Huge...but that's alright cuz one day I would grow into it.

"But we're in the championship game. The series is a tie-one game to one. We're in the bottom of the seventh. We only played seven innings then and we were in the bottom of the seventh with the scores tied 1-to-1. The series is also tied 1-to-1 and it's the best two out of three.

"I lead off. I get a base hit. 'Yeah!' but now I'm on first base and I'm thinking, I'm going to be the hero. So, I look at my coach whether I should steal and go to second. He gave me the signals that said, 'stay where you are,' and I didn't go.

The next guy up struck out. So, I looked at my coach again. He gives me the signals again. Don't steal.

"Next guy, pop-up to the pitcher—it's two outs. I'm still on first, and my coach is playing it safe. Alright. So, this is little Jimmy with the Big Head. Knowing that one day he's going to be interviewed by Clifton on his podcast, motivational speaker. He needs a story.

"So, I ran, and I stole second—safe! And the coach gave me that look. I'm on second, I'm in scoring position. The coach is admonishing me not to try to steal third. The next guy came up, he crushed it! On a line-base hit the center field, one hop. The center fielder picked it up and motioned himself to throw into home.

"Now, I'm rounding third, and my coach said, 'No!' and I had to give him one of those 'Whatchu talkin' bout Willis?' looks as I rounded third, and I'm running for home. Now, Clifton, I see the ball beat me, and the catcher has the ball, and I'm halfway there. Now, here's where I digress; this is age ten to twelve. Their catcher looks like he's twenty-five. He has a moustache; he has a little beard. He's like six-two; his chest protector doesn't fit; he doesn't have any lay guards on, and he looks like Shaquille O'Neal's son. He was Baby Shaq. Throughout the season I would always tell my coach, 'Get his birth certificate. He's old!'"

"So, I'm rounding third, coming in Baby Shaq has the ball looking like he's thirty-seven years old, and I knew that if I slid, I was out. If I just slowed up, I was out. This man looks like my grandfather. However, the only way I can conceivably create an opportunity for me to be safe is to knock him down.

"Again, about twelve years old, I'm skinny Jimmy with the Big Head, but I got Baby Shaq in front of me. But Clifton, I ran in almost like a Rocky movie, and I ran into him like ice cream on a sweltering day running down an ice cream cone. I just slithered down: fell down. I was in major pain and called for the ambulance and my teammates said, 'Touch the plate, touch the plate!' So, I touched a plate. The umpire came over and said, 'You are safe!' "What? What happened?" Dr. Smith said looking around.

"What happened was," he continued, "Baby Shaq, upon my feeble impact, dropped the ball. Wow. So, I was safe. We won the game and the championship; I'm the hero. That story in itself describes how I live my life. I go hard. Where there's an obstacle, I see an opportunity; where there's a problem, I see a possibility and I go in and we'll see what happens and that was at twelve years old. I'm fifty-nine and I haven't changed my approach. I'm going in hard to create possibilities for myself. *It's what I do*.

Pulse Check: Recognizing the Abundant Factor *Dr. Smith*

Okay, last point before we see how *problem-solving* connects to Step #1: *Recognize Your Abundant Factor.* No tricks this time–I promise. Can you identify from what we have covered so far of what Dr. Smith's abundant factor is? What do the two stories about skinny Jimmy with the Big Head expose? Let's unpack this—shall we?

Dr. Smith's *passions* were revealed in his love for speaking as an elementary school student. He also had a *pattern* of being funny, respectful, and a good student. Overtime, he found that these two qualities led to a *proficiency* of being able to lift people up and as he put it "elevate them" as he began "modeling a message." This story uncovered three of the 5P Framework in his elementary school class, but what about on the field?

Here is where we will find him personifying one of my favorite quotes by Leonard Ravenhill, "the opportunity of a lifetime must be seized within the lifetime of the opportunity." As he is standing on base in the last game of a championship series that is tied one-to-one, he understood that although his coach was playing it safe, there was a moment that measured his instinct and ability against the opposition at hand.

Obviously, his primary opposition was against the other team, but in this moment he was also up against his coach's decision to have him remain on the baseball plate.

Some may see this as defiance; however, I believe it was the birth of his entrepreneurial mindset up against an early indication of what one may have to do when confronted with an opposing force standing between them and their opportunity. Do you run towards that goal or play it safe? We will flesh this point out further in Step # 4 *Specialize in offering what is helpful to others but unique to you* and Step # 6 *Organize the delivery of your niche to a wider audience,* as we continue through the *Life Cycle of Excavation* later.

However, when he circled third base and ran into the catcher, it was more than just two bodies impacting one another. No, it was at this very moment that his passion to pursue his goals, pattern of exposing his unique abilities and proficiency of uplifting others—in this case his team—also collided. These qualities from times past are what helped to shape the fifty-nine-year-old version of himself that, as he put it, is "still making it happen." My next guest, Dr. Owen Legaspi, helped to reveal the last important quality of the Niche Finder Framework of *problem-solving*.

Excavation Exercise #2: *Proficiency*

Here is another commercial break on this point. Let us see how this principle applies to you. Dr. Smith's section covered *Passion, Pattern and Proficiency.* However, you only have to complete proficiency being that Excavation Exercise #1 covered the other two. Take a moment to complete this exercise, follow the instructions, and include those whom you feel will help to provide honest and supportive feedback. Save your score to reference alongside later sections.

Instructions	Quality Scoring Grid Directions				
• List 1-3 qualities you believe is—or has been—associated with you. These characteristics can be your opinion or statements that others have said about you relative to that particular 5P niche category. The qualities do not have to be written in any particular order.	Place a ranking from **1-5** (1 very weak quality; **5** very strong quality) for each quality you believe you have in you.				
	Quality Scoring Grid Result Range				
	Strength Likelihood	Self	Family	Friend/ Mentor	Overall
• Complete the "self" segment on the quality scoring grid using the noted criteria.	Very Strong Quality	4-5	4-5	4-5	<u>12-15</u>
• Ask a family member, trusted friend and/or mentor to give a score for each quality you have identified. If anyone adds a quality that you missed, you will need to place a score for that on the "self" segment.	Strong Quality	3-4	3-4	3-4	<u>9-12</u>
• Once complete, add up the totals for each quality. Use the Quality Scoring Grid Result Range to obtain the niche with the greatest quality concentration.	Moderate Quality	2-3	2-3	2-3	<u>6-9</u>
• Note: Your responses may repeat between categories. This may be helpful as it could be a strong quality. Your family, friend or mentor will confirm this for you if the score they provide you is also high.	Weak Quality	1-2	1-2	1-2	<u>3-6</u>
	Very Weak Quality	0-1	0-1	0-1	<u>0-3</u>

PROFICIENT: What do you do well that comes easy for you? (i.e.: Writing, public speaking, getting preschoolers to respond to your instructions, etc.)		Self	Family	Friend/ Mentor	Total
Qualities	1.				
	2.				
	3.				

Unpacking The 5P Framework: Problem-solving
We Now Welcome *Dr. Owen Legaspi*

We initially met because a torn meniscus in my right knee led to poor body mechanics that eventually threw my back out. I was referred to Dr. Owen Legaspi by another physician who highly recommended him. He and his practice not only helped me to recover but also helped me to become stronger with a greater awareness of my body than I ever had before. I was grateful to have him as one of my guests on the Niche Finder podcasts to talk about how he got into his field. At the time of the interview, Dr. Legaspi had established three successful physical therapy practices, received the George J. Davies James A. Gould Excellence in Clinical Inquiry Award, and was a serial entrepreneur.[20]

In this interview, he shared how he grew up poor but didn't realize that he was because his parents created such a nurturing environment for him and his siblings. About fifteen years earlier, at the age of twenty-three, his entrepreneurial fervor had him in business for himself with three successful businesses in operations under his belt. This success is what brought him to a moment where he was seated across the table from his accountant who asked him one simple question: What do you want to do in life right now? We pick up at this point of the interview with his response.

Fight the Big Guy

"My accountant pretty much said," Dr. Legaspi remarked as he adjusted the angle of his laptop to improve the view of the screen, "'what do you want to do in life right now? You're doing well for a twenty-three-year-old, if you want to just take in the passive income, you'd be well off.' I said to myself, you know what? I think this is my chance to technically do something more fulfilling rather than just being monetarily or financially driven.

"So, I said, maybe helping people through medicine may be the route for me, since I'm going to have a passive income anyways. I want to be fulfilled…. people always say, 'I want to help people.' However, I think part of helping people is also self-fulfilling for myself, because there is much gratitude and accomplishments in helping humankind in general."

This conversation helped to expose what I liked about Dr. Legaspi as he was both sincere and transparent. To drill deeper into the topic I then asked, "What were you strongly interested in when you were starting your journey?"

"Once I became a Doctor of Physical Therapy," Dr. Legaspi replied, "I definitely applied some of the knowledge I had in business. The first question I asked myself was, how do I become good in medicine? So, I told myself that I'm going to work in a hospital for a couple of years, get a chance to see the worst cases ever, and not be afraid of it.

"Once I got hired in the hospital, I sought for the hardest cases. I was hungry for that. I thought that if I can fix the people in the hardest cases, then I could fix anybody. My co-workers would shy away from that because they didn't want to spend their days dealing with those kinds of people. They wanted a nine-to-five.

"This was the difference between me and them. That's what eventually allowed me to move up into the hospital hierarchy. I also had a lot of the physicians telling me they wanted to send me their patients because I wasn't afraid of the challenge and that I would get them better. Now, how did I get them better? Hard cases. Hard cases made me learn; because they're the people that you need to put your heart and soul into: your clinical, academic training, and everything else in. Now when *they* get better, it's more rewarding.

"When I was a young kid, I was a little bit of a fighter. I did a little bit of mixed martial arts or MMA. I loved fighting big guys and I always told myself, if I fight the big guy, and he knocks me out, it's supposed to happen. I'll get in there and fight the big guy. If I knock him out, I'm a *victor*. It's the same when it came to the hospital. I wanted the hard cases and if I didn't do anything better, at least I made my best effort—it wasn't expected.

"But if I fixed them, then that would be super impressive. The doctors in the hospitals then encouraged me to start my own business. I did, and now I have a following."

I found myself nodding in agreement and remarked, "Sounds like your passions sort of tied into your willingness to want to help the people who needed the greatest help. As if you wanted to be a great resource to their great need. That's what I'm hearing you say. Is that correct?"

Dr. Legaspi replied, "For me, if you want to be great, you got to think of the hardest challenges. I think that was ingrained in me earlier on in my life. I came here from the Philippines. I was a skinny kid. I was picked on…. though I was picked on, at one point or another, I had to wake up and forget the excuses.

"I took my punches and I got something out of it. I learned from it. In actuality, the same people that used to beat me up became my buddies because they knew [if I got knocked down I would] get up and stand up. It's not how you fall. It's how you get up."

Pulse Check: Recognizing the Abundant Factor *Dr. Owen Legaspi*

So here we go, let's put our REMBA thinking cap back on or as Farrokh would say, "Stay with me here." So far, we have identified the different components of the 5P Framework and how each of the five elements relate to Step # 1: *Recognize Your Abundant Factor*. We uncovered Step #1 with Dr. Manning-Gibbs underscoring *Passions* and *Purposefulness*, while Dr. Smith's story of *Little Jimmy with the Big Head* highlighted *Patterns* and *Proficiency*. Now, let's spin our drill a little further into Dr. Legaspi's interview. As you were reading, did you come across any rumblings of a potential geyser here? By that I mean, were you able to see Dr. Legaspi's abundant factor? Before you go back and take a quick look, let's take a commercial break on this.

I think by now you see that we have a bit of a theme happening with our interaction. In brief, the goal of these exercises is to establish that if we can tighten the lens on the journey of others, we may be able to bring our own qualities that cross connect with these experts into clearer view. We will shine a brighter light on this landscape when we pick up the conversation with Miss Charlie and cover *Step # 3 Summarize Your Comparative Advantage*. With that said, let's go back to the pulse check of Dr. Legaspi.

We have learned thus far from Dr. Legaspi's story that he was a twenty-three-year-old entrepreneur who went into medicine and had a brief stint as a fighter in mixed martial arts. Although I had the *problem-solving* topic listed on my interview sheet to ask Dr. Legaspi, he beat me to the punch with that question. That is not surprising considering his Mixed Martial Arts (MMA) background.

However, what is his abundant factor? Is it business management, medicine, or MMA? Let's fast-forward to the end that none of these are his abundant factor for reasons already established in prior pulse checks. What made these areas successful? If we start with MMA, his journey towards becoming successful was having the desire to take on the *big guy*—or the greatest available challenge. He also carried this mindset over to medicine. This benefited him in two ways: First, it caused him to work harder—through research and honed techniques—at helping people and secondly, it caused him to stand out from his peers who sidestepped these cases.

So, in short, the way he contends against challenges is his abundant factor. This is confirmed when we see the picture of his younger self fighting against the big guy, getting knocked down but rising again. As he put it, "It's not how you fall. It's how you get up." It's no coincidence that physicians encouraged him to pursue opening his own practice, as well as rivals becoming friendly with him after seeing this mindset.

After all, who doesn't want to root for the skinny kid who gets knocked down but rises again? Now that we've established the value of recognizing your abundant factor, let's see how to benefit from *optimizing where that niche is used intensely.*

Excavation Exercise #3: *Problem-solving*

Okay, last segment of the 5P Framework. Please take a moment to complete this exercise, follow the instructions, and include those whom you feel will help to provide honest and supportive feedback. Save your score to reference alongside later sections.

Instructions	Quality Scoring Grid Directions			
• List 1-3 qualities you believe is—or has been—associated with you. These characteristics can be your opinion or statements that others have said about you relative to that particular 5P niche category. The qualities do not have to be written in any particular order.	Place a ranking from **1-5** (1 very weak quality; **5** very strong quality) for each quality you believe you have in you.			
	Quality Scoring Grid Result Range			
• Complete the "self" segment on the quality scoring grid using the noted criteria.	Strength Likelihood	Self	Family	Friend/Mentor	Overall
• Ask a family member, trusted friend and/or mentor to give a score for each quality you have identified. If anyone adds a quality that you missed, you will need to place a score for that on the "self" segment.	Very Strong Quality	4-5	4-5	4-5	**12-15**
	Strong Quality	3-4	3-4	3-4	**9-12**
• Once complete, add up the totals for each quality. Use the Quality Scoring Grid Result Range to obtain the niche with the greatest quality concentration.	Moderate Quality	2-3	2-3	2-3	**6-9**
	Weak Quality	1-2	1-2	1-2	**3-6**
• Note: Your responses may repeat between categories. This may be helpful as it could be a strong quality. Your family, friend or mentor will confirm this for you if the score they provide you is also high.	Very Weak Quality	0-1	0-1	0-1	**0-3**

PROBLEM SOLVING: What pain points do others call upon you to fix? (i.e.: Taking the appropriate lead on things, people confide in you for advice, volunteering, etc.)		Self	Family	Friend/Mentor	Total
Qualities	1.				
	2.				
	3.				

Chapter 4

Step # 2: Optimize Where

Your Niche Is Used Intensely

Change The Frame

A t first glance when you look at the following pictures, which one do you believe has the highest value? I'll give you three clues. The first hint is that they are both pictures by famed artist Claude Monet. The second is that both images displayed have a noteworthy price tag: one is valued at $40,000-$50,000 and the other sold for $110.07 million dollars. Lastly, I took the liberty of digitally adding frames to each photo. Now, look at both pictures. Can you tell which one was valued higher?

Example A

Example B

As you think about it, I'll explain the point of this exercise and reveal the answer to the question. At the start of the book, we touched upon breaking the jar or adopting a mindset that is conducive to growth. This is somewhat the same coin, just a different side.

Changing the frame is about how we see the value that we have to offer. Going back to the pictures exampled above, there are two sets of values that can be placed on each example. When you look at them, there is the value of the painting and the value of the frame. In Example A, the frame was randomly selected by me off Target.com and I digitally placed the image in it.[21]

However, the 1890 "Meules" original oil painting by Claude Monet sold for: $110.7 million at Sotheby's (May 14, 2019). Example B's frame, on the other hand, was more expensive. Brad Shar, Vice president of Julius Lowy Frame and Restoring Company in New York, noted it as being "a rare 16th-century Italian frame with delicate gold stenciling against a black finish, is itself valued between $40,000 and $50,000."

Illustration 1

Leonardo da Vinci's 'Salvator Mundi'[22]

In fact, this particular black frame once housed Leonardo Da Vinci's *Salvator Mundi,* which at the time of this writing, was the most expensive art work ever sold at an auction.[23] On November 15, 2017, the work of art sold at Christie's for $450.3 million. This far exceeded Pablo Picasso's, *Les Femmes d'Alger* ("Version O"), 1955, which sold for $179.4 million at Christie's (May 11, 2015). This is about seven decimal points outside of my taste, but not so in environments where art lovers have the money to spend. After all, there are only twenty art pieces by da Vinci known to be in existence.

Illustration 1 is the original depiction of that painting inside of the $50,000 frame I took the liberty of using for Example B. However, the picture of the canvas print that I digitally placed in the $50,000 frame was available—at the time of this writing—for $69.00 at Target.com. That canvas print of Claude Monet's 1916 *Water Lilies* painting is shown in Illustration 2 below. Incidentally, if you are one of the art lovers with a bank account that supports 7 decimal point taste, you may be pleased to know that one version of Monet's water lilies oil painting did hit the auction block. *Nymphéas en fleur* (Water Lilies in Bloom), 1914-1917 sold on May 8th, 2018 at Christie's New York for $84.6 million dollars.[24]

Illustration 2[25]

I digress but the point here is this: If you put an expensive piece of artwork inside of an inexpensive frame, an untrained eye may devalue the overall perception—or perceived value—of that piece of art. As we get back into the flow of the Discover phase of the *Life Cycle of Excavation*, I want to encourage you from the onset of Step # 2 *Optimize Where Your Niche is Used Intensely*. The value that you have to offer is important. However, it is equally important that it is framed in environments that also appreciate its perceived value. I liken this matching of inherent worth with complementary environments to the method curators used for framing artwork starting in 1994. Frame conservator Gene Karraker for J. Paul Getty Museum noted, "Even at that point, the reasoning by the curators and the conservators is that when reframing was done, they wanted to fit the period of the frame with the period of the painting—either by country, by region, by date,"[26]

So, were you able to match the correct value point with the right picture? If you did, great. If you didn't, don't worry the goal of the exercise is really to shape our perspective. Breaking the jar at the start of the book was to lay the groundwork for putting in the work from the beginning with a mindset positioned for growth. Changing the Frame is understanding that what we have to offer is important enough to place in environment(s) that can appreciate—and highlight—its worth. As we enter back into the *Life Cycle of Excavation* let's see how an insurance salesperson benefited from optimizing where his niche was used intensely.

"I was born tonight."

–Steve Harvey

On October 8, 1985, an insurance salesperson named Steve Harvey went to an event that changed the trajectory of his life. It happened at a comedy club where his friend Gladys dared him to perform. Steve Harvey stated at that point in his life that he did not even know what a comedy club was, but Gladys urged him to go with her to perform at the open mic as she believed he was the funniest person she had ever met.[27]

At that point in his life, he was miserable going to a job he did not like and felt as though he had no purpose. When he walked into the comedy club for the first time, he put his name on the open mic list for the following week once he saw that they had the ten comedians listed for the night.

He was twenty-seven at the time, and although he felt he was funny, he wanted to see what he could learn from those who were more experienced in this unique environment. He sat through nine of the comedians but did not find any of them entertaining. He knew the punchline before they gave it, thought of an even better punchline that was much funnier, and began wishing that he could be up on the stage entertaining the audience.

When the time came for comedian number ten—the last comedian of the night—to do their set that person was nowhere to be found. When the comedy club amateur night host called the person's name, he was no longer there. The host then decided that he was going to go to the sign-up list for the next week. He then called his name, "Steve Harvey come up to the stage." Steve Harvey took the stage, and his performance was amazing as he nailed his jokes and walked away as the winner of that night's comedy club competition. On the 45-minute ride home with Gladys, Steve Harvey said that he could not stop crying and Gladys could not understand why he was getting so emotional over winning $50. However, the emotion was not because of the money but resulted from him seeing what he wanted to do as a career.

He responded, "No, no, you don't even understand. I was born tonight. I now know what I'm supposed to do." The next day on October 9, 1985, Steve Harvey walked into the job that he worked at as an insurance agent and handed in his resignation with only $50 to his name in his pocket.

Can others help you to see where your abundant factor is used intensely?

The decision to quit his job and pursue comedy had Steve Harvey living out of his 1976 Ford Tempo for the next three years.[28] He worked odd jobs and slept in his vehicle when he did comedy gigs that did not provide a hotel room for him. Additionally, when hotel facility bathrooms were not available, he would wash up every other day at gas stations or public pool showers.[29] Although discouraging at times, this rough patch of his life did not deter him from pursuing these comedy clubs and talent show environments where his abundant factor was used intensely. His friend Gladys saw something in him that compelled her to encourage him to take the stage.

When he quit his job on October 9th, 1985, Steve Harvey's boss initially talked him out of quitting once he found out that he was leaving to pursue a career in comedy.[30] Steve Harvey's coworker, Russell Middlebrooks, saw him walking back to his desk with belongings in hand and looking dejected. Russell walked over to him and said, "Aey Harv, I thought you were quitting today, man?"

"Nah," Steve said, "I talked to Tom, and he said that I wasn't funny."

"He don't know you," Russell replied. "Dawg, you the funniest dude I know… I can't believe you letting him tell you what to do." Steve eventually agreed with him and went back into his boss's office to resubmit his resignation for the last time. Russell saw something in Steve that his boss didn't because that environment did not use his abundant factor intensely. In fact, Steve's boss, Tom, had never even heard Steve Harvey say anything funny. Russell, on the other hand, saw that Steve had an abundant factor that needed to be placed where it was used intensely.

Step #2 Optimize Where Your Niche is Used Intensely:
Steve Harvey

So, what is the significance of connecting our niche with an environment that utilizes it intensely? Let us quickly look at this aspect of Steve Harvey's journey to see if we can uncover the answer to this question. Before becoming an American actor, bestselling author, television and radio personality, Steve Harvey took the leap into the area where his niche was used intensely. Prior to that leap he tried being a mail carrier, boxer, and insurance agent. None of the latter areas used his niche intensely. However, that first amateur comedy night win ignited a passion in him to seek more venues where his abundant factor would be on display. He did as many comedy clubs and talent shows as he could.

During that season of his life, Steve Harvey said that only one of his family members believed he could make it in comedy. That one person was his father. He was funny himself but, in those days, venues that used his father's talents intensely were not as accessible for Blacks. He was born in 1914 and his father—Steve Harvey's grandfather—was a slave until he was twelve. It was a different time where becoming successful at something as specialized as comedy was a long shot. However, Steve's father encouraged his pursuit by saying this, "Son, if you think you can make it, get on out there and get discovered."

Did you see it? The answer to the question? *What is the significance to placing our niche in environments that utilize it intensely?* If you look back, it's right there in Steve Harvey's father's response, "Son, if you think you can make it, get on out there and get discovered."

Okay, maybe it wasn't blatantly obvious but the wisdom behind increasing the possibility of success by placing what we have to offer in an environment that best appreciates it, is enveloped in that statement. If we look back to the twenty-seven-year-old Steve who felt he had no purpose, what do we see? There you will find a man with untapped potential inside of an environment which did not use his abundant factor—or niche—intensely.

As an insurance agent, Steve Harvey's coworker, Russell, saw the mismatch between Steve's talent and being an insurance agent. Gladys also discerned that

Steve's talent needed to be in an environment that would fully appreciate it. It wasn't until Steve stepped into that environment that he realized what he was born to do. If we burrow deeper into his statement of being born tonight, we will find one word that encapsulates why that moment happened and it's: Resonance.

The Law of Sympathetic Resonance

Let us stop drilling for a moment and shift our attention to a phenomenon that happens in music. I first learned about the principle of sympathetic resonance from Pastor AR Bernard of the Christian Cultural Center located in Brooklyn, New York. Earlier on in my leadership career, I would listen to his messages on my way to work as they provided both spiritual understanding and inspiration at the start of my day. We will delve into this principle of being ignited in Step # 6 *Organize the Delivery of Your Niche to a Wider Audience* when we cover the I.D.R.E.A.M. principles.

Dr. Bernard was a skillful orator who made his Biblical lessons practical and understandable. On one occasion, he shared the law of sympathetic resonance, and the topic caught my attention. In this example, he explained what happens if you have a room of stringed instruments and only one of these instruments strings is plucked. He said the other stringed instruments would begin to resonate at the same frequency that was played even though they have not been touched.

Fascinated by this principle, I scoured the internet looking for more information on this topic. I found one musician who shared an example of sympathetic resonance where he used his left index finger to slowly depress one of the keys on his newly tuned piano.[31] He did it in a way to ensure that the piano did not play the note that he was holding down. As the musician continued to depress that piano key with his left hand, he used his right hand to play random notes on the keys to the right. When he stopped playing with his right hand, there was a hum of several notes coming from the one string that was connected to the key being depressed by his left hand.

The musician then played notes to the right of that key, which were higher tones and played at random. When he took his right hand off the keys the key that was still depressed with his left finger began resonating the sounds of the keys that were just played, although he had not played a note on the depressed key.

I believe this phenomenon happens to us as individuals as well. For instance, place random people in a room that's being provided a single inspiration to the audience. Even if you have—for example—an artist, an architect, and an athlete in that room, the inspiration furnished will resonate with everyone at the frequency that person is in tune with. That single inspiration can motivate the artist to paint a picture, an architect to create an innovative design, and give an athlete motivation to play her best game. Although they were not physically touched, there was something that resonated within them.

On the same topic of sympathetic resonance, I uncovered another video of a scientist explaining this principle with a tuning fork that was tuned to the frequency of 440 Hertz.[32] When he struck the tuning fork with a rubber mallet it began making a humming sound. He then dampened that sound by placing his right hand over it and stopped the hum.

Shortly thereafter, he brought another identical tuning fork that was tuned to the same frequency within proximity of the one to his right that he had just dampened. He struck the tuning fork to the right, and it began humming again.

However, this time when he used his hands to stop the sound of the tuning fork to his right, the tuning fork to his left—that had not been touched—continued humming. Because both tuning forks had the same 440 Hertz resonant frequency, when he dampened the tuning fork to his right although it stopped making a sound the tuning fork to the left that was not touched hummed the sound of the original tuning fork. Was this principle on display in Steve Harvey's example when he found an environment that used his abundant factor intensely? Possibly, yes.

A quote that Steve Harvey often states by Albert Einstein helps to paint a clearer picture. Einstein said, "Your imagination is everything. It is the preview of life's coming attractions." Could it be that inspiration has a frequency that is tuned to the same frequency of our imaginations? We may all have different pictures that get painted from that frequency as in the depiction of the artist, architect, and athlete example. The pictures may differ, but the principle behind resonance providing a glimpse of where our niche could be used intensely may still be there. To help us understand this aspect a little more, let's head back to the early 1990s to speak about a few guys name Mike.

Like Mike?

In the 1990s, there were two men named Mike who dominated the sports arena at the start of the decade. They were Michael Jordan in basketball and Mike Tyson in the boxing ring. Although at this time the two men rose to the top of their sport, their teenage journey into their respective field

117

of play was starkly different. The basketball phenomenon known as Michael Jordan was infamously denied a spot on his high school varsity basketball team.

The 5-foot 10 inch fifteen-year-old Michael initially responded to that rejection with tears of frustration, but his desire to have his talents displayed in an environment that used them intensely seemed to reverberate a deeper resolve within him. [33] After missing out on the only varsity slot available that year, he feverishly worked twice as hard to play at his best on a junior varsity team. As a result, there were times where he scored 40 or more points in a game.

He remarked in an interview with ESPN, "Whenever I was working out and got tired and figured I ought to stop, I'd close my eyes and see that [varsity basketball player] list in the locker room without my name on it," Jordan said, "and that usually got me going again."[34] Michael Jordan's abundant factor of tenacity coupled with his athletic abilities attracted the attention of many once they were placed in an environment that used them intensely. That sophomore year drew the attention of local fans packing out junior varsity high school gymnasiums.

The following year he not only made the varsity team but his twenty points per game average also caught the eyes of the collegiate basketball community.[35] Before the start of his senior year of high school, he had been recruited into the

North Carolina University basketball program where he would go on to play three years and made history by bringing the school their first National Collegiate Athletic Association (NCAA) championship with Jordan scoring the winning shot.

Before becoming the National Basketball League's (NBA) Rookie of the Year in 1984, 6-time NBA champion with a record 6 NBA Finals Most Valuable Player Award, and hold the standing record of having 10 NBA scoring title awards—just to name a few—Michael Jordan tuned into the frequency of the environment that utilized his niche intensely.[36] Many teenagers with similar aspirations as Jordan could have given up on their dreams of playing varsity basketball after being rejected out of sheer juvenile frustration. However, Michael Jordan persisted so that even when that high school motivation was dampened—just like the tuning fork—his career carried the tune that has become a source of inspiration to individuals around the world.

Where Michael Jordan's initial high school varsity rejection came in conflict with his internal motivation, Mike Tyson's teenage journey into boxing was opposite in comparison. In an interview with GQ sports, Mike Tyson noted online reports of him being discovered at the Tryon School for Boys in Johnstown, New York by Bobby Stewart as being true.

At that point in his life, Tyson had been arrested thirty-eight times by the age of thirteen but the counselor, Bobby Stewart, saw something special in him.

Tyson remarked, "Bobby Stewart was the first person that ever discovered that I had any kind of talent and showed me that I had ability to do anything...as a young kid I didn't think that it was anything I was capable of doing. I didn't think that I had a purpose in this world. I didn't really care about being in this world at that time in my life. He introduced me to [Renown boxing trainer] Cus D'Amato and I started going to school and started improving as a person...boxing gave me the confidence to do things that I never believed that I could do before."[37] That confidence helped to make Mike Tyson the youngest heavyweight boxing champion at the age of twenty-year. His 5-feet 11 inch 218-pound frame was homed by his trainers in a way that highlighted his natural abilities while in a ring that utilized them intensely.

Mike Tyson serendipitously ended up in the right environment, but that environment began to resonate a sound that made him want to echo greatness. As a result, he is known as one of the top ten greatest heavyweight boxers of all times.

Which Mike Example Would You Choose?

So, out of the two examples shared about Mike Tyson and Michael Jordan which one would you choose? Would you want to use inspiration as a driver towards success or would you prefer someone pointing out your potential to help push you in the right direction? Neither are better or worse; simply different.

Between these two divergent paths, however, there is one key similarity: when given the opportunity, both men optimized their abilities in the environments that used their abilities intensely. Both worked hard at honing their crafts within their respective field in the pursuit of mastery. Although they both were ushered into their opportunities differently, these environments gave them a chance to display that excellence.

This is incidentally supported by scientific evidence. We will cover this at the end of Step # 2 in the section entitled the *Science Behind Inspiration*. When inspired, what image is painted for you of your future? Do you see yourself hitting the game winning shot, having bestselling author at the top of the cover of your book, or are you the one holding the scalpel to begin a lifesaving surgery? Whatever that picture may be, which Einstein called *a preview of coming attractions,* it is our responsibility to ensure that we put in the work. After you have *Recognized Your Abundant Factor* in Step # 1, when you get to Step # 2 it is important to put in the work and *Optimize Where Your Niche is Used Intensely*. According to Dr. James Smith, this is important to prevent us from handing out bullets.

From Resonance Back to Energy

"...don't give people bullets because they already have guns." –Dr. James Smith

Dr. James Smith shared further insight during our interview that embodied this point of matching diligence and effort with environments that utilize our niche intensely. He said he learned a valuable lesson from his mother about work ethic. Dr. Smith remarked, "A long time ago that person I said poured into me: My Mom. She said, 'don't give people bullets because they already have guns.' Which meant to me, don't give them reasons to say you can't be on the team. You can't be on the project; you can't move forward with us. So, one of my patterns is never to make an excuse; never to be late. Never to not fulfill every assignment that I've been given. Not to do what I've been asked because if I do that, I'm giving them bullets. I'm not going to give you a reason to exclude me.

"Number two, a pattern has been to not only be there early, be in the front row and tilt the room when you walk in." Dr. Smith lifted his hand palm facing down before him and leaned his body to one side as he said this. "Where they know you're there. In life they say some people light up a room when they walk in; some people light up the room when they walk out. I want to be that person who lights up the room, who tilts the floor, who makes a *difference*—upon entry. You're gonna feel me, that's another pattern.

"And you know Clifton," Dr. Smith continued, "I know that:

"I know where I live.

"I know organizations.

"I know that institutionalized isms are there.

"I know that some people are intimidated by virtue of what I look like—what I sound like. [So, I want to be the type of person] to not just make them feel comfortable but make them feel safe to want to pour in, want to ask those questions. There are so many things operating during meetings, training, podcasts, Zoom calls or webinars, I'm working overtime during the session and working overtime after the session. But there are a lot of things [like] emotional intelligence, social intelligence that are going on to get people open to receive my gift.

"…Want to embrace it and want more from it. So those are the patterns. I know that the world is not equal. Darn? What am I going to say: here are the cards that I have—play them. This is the hand that I've been given—play them. If I go 'victim' or 'woe is me,' I'm not taking advantage of the opportunity that's afforded."

Dr. Smith's story here highlights the fact that even when inspiration comes to us, we then have the option of not only acting upon that motivation but pursuing mastery after we have been stimulated. When you are inspired to the point of resonance, are you acting on it or do you dampen the sound? As I continued to boar into the subject of inspiration, I came across research that supported the work ethic Dr. Smith admonished: "*...don't give people bullets because they already have guns.*"

The Science Behind Inspiration

While researching the topic of inspiration, I came across an article in *The Harvard Business Review* (HBR) entitled, "Why Inspiration Matters." It highlighted the research of psychologists Todd M. Thrash and Andrew Elliot who created the Inspiration Scale (IS). Where the term inspiration traditionally has been seen as something subjective or elusive, these researchers dove deep into this topic and helped to put some meat on the bones of what we covered in this chapter.[38]

This article defined inspiration—based on the research of Thrash and Elliot—as being both "inspired by something and acting on that inspiration."[39] If we tie this back to the law of sympathetic resonance, this is like having both tuning forks being tuned to the same frequency. The frequency leaving tuning fork A that hit tuning fork B had an affect that the high school version of Michael Jordan depicted. He was *inspired by* the reality that he didn't make his varsity team that sophomore year. Visualizing his name not being on the varsity basketball list for the coming year motivated him to *act on* that image by working hard to achieve that goal. However, the teenage selves of Michael Jordan and Mike Tyson epitomized the other principles of the research indicative among those inspired as well: (a) mastery of their work (b) absorption of tasks (c) increased creativity (d) perceived competence (e) higher levels of self-esteem and (f) greater sense of optimism.[40] Although mastery of their work could lead one to believe that being competitive was tantamount in fulfilling the evoked inspiration, the research states otherwise. The HBR article further stated "[i]nspired individuals also reported having a stronger drive to master their work but were less competitive.... Inspired people were more intrinsically motivated and less extrinsically motivated, variables that also strongly impact work performance."[41]

Although both Mike Tyson and Michael Jordan were known as fierce competitors, the inspiration they received at that point in their lives focused their attention on mastering *themselves* before they even stepped foot in front of a competitor. They were ready for their moment, but they also showed the importance of Step #3 on the Life Cycle of Excavation *Summarize Your Comparative Advantage.*

Chapter 5

Step # 3: Summarize Your Comparative Advantage

Here's the way you identify your gift: Your gift is the thing that you do absolute best with the least amount of effort.
–Steve Harvey[42]

Comparative advantage is an exchange not a competition.

Heading back into the REMBA classroom, Professor Farrokh Langdana stood before us at the start of our second class for our last week in residency. He had a relaxed pose as he leaned against the podium next to him. As my classmates and I settled into our seats, one of them mentioned to Farrokh how she was looking forward to Professor Ben Sopranzetti's financial strategy class.

To which Farrokh replied as he began powering up the class for the lesson, "I never forget once Ben was with me in China and I was telling him, 'Man you look great!'

"And Ben said, 'Dude, you gotta meet my trainer. She's amazing.'

"And I said, 'Ookkkaay?'"

"And he said, 'In *six months*, I can have you looking like me.'"

The class giggled at the story as Professor Ben's class was one we all appreciated and I'm sure many of us could picture our beloved professor saying that.

Farrokh continued, "So anyway, when we were in China the guy, who runs the program site, and I somehow got to talking and he said, 'Ben said that to you?'

"And I said, 'yeah Ben said that to me.' Then the guy's face looked stricken. He then said, 'I had the same conversation with him but when Ben said meet my trainer, he then said in *twelve months* I can have you looking like me.'" Farrokh broke out in laughter with the class and remarked, "Man, then you are in worse shape than I am."

He then turned to the white board as he grabbed his dry erase marker and said, "Okay, here we go."

That is a classic Ben story. He is ranked as one of the top professors in the U.S. and we are fortunate to have him.

"Okay, what does it mean to have a comparative advantage?" Farrokh said with a contemplative look on his face. "Comparative advantage...?" he continued.

"—in what?"

"—of what?"

"What exactly is that—comparative advantage?

"Basically, it's making "X" in terms of "Y" within a country. It is an internal thing.

"Now, what drives comparative advantage? Remember folks its com-pa-ra-tive not com-pe-ti-tive advantage...."

On this point it is important to note that comparative advantage is not a competition. *Competitive* advantage has a strong emphasis on how one can obtain an upper hand on arrivals within a particular market. We learned in class that *comparative* advantage, however, has a country looking within itself to find what factors they have in abundance that could provide a benefit to another country that has that same factor in scarce supply. Although Farrokh noted that trade is not a panacea, in a roundabout way, the two countries who partake in these exchanges both end up better off.

"So, what I'm going to do," Farrokh continued, "is each time I give you a piece of international trade theory, I'm going to give you an anti-Langdana comment. We will be critiquing it at every point.

"So why trade," he said jumping into the character of a cynic that he pitted against himself, "with a country that has a lower standard of living?

"We will be going down to their level—*what the heck?* How do you answer that?"

"We will have a comparative advantage," my classmate Rich said in response, "in producing certain goods while the other country will have comparative advantage producing other goods. So, we will both be able to increase our consumption of the other countries product that we were lacking and increase our efficiency of producing what we have in abundance to supply for their needs."

"Both countries will then be better off," Bala added.

"Exactly! Thank you," Farrokh said. "Both of us will consume more of both goods and both countries will be better off.

"Any questions? Okay, open your textbooks," Farrokh said. The textbook that we used in class was the *International Trade and Global Macropolicy* that he coauthored with Peter T. Murphy. For some, macroeconomics could be a dry subject, but Farrokh wrote his book in a way that expressed the same voice he had in class. This technique made the teaching come alive and pair together seamlessly with his lectures.

"Now, let's look at page sixteen," Farrokh said to the class. "Please note there are answers on page eighteen, but don't turn and look at them. Work with me here. Let's work this through in class." He began going through different trade policies statements in the book that were expressed in plain language and the class had to let him know which macro policy was being referenced. He started the exercise at statement (a) but we will pick up at the question for (c) and the conversation as it unfolds.

"Look at (c)," Farrokh continued. "Colombia is willing and able to do excellent manufacturing…what is that?"

Random murmurs issued from around the room. Farrokh looked at each of us probing for the correct answer.

"Specialization."

"They have the resources."

"They have the capital."

Then he stopped on one of my classmates and pointed at him.

"Wham, nothing but net," Farrokh said as he waved his hand in front of himself depicting something flying by. He then gestured with his hands to beckon for more and said, "Louder."

"They have identified their comparative advantage," Bala responded.

"They have comparative advantage in manufacturing," Farrokh agreed. "You've got to start talking trade back to me. In fact, if you remember, Colombia is a manufacturing giant in more than just coffee.

"Also, long stem roses—one of the biggest exporters of roses is Colombia. So, the Valentine's Day flowers, a majority of them come from Columbia. Remember the product is not the abundant factor. "

As we peel back the initial layers of Sep # 3 *Summarize Your Comparative Advantage* keep a mental note that your comparative advantage is what is easily offered by you to a given opportunity. The 5P Framework list that was compiled in Step #1 is pulled out here so you can look at your described quality with the highest score that also has the lowest opportunity costs. In the coming pages, we will go through this exercise of *Summarizing Your Comparative Advantage* with a few individuals to give examples of how this unfolds. The 5P Framework hopes to make this answer more transparent as you would have already recognized the qualities that you have been successful with in times past and placed a score on that line item, which would indicate that it is a high or low quality. Now we have looked at that summarize list, which one of these items would be the easiest for **you** to implement with the lowest opportunity cost? Again, this is an individualized approach to helping you pull out what is unique to *you*. When you look at the summarize list you completed on the 5P Framework, out of the ones with the highest score, remember to consider your opportunity cost.

Briefcase

What do you have in abundance within you?

My mom and dad were both born in Jamaica but met for the first time in Bermuda. After a brief courtship, they were married, and shortly afterwards my mom gave birth to me. Eventually, our family relocated to the United States to live in New Jersey. From the time my dad arrived in New Jersey he had a briefcase. Originally, this briefcase was used for all his important documents that he needed to travel with from Bermuda to the United States, as well as some other memorabilia he had from his childhood days in Jamaica. However, when you grew up in our household, this briefcase became a time capsule because anything we did as kids that was worth cherishing went into the briefcase. It could be that third-grade piece of artwork that we made for Father's Day's; Dad would take it –give us some love for it—and then stick it in his briefcase. Even those class assignments that my sister and I did exceptionally well on, Dad would take it –give us some love for it—and then stick it in his briefcase.

So, here we were nearly forty years later, and I was telling my dad about wanting to finish *Dream Octane*, at which point he reminded me of his briefcase.

"I'm so proud of you," Daddy said. "You know what, Cliff? You have had this thing—since you were a kid—where you just loved writing. Your entire life you've been this way. I still have some of your first handwritten book reports from when you were in the first or second grade that you received As on that are still in my briefcase."

So, maybe you don't have a briefcase, but I'm sure you have a briefcase story in your own family, or if you don't, you may have heard examples of influencers sharing their stories online, or celebrities mentioning similar stories of how capturing that award seemed to validate some inherent quality they had that led them to walking up on stage and receiving that recognition. The journey that is shared often ties back to some inherent quality seen in times past that connects to their current success. It is often something that they saw in themselves, or someone saw in them back in the day before they found themselves successful. In his book, *Strength finder 2.0*, Tom Rath highlights a twenty-three-year-old longitudinal study from New Zealand that began with 1,000 three-year-olds and ended when the kids turned twenty-six. The study showed that personality traits at age three were remarkably similar to the personalities traits at age twenty-six. Tom Rath concluded from this study that the elements of our personalities that are least likely to change are our talents.

It is important to note here that the briefcase doesn't need our help. My dad never asked me if he could tuck away my accomplishments. He merely memorialized these moments within the time capsule he kept.

What is being placed in your briefcase? What experiences have you had that would cause someone to stop, take note, and stick those moments in the briefcase? We see this in scripture as Joseph, Mary, and the twelve-year-old Jesus take their annual journey during the feast of the Passover. Scholars have said that this travel was done with friends and family typically, so it was common for their son Jesus to not be with them as they traveled back to Nazareth. This time mentioned in the book of Luke chapter 2 verse 41 was different though. The group thought that Jesus was with them but could not find him, so they went back to Jerusalem to look for him.

The next day, they found him listening to and challenging scribes with conversation, which left these teachers impressed with his level of understanding and wisdom. When Mary and Joseph found him, I'm sure they were relieved, but as any parent would do they reprimanded him and Mary stated, "Son, why have you treated us like this? Your father and I have been anxiously searching for you."

He [Jesus] said, "Why were you searching for me?" he asked. "Didn't you know I had to be in my Father's house?"[43] Although they didn't fully understand what he meant by that, the very next scripture stated that Mary *treasured* these things in her heart. This may have even taken her back to the memory of when baby Jesus was lying in a manger, surrounded by animals while the shepherds told prophesied stories about him. Here again scripture states "But Mary treasured up all these things and pondered them in her heart."[44]

Now I get it: trying to follow a divine example might be somewhat unfair. In Mary's example, her briefcase was her heart. If you take a retrospective look at your life, what's in *your* briefcase? What significant event is *treasured* in the briefcase of your—or individuals who know you best—heart? What have you done that is worthy enough to be encapsulated within time? Think about it as these are the moments that make summarizing your comparative advantage E.A.S.Y.

Make it E.A.S.Y

One technique for summarizing your comparative advantage is to make it E.A.S.Y. By E.A.S.Y I do not mean that it is effortless. As a matter of fact, each section on the *Lifecycle of Excavation* is best facilitated when combined with the following behaviors: discovery needs diligence; development requires discipline; and delivery necessitates determination. No, the E.A.S.Y method is best applied when you are prepared for a moment but still feel unqualified to render what you have prepared to share. There may be times when others impose their opinion upon you that may imply that you are not ready for the opportunity. However, just because others may believe that you're not ready for the moment, it doesn't mean that you are not *designed* for it. The E.A.S.Y method is intended to work like a cross-check. Once you look back to what has worked well in times past, you will be able to see what transferable qualities were displayed. This perspective could help to reveal that although the opportunity may be placed in an unfamiliar environment, what you have worth sharing is something that you are acutely familiar with. To unfold this acrostic simply ask yourself: *When has success come from…?*

E-<u>Exposure to useful information</u>: These are times when you were able to cross a hurdle by either knowing— or learning—what to do. The late Zig Ziglar told a story of a time at a conference where he spoke to and taught leaders of Fortune 500 companies. After the conference was over, he drove home and got his car stuck in mud. Zig called a tow truck company. When the tow truck guy arrived, he appeared to be a friendly man who enjoyed what he did, but Zig assumed that based on the man's broken English that he wasn't high in the IQ category.

Zig watched as the tow truck guy got into Zig's vehicle. He put Zig's car in reverse, turned the wheel, tapped the gas and in a fluid motion—as the car rocked back—he put the car in drive, gave it more gas, and rocked it forward a little further. He did this technique a few more times before the vehicle eventually rocked out of the ditch. The entire exercise took a few minutes.

Did the tow truck guy have a degree? Not likely. Was he able to teach other leaders of Fortune 500 companies like Zig Ziglar did earlier in the day? I highly doubt it. However, he was able to solve Zig's problem because at some point in his life he was exposed to useful information that he could use to overcome this dilemma.

Zig Ziglar learned from that experience that it does not take a genius to problem-solve. It is about knowing what needs to be done to accomplish a task and this can come from previous knowledge or life experiences. So, people can come to you and say, "Hey, how do you do this?" and you can provide a solution, even if they cannot because you have encountered this problem before.

Experiential exposures may not be inherent qualities or natural abilities but knowledge that is gained along our journey of life. However, when we look back, we may find a technique that could be helpful—like Zig Ziglar learning how to get a car out of a ditch from watching the tow truck guy. You may find there is one thing that you can look back on and say, well, every time I'm asked about this particular thing—whatever it is fill in the blank—I'm actually pretty good at it. In the future, someone might come to you if assistance in this area is needed.

A-Accelerating change: The next part is uncovering areas where you have accelerated change. This part of the E.A.S.Y method is the 5P Framework that we have reviewed in detail thus far. This is where the five questions come into play. Think about the moments in time where change has been accelerated for you, or you've maximized some benefit in trying to achieve a goal. It could have been finishing your degree or being presented with a challenging assignment, but whatever it was you were able to get through it. What helped you to get from the point the challenge began, to where you fixed a problem or received a recognition for it? There was something unique about you that helped to get you through it. What was it?

Looking at this through that lens, use the 5P Framework to document that. What are your *Passions*? What do you do—or have done—that you enjoy so much that you lose track of time or you would do it wholeheartedly free of charge? Next, what have you done that feels *Purposeful?* In other words, what do you do that makes you say to yourself: I feel like I was born to do this

_____ thing? Now let's look at your *Proficiencies*. What have you learned to do well over time? Epiphanies also count in this area. So essentially your Es in the E.A.S.Y method could become your As under this category. *Patterns* are the other side of the proficiency coin. This is what you do naturally well. Maybe you are naturally gifted at sports, writing, comedy or whatever. Patterns are often overlooked, as you will see in Step # 4 in Dr. Ohmslaw's story, but they have been helpful in some way.

Lastly, we drill down on *Problem-solving*. What do you do that helps you solve a problem for someone? What do people come to you for help with? We will soon go through these questions again in the coaching session with Miss Charlie at the close of this chapter. However, all these examples contained in the 5P Framework are intended to bring to the forefront the times where you accelerated change. These principles are important as they have the potential to accelerate change by altering someone's trajectory for the better.

How many people have we seen operate with *Passion* or in a way that is *Purposeful* in areas we admire, and that motivates us to be better at that thing? How often have we used *Problem-solving*, a *Pattern* of behavior or *Proficiency* for executing a task that helps us overcome hurdles? These were all examples of how your niche accelerated change.

S-<u>Studying best practice</u>: Once you figure out what you have the most experience with, think about those areas in which you excel. Then, you want to capture information from others who are successful in this area. This is where you start to study and refine what you have in mind. When have you acquired best practice information, applied it, and had a successful outcome?

For me, the value in the application of capturing information began early on in my 20-year career in healthcare. As I stated, having just my Associates degree in Applied Science brought me to a pivotal point in my career. I could have used my insecurity of not having an advanced degree to make excuses for any failings. However, I found books and attended leadership development seminars that would help me in the areas where I saw opportunities to improve. John Maxwell's, *21 Irrefutable Laws of Leadership*; Steven Covey's, *Seven Habits of Highly Effective People*; *How to Win Friends and Influence People* by Dale Carnegie to name a few; and daily reading of biblical scripture in particular the book of Proverbs helped to shape my leadership decision making a few years into my career.

Additionally, seeing the likes of Zig Ziglar, Collin Powell, and other great leadership trainers through

Steven Covey's Franklin institute on stage also helped to provide best practice ideas I was able to pull from. Overtime, things began to make sense as these disparate learning moments started to coalesce in my mind as helpful advice for myself and others. I also saw as I applied these best practices that I began having ideas of my own, which I created frameworks for to better use them. These constructs are what I gave to others who sought my help with problem-solving. I tweaked the concepts each time I used it and repeated the process with a more refined framework, which made overcoming the problem easier the next time around. We will cover in greater detail *give, tweak,* and *repeat* in Step # 4 *Specialize in Offering What is Helpful to Others but Unique to You.* In short, I then noticed that the models yielded results and developed my expertise.

Y- Yielding results from your expertise: Then the last one is, your expertise. So, after you've recognized the value of your experiences, identified areas where you have accelerated change, and have assisted in solving problems from your study of best practice, we can now include your frameworks. The Y in E.A.S.Y is what will eventually help you to become the expert in the room. This ties back to the delineation made back in Step # 1 when we mentioned Michael Mauboussin's paraphrased quote of psychologist Gregory Northcraft "the difference between *experience* and *expertise* is that *expertise* is having a predictive model that works."[45] I learned the true value of having a predictive model that works when I worked as the Director of Radiology at a community medical center in New Jersey. I had an Excel spreadsheet that I brought over from a previous position, which included some key performance indicators that helped me to manage my department. This dashboard included monthly monitoring of my patient experience scores, my equipment repair cost broken down by imaging department, staffing productivity, and a few quality measures we needed to keep an eye on.

I modified what I used from my previous location because I saw that it worked for someone else, and I tweaked the idea to fit my departmental needs. Both the Vice President and Physician Chairman who I reported to, appreciated this dashboard as it helped to make discussing the strength and weaknesses of the department *easy*—no pun intended. Eventually, the recognition led to a promotion to an Executive

Director position over the imaging service lines of three hospitals. It was an outsourced position that had me working in the same system I was the director in, but I reported to individuals who were in a joint venture with the hospital.

The first order of business for me was to now show the three directors who reported to me how this predictive model worked. Overtime, as they used a modified dashboard, I had created for them, they became just as proficient at managing their department as I did.

About a year and a half into that corporate position, disruption happened between the company I was working for and the hospital system we were working with. They eventually began a separation that was like a divorce. Out of the hundreds of workers, the outsource company had the hospital system only retain a handful of people and I was fortunate to be one of them. I took an open position as manager but was promoted to director in a relatively short time. However, what was fascinating was less about what occurred with me and more about what happened to the other two managers who no longer reported to me. They both continued to use this model for managing their operations and eventually both received leadership awards for their department a few months later. This was amazing considering that they worked at different hospital locations, and it was the same award that I won previously while using that predictive model.

My encouragement to you is that whenever you feel that you are about to step into a moment that's bigger than you, if you feel unqualified confront that moment with the E.A.S.Y method. Again, just because you may not feel ready for that moment doesn't mean that you are not made for it. I soon found while working with Miss Charlie how the *A* in E.A.S.Y helped to guide her through the process of finding her niche as we used the 5P Framework tool to do so.

Applying Step # 3 *Miss Charlie Why would the audience have a vested interest in your backstory?*

Let's take a step back as we move to the last stage of the discover segment on the *Life Cycle of Excavation*. As this framework first came together, I shifted my attention from experts to those seeking the expertise of others. There was no better example than that of Miss Charlie. The goal was to balance resources found in successful people with the needs of those striving to uncover the value they have to offer others with their niche. I began my Zoom call with Miss Charlie with this statement, "So, tell me about your backstory and give the audience insight as to why they would have a vested interest in your journey."

"Okay," Miss Charlie said as if her words left her lips like an Olympic track athlete jumping out of her block after hearing the shot to start the race. "With that question, how it feels to me is because I'm not an expert yet, or I'm not where I need to be. The backstory is me saying to the audience: Are you sick and tired of being sick and tired? For me it's more [than that]. My backstory is that I'm here, thirty-four years old, and I am nowhere near where I want to be, where I thought I would be [in life]. For me, the audience is anybody [who] wants to live a better life. Do you want more for yourself? I think [about] why [they] should be invested in me....One, to come together and connect. But two, aren't we all tired? If there were people around us, [I would say] raise your hands if you're happy where you are in life.

"I'm a girl [who] grew up with Haitian descendant parents who were very successful, and I am nowhere near where they were. It's like [going] on a quest to be more; I gotta do more. There's gotta be more out there and I think...I need to look for people to help me, and [Cliff] that's where you come in at. People with a strong personality sometimes hold [themselves] back. Obviously, I don't have it together, and I do need some help, and I do need some support. This audience is for anybody that's not happy [in] their situation and more likely, most of us are not happy. We're not fulfilled. We're not living in passion. We're not living in purpose. We've given up...

"Let me get with the people that can help me; let me become coachable; I'm not a know-it-all. Just because I have great rebuttals and act tough doesn't mean I know everything...I need to listen. I need to seek...I need help...

"Just because I know a lot, I know nothing at the same time. For me, it's humbly coming back to terms. I got a long way to go, but let's do it differently this time...

"When [I] think about where I hope to be in five years, I hope to say I was at a place in my life at thirty-four that didn't consist of me just working different jobs. It's going to be the same thing over and over if [I] don't make a change, if [I] don't take a step.

"I am scared, and I do feel stagnant, but I know there's a way, and I know there's people like you; that's what resonates with me."

"You know I'm encouraged," I said in response to Miss Charlie, "because there's so much to unpack there, and that's why I appreciate these conversations. I think that success has a multitude of things, but let's just focus in on two: It's the information on what to do, and the application of that information so that you model it correctly. I think you have framed it perfectly. Yes. People who want to accelerate aren't people who say, 'I know it all.' As a matter of fact, the people who succeed and want to accelerate their progress are the ones who have more questions than answers. So, your awareness about humility I think is so important and it's even scriptural. It was just today that I sent out a group email to a cohort that I have been working with as encouragement that had a line: 'Humility is the springboard that God uses for elevation.' It was based on the scripture from Matthew 23:12 NIV. For those who exalt themselves will be humbled, and those who humble themselves will be exalted."

The purpose of this meeting with Miss Charlie was to help her through the *Life Cycle of Excavation* as a pilot program of sorts. She encapsulated the thirty something year old who many would call a success. Rightfully so: She graduated from college, furthered her education by obtaining her master's degree, and began teaching undergraduate courses. However, although she had two jobs—one teaching and the other working as a patient navigator in healthcare—she said that she felt unfulfilled.

Turning my attention back to our interview I asked, "What do you want to accomplish on this journey of discovering, developing, and delivering your niche? I think knowing this answer will help me to better understand where I can be most helpful. Does that make sense?"

Miss Charlie replied, "It does and to explain my story on paper, I sound pretty okay. To someone who hasn't been to college—if you've never experienced it—college is going to seem like the most amazing thing, and while college is very valuable, one thing I've learned, and I pass down to my students... all these things are beneficial, but you still need guidance.

"I was not a kid that took to guidance. I was a very know-it-all type of person. While I was doing these things, I always just thought, no, my way is the best way, and I'm going to figure it out. Does that make sense?

"So, I can still see I'm a success, no way do I think I'm a loser, but I know there's better. Moreover, after getting my masters and then teaching, while there are some things I love about my life, there are some other things that I can't help but to say, no, I need to do this, and I need to do it now—or in a better way. So, when you say help me, I think: What am I trying to get?

"When you said something about application, I want to start doing things that make sense for me. It's so funny because as much as I want financial freedom—and that's a part of it—I also want to be satisfied. I also want to feel like it's a meaningful life. I also want to feel like I'm making a difference in the capacity that I know I can. There's something internally burning inside of me that says, no, there's so much more for me to give that can be so beneficial to the world or a group of women or a group of people. I don't know yet. When you have that calling on your life, that feeling that you know your energy, the person you are, can be applied in so many different ways that would bless people.

"It's not having the degrees and the title. The title is one thing, but it's like when you're walking in your calling in something that you feel is your purpose. That's where the satisfaction comes [from]. The money is great, but that's one aspect. It's like, here I am at thirty-four, and as an example: I'm not married; I don't have kids. Some people look at family as a very accomplished life; they look at their kids as accomplished life. So, because I'm a strong believer in God I know he's ordering my steps. Therefore, if it didn't happen or it never happens, I know it's for a reason, but all I can control right now is me, Miss Charlie, and what I'm going to do.

"It's like, you're trying to chase a better day. When you get older and you've lived a little bit of life, it's different. I know every day can't be perfect, but to make a difference and to feel like this is good; if I died today, and this is what I did, I'm happy. So, that's what I need help with developing and putting that goal in real language. Real talk real time. I don't want to just say I want to help. I want to really get into, how am I going to help? What am I going to do? What is the area of focus? What more training do I need? Do I need to develop more of this skill? Or do I need to go to this thing? Or how do I network? Just saying, that's what I need help with. Whatever is inside of my mind [is] inside of my heart. I want to get it on paper and get it as close to making the vision so plain and easy for myself. How does that look? The practicality, that is what I'd like help on."

Applying the Niche Finder 5P Framework to derive your comparative advantage

"Yeah, I hear what you're saying and it's all great stuff," I said. "In speaking to this point, I think Miles Munroe said it best: 'Success,' as he puts it, 'is predictable.' But I would add to that and say as a result, your talents, your gifts, your abilities, are transferrable." I then gave her a high-level synopsis of the seven steps that make up the *Life Cycle of Excavation*. After going through each step, I then took her back to the beginning of Step # 1: *Recognize Your Abundant Factor* through Step # 3 *Summarize Your Comparative Advantage,* and reviewed the answers she provided to the five questions that made up the Niche Finder 5P framework.

During the Zoom call our cameras were off, so I asked,

"Do you have the worksheet in front of you?"

Dream Octane® *Niche Finder 5P Framework*™

Instructions

- List 1-3 qualities you believe is—or has been—associated with you. These characteristics can be your opinion or statements that others have said about you relative to that particular 5P niche category. The qualities do not have to be written in any particular order.
- Complete the "self" segment on the quality scoring grid using the noted criteria.
- Ask a family member, trusted friend and/or mentor to give a score for each quality you have identified. If anyone adds a quality that you missed, you will need to place a score for that on the "self" segment.
- Once complete, add up the totals for each quality. Use the Quality Scoring Grid Result Range to obtain the niche with the greatest quality concentration.
- Note: Your responses may repeat between categories. This may be helpful as it could be a strong quality. Your family, friend or mentor will confirm this for you if the score they provide you is also high.

Quality Scoring Grid Directions

Place a ranking from 1-5 (1 very weak quality; 5 very strong niche) for each quality you believe you have in you.

Quality Scoring Grid Result Range

Strength Likelihood	Self	Family	Friend/ Mentor	Overall
Very Strong Niche	4-5	4-5	4-5	**12-15**
Strong Niche	3-4	3-4	3-4	**9-12**
Moderate Niche	2-3	2-3	2-3	**6-9**
Weak Niche	1-2	1-2	1-2	**3-6**
Very Weak Niche	0-1	0-1	0-1	**0-3**

5P NICHE CATEGORIES / Quality Scoring (1-5)

PASSION: What do you love to do that ignites and/or excites you? (i.e.: Skillful at playing music, sports, doing well academically, etc.)

Qualities	Self	Family	Friend/ Mentor	Total
1.				
2.				
3.				

PURPOSEFUL: What do you do that adds value to others and/or a particular environment? (i.e.: Serving others at a food pantry, mentoring, teaching, etc.)

Qualities	Self	Family	Friend/ Mentor	Total
1.				
2.				
3.				

PATTERNS: What practice has been consistently successful for you over the years? (i.e.: Exercise, being calm in stressful situations, humor that puts others at ease, etc.)

Qualities	Self	Family	Friend/ Mentor	Total
1.				
2.				
3.				

PROBLEM SOLVING: What pain points do others call upon you to fix? (i.e.: Taking the appropriate lead on things, people confide in you for advice, volunteering, etc.)

Qualities	Self	Family	Friend/ Mentor	Total
1.				
2.				
3.				

PROFICIENT: What do you do well that comes easy for you? (i.e.: Writing, public speaking, getting preschoolers to respond to your instructions, etc.)

Qualities	Self	Family	Friend/ Mentor	Total
1.				
2.				
3.				

"Yes, I have it right here," she replied.

"Okay, great," I said.

"So, now that you are familiar with the seven steps, let's go back through it as a lightning round, and let's look at this as it relates to you. Now, we may not have all the answers at this very moment, but I think it's a good exercise to at least get the brain juices flowing around it. So, what do you believe your abundant factor is? Let's recognize it from the five questions you have in front of you.

"Okay, here are the sections in a nutshell:

"Passions: what do you have strong interests around?

"Purposefulness: What do you do that feels meaningful to you?

"Patterns: What do you do naturally well, that feels almost second nature?

"Proficiency: What have you learned to do well? This is what you have learned to do well over time and then the last one...

"Problem-solving: What challenges do people bring to you, because they find you to be a good resource for solving— or fixing—that issue?

"Now what did you have down for passions?"

"I would say giving advice and making people laugh," Miss Charlie replied.

"Where did this fall on your sheet?" I said in response. "As far as giving it a number from one to five—with five being a strong quality and one being a lesser quality. What number would you give each?"

Miss Charlie replied, "I would say, giving advice is for some reason, always number one. So, if I have to score it, giving advice will be five; making people laugh would be four. Sometimes I feel like its neck and neck, but people mainly come to me for advice and then I make them laugh—it's weird. I feel like it's a tie, boss, it's so hard because if I'm in the atmosphere with somebody and they're not asking for advice, we're laughing and we're good. And then other than that, everybody comes to me for advice like I'm a therapist."

She could not see me, but as the tenor of our conversations began gaining momentum, I started smiling to myself like a mad scientist addicted to eureka. "Could it be that people come to you for advice because they anticipate, although they feel burdened when they come to you, that somehow you will give them great advice and make them laugh?"

Miss Charlie replied, "I think there is comfort in making them laugh…they get more out of it. Absolutely."

"Okay," I responded. "Now I got that. If you want to put fives down for both, don't struggle with it. Just do it. Put the first thing that comes to mind. That's the easiest way to tackle this. So now, just to clarify, did you put giving advice and making people laugh on the same or different lines?"

"They're two different lines," Miss Charlie said.

"Five for both?"

"I put five for both."

"Perfect," I said. "Now what's the next question you answered?"

"It says Purposeful," she replied. "What do you do that adds value to others and/or a particular environment? The examples are serving at food pantries or mentoring? Teaching? I say teaching is one. I put giving advice.

"Giving advice, I put that at five, and then the teaching I put a moderate because all the reason why I wanted to teach was because I was afraid of public speaking, and I knew that was a way to get rid of that fear. To me, my classroom was a stage and I just told jokes all day in class. Anyway, if you look even at all these, like all I was doing was teaching and making them laugh at the same time. So, to me, teaching was like a three. Yeah. So, advice was five and then teaching was a three."

"All right," I said. "So, here's what I would say very quickly on this point. I would liken your teaching to be Step # 4 *Specialize in Offering What is Helpful to Others but Unique to You* step. This is the step where we cover how to master your microcosm."

"Teaching is my Step # 4?" Miss Charlie said seeking clarification.

"Based on what you are telling me, teaching for you is an environment. It is *not* your abundant factor. You are using it as a forum to develop. If teaching others was your abundant factor, it would be ranked higher by you and would be Step #2 where you discover that you're using it intensely. The difference between Step #2 and Step #4 is that Step #2 is part of the discovery process where you explore your resolve for your abundant factor. However, Step #4 is the environment where you refine what you are offering to others. Or, in other words, Step # 2 is drilling for oil and Step # 4 is refining it."

"Right," Miss Charlie said in response. "I just needed to get rid of the fear of public speaking."

"Getting rid of that fear may also have some elements of Step # 5 *Neutralize Barriers Blocking You From Fulfilling Your Dream*. In this step, we touch on eating your scorpions, but we will unpack that later."

"What about purposeful?" I said. "What did you have on your list for that?"

"Okay," she replied. "Under purposeful I put the same two responses—giving advice and making people laugh.

"The next column was patterns. The question to be answered for that is: What practice has been consistently successful for you over the years? I put active listening has been awesome for me. I get so much from listening to people attentively."

"What number did you give it?" I asked.

"Active listening, I scored a four. Humor was five again; humor was first on my list and then active listening. That's what I put there.

"Then the next one is problem-solving: What pain points do others call upon you to fix? It's always been people confiding in me for some advice. Something to do with their relationships; [their] job; what they should choose; which way they should go. They often ask me what I would do and so on. That goes back to the advice giving.

"With problem-solving I can always come up with a solution, what to do, who to call. I'm very resourceful. So, problem-solving comes easy to me when it applies to others but when it's my situation the problems aren't that simple to solve. But somehow when others come to me, I'm like a traffic cop: Go back here…do this…do that. I say in those moments," she said through laughter, "look here, we're going to make this work. That's how I problem solve."

"Did you give problem-solving a number?" I said.

"The number I gave it was four to five," she replied.

"Ok," I said in response. "What did you put down for the last one?"

"The last one was proficiency," she said. "What do you do well? That's when I had to learn public speaking. I had to get rid of that fear. I took like maybe three communication classes in college. I knew I was striving to be a professor so there was no way I could do that with the fear of public speaking.

"[I became proficient at writing when] I took some writing classes. Just to improve in this area and better express what I wanted to say. So, public speaking and writing communication was very big for me in college because I was incredibly shy. I had a big personality, but I would shut down [around] large crowds and I would shut down around people.

"I remember my father saying, you are going to go absolutely nowhere…if you keep trembling in front of people," she said while giggling. "So, that resonated with me as a kid."

Commercial break on this as I don't want you to miss the proverbial tuning fork that was struck by her father here that moved her to action. Now, let's see what the impact of the resonance did for her. Okay, back to the program.

"So," she continued, "in college I made sure to take two or three communication courses aside from the ones that were required. I made sure to take public speaking…and I made sure to just get myself out there because I knew in the real world, there was going to be a time where I would have to speak up."

"Well," I replied, "I love your story right there. You know why? This is just another example of eating your scorpions in Step # 5 *Neutralize the Barriers Blocking You from Fulfilling Your Dream.* Later, when we get to *neutralizing* your barriers, I will remind you about what you did to become proficient. I think it is good and may provide you motivation. But, now let's look at your scores. Alright? Which one has the highest score?"

"Making people laugh," Miss Charlie said, "giving advice, and then active listening. Making people laugh I gave a five; giving advice a five or a four, depending; and active listening was a good four as well."

"Wow!" I said "Okay, now with [that], can you come up with three different areas where these three qualities are used intensely. So, for Step # 2, what area uses all three?"

"I know counseling could," she said "...or a therapist could. I think any type of host –talk show hosts—could use that too. I can't think of three. Let me see. I mean, when you think about advice, it's definitely counseling, therapy, a coach, you get to listen and offer advice. I feel like a talk show depending on how you formulate it, and especially with the way the world is nowadays. My innovative spirit feels like there is a niche for me in that. Where people can call in and I can help them. It may not be a now thing, but I definitely think that's possible."

"Okay," I said in response, "I think this was very valuable. The reason that I wrote this book about how to find your niche is because I spent fifteen to twenty years trying to uncover how one person can deliver this value that they have with [what is] inside of them. So, I have all of this information to be able to write this book; come up with different materials; host interviews; do all of this content creation because I had this tenacity of trying to just immerse myself in this experience of, how do I answer this question. Now, I kind of feel like you are on the same journey of trying to find this out as well. Based on my study of those who have succeeded, once this is discovered and effort is put behind bringing that quality out, they often simultaneously uncover the *one thing* that comes easy to them. This makes it *easier* to develop content when you get to Step # 4 *Specialize in Offering What is Helpful to Others but Unique to You.*"

Summarizing your Comparative Advantage

"Now, let's talk about your comparative advantage," I said. "So, you have identified your abundant factor of being funny, people finding you an easy person to talk to, and being resourceful. These are three good qualities that you're saying could be in counseling, therapy, coaching, or possibly a talk show host—did I summarize that correctly?"

"Yes," she said.

"Okay, that's Steps # 1 and # 2," I responded.

"Now Step #3 is what would be the *easiest* environment for you to express *your* abundant factor with the least amount of effort, but with the **lowest opportunity cost**? Let's think about the first one: counseling. For you to do counseling, what would have to happen? I would imagine you have to go back to school to get the necessary training—no?"

"Okay. No," Miss Charlie interjected.

"Okay. Tell me what you mean by that," I responded.

"I'm not going back to school right now," she replied.

"Okay, so that has a **high opportunity cost**—yes?" I said. "Alright. So, let's put that one to the side. **If it has a high opportunity cost, it cannot be your comparative advantage then**."

Let's take a commercial break on this. Remember as you look at the list you created with the 5P Framework, summarize those that have high opportunity cost versus those with a low opportunity cost. Prioritize the highest quality score from the 5P Framework with the lowest opportunity cost. If you need more clarity around the topic of opportunity cost, don't worry we will cover it in greater detail before closing out this chapter.

"Now, the next one that you called out—talk show hosts. What does it take for you to be a talk show host?"

"I mean," she replied, "honest to God, I don't know, but I'm thinking maybe start a YouTube channel? Start giving advice. Start being funny. Start looking up stuff to try in jobs or side gigs. I don't know... that part I'll have to research but find a way to put yourself out there and somehow see what that industry looks like relative to what you have? That's what I'm thinking."

I smiled to myself and said, "Based on what you are telling me this is something that you can do right now—even after you get off the phone. A microcosm to being on the talk show as a host is doing your own podcast. You know what I mean? It has all of the elements that you just mentioned."

"That's it. Alright," she replied.

"This is where I would say you can start," I continued. "I can even discuss possible resource connections around this. I do this now myself.

"You can start a YouTube channel immediately, as well. All those arenas are a nominal cost. Now, how do you begin? Who do you interview? Step # 4 is where you will master your microcosm. You start to interview people who you are closest to; people who you find interesting; who would love to invest in this journey of yours. After you have started with you, continue the journey by looking at your abundant factor through their eyes. Alright? So, now what you just said, we identified a comparative advantage is in these spaces of you doing YouTube and podcasts right now. What you will be doing then is *specializing.* **Specialize in offering what is helpful to others but unique to you.**"

LeBron James High School Decision and the Opportunity Cost (OC) Grading System

Before LeBron James became the basketball phenomenon that we know, possessing four NBA championships, 18 All Star appearances, and being regarded as one of the greatest athletes to play the sport, he had a decision to make. As a 6-foot-8 232-pound teenager with a 44-inch vertical, playing both basketball and football were options for this junior heading into his senior year at St. Vincent-St. Mary's High School in Akron. As a high school football player, he had racked up impressive stats his sophomore and junior years that totaled: 103 catches that amounted into 2,065 yards gained and 23 touchdowns.[46]

On the basketball front, his talents were just as evident leading his freshman and sophomore basketball teams to 27-0 and 26-1 records respectively with each culminating in state championship titles. His junior year ended in a state championship loss but having a team record of 23-4, average stats of 28 points, 8.9 rebounds and 6.0 assist per game were still enough for him to be named *boys' basketball national player of the year.*[47]

So, here he is at the end of his junior year with arguably both his basketball and football abilities equally matched from a talent standpoint. However, his senior year he opted to play basketball and forgo football for this reason: His basketball teammates assured him that if he played football his senior year, they would beat him up after every practice until he stopped going[48]. LeBron James' friends adding in that variable of causing him bodily harm if he chose to play football also added a high opportunity cost to the decision to play that sport.

As we close out Step #3 and head into the *Develop* section, the goal is to start the refinement process of Step #4 with your *one thing*. If you have more than one abundant factor—or niche—I want you to see opportunity cost as a grading system. By grading system, I mean like the type of letter grade teachers use to provide high school students insight into how well they were applying what they learned in class: A-Excellent, B-Very Good, C-Average, D-Below Average and F-Failing.

When it comes to adding in an opportunity cost (OC) grade into your decision, use this grading system to help you pick your one thing if you have more than one quality with the same high 5P Framework score:

- **A-** Low OC / No foreseeable penalties or added obstacles if selected/ Highly beneficial.

- **B**- Somewhat Low OC / Unlikely penalties or minor obstacles if selected / Very beneficial.

- **C**- Moderately Low OC / Some foreseeable penalties or added obstacles happening occasionally if selected/ Average benefits.

- **D**- Somewhat High OC / High likelihood of having foreseeable penalties or added obstacles happening if selected/ Below average Benefit.

- **F**- High OC / Inevitable penalties or added obstacles happening if selected/ Little to no benefit when measured against the penalties.

If we look back at LeBron's high school decision, having the ability to play football and basketball would have both been—in *Dream Octane* terms—a 15 on the 5P Framework for each. However, choosing to play football his senior year while getting beat up after every practice, would add an OC grade of "F." The fact that his senior year of basketball was going to be nationally televised on ESPN and there was no foreseeable added bodily harm being inflicted on him would add an "A" to his 5P score of 15. This would amount to him having a 15F for football and a 15A for basketball. In this modeled, choosing basketball would be the most advantageous selection, which he did of his own volition. As a result, his team won its 3rd state championship that senior year and after graduating high school he became the #1 pick in the NBA draft that year.[49] Now that you have your one thing, we are ready to have you head into Step #4: ***Specialize in Offering What is Helpful to Others but Unique to You***.

Develop
Section

Keep Giving….

Chapter 6

Step # 4: Specialize In Offering What Is Helpful To Others But Unique To You

"You can have everything in life you want, if you will just help enough other people get what they want." Zig Ziglar.

'Look, it's not about you, Cliff.'

The purpose behind finding one's niche is the key to uncovering how our value adds value to someone else. Identifying that you have something of value—your abundant factor—is important but giving it away is what makes that potential special. In his book, *Understanding Your Potential,* Myles Monroe shares his perspective on the wealthiest place on Earth. Surprisingly, he remarks that it is not the oil fields in Iraq or Saudi Arabia. Nor is it South Africa's gold and diamond mines or the uranium enriched soil found in parts of the Soviet Union.[50]

The richest place on the planet—as he put it—may not be far from our own homes. As a matter of fact, we may even ride by it on our way to work every day. It is the graveyard. It is in these solemn grounds that you will find songs that were never produced, best selling books that were never written, and billion-dollar business ideas that were never acted upon. He is right. It is a sobering reality to think of the number of gifts that started as a passing thought but ended with that individual when they passed away.[51]

Some years ago, I worked at a level 2 trauma center in the heart of Jersey City. To help build morale among the staff, we had potluck days where staff would bring in a favorite dish to share with everyone else. These were welcomed events and one of the maternal figures in the department helped to coordinate all the activities. We affectionately called her Mama J. Although Mama J was close to retirement age, she was energetic and could run laps around the most junior person in the department. She had two jobs, was involved with church activities, and consistently went to the gym four to five times a week. So being able to coordinate five imaging department staff members to bring in dishes and set everything up while minimizing any disruption to patient flow, was right up her alley.

Now, Mama J took me under her wing and treated me like her son. At that point in my life, she knew that I could eat the amount of food for someone who was twice my size. So anytime we had potluck and I was working in the office, Mama J would always bring me a plate of food. She would make sure that I did not have items on my plate that was on my short list of foods I did not eat, such as red meat, pork, and a few other things.

Her selections were always spot on, and the portions just right. Now, let's fast-forward to a period of time later where I'm at a different hospital and my Momma J wasn't there. I started a new role as Assistant Director for Radiology and decided to do a potluck. I happened to swing by the office of the person who was coordinating the menu for the potluck. She started to run down the list of what she had and most of the items were either red meat or had pork in it: roast beef, antipasto, pork chops, and the like. When she mentioned there would be roast beef I asked if anyone was bringing a chicken dish. I also audaciously questioned if antipasto was ever made without ham and inquired if the person making the baked Ziti was doing so with ground turkey.

Now, maybe my attempt to ensure that I would be able to enjoy a variety of foods that I liked to eat fell short and came across instead as a self-centered display. However, the organizer's response at that moment made things abundantly clear when she responded to my questions with, "Look, it's not about you, Cliff." She was right.

If we just ate what my appetite wanted, the group might not have been satisfied. So it is with finding and delivering your niche. The true value of your unique ability can be found in how helpful it is to someone else but note: *It's not about you*. Now that you have uncovered the value you have to offer while quarrying your way through the *Discover* section of Steps # 1-3, we are ready to *Develop*. This section introduces Step # 4 *Specialize in Offering What is Helpful to Others but Unique to You* and Step # 5 *Neutralize Barriers Blocking You From Fulfilling Your Dream*.

Ultimately, Steps # 4 and 5 are intended to help position you for the final section of *Deliver*. Here is where Step # 6 *Organize the Delivery of Your Niche to a Wider Audience* and Step # 7 *Maximize Your Abundant Factor* will guide you with methods that can help to deliver your niche to a larger audience. However, we *Develop* Step # 4 *Specialize in Offering What is Helpful to Others but Unique to You* through the refinement process of service.

I hasten to add to this point that the goal of Step # 4 is less about being a **go-getter** and more about what you are **going to give**. Step # 4 is about caring enough about your audience that you refine what you are offering until it is distilled into a form that is most helpful to them. You will know when it is refined because it has helped to fuel the ideas or progress of others. But even when you get to that moment, I would still argue that: *It's not about you*. Why wouldn't it be about you now—you ask? After all, you are the one offering this great thing—your niche—to this smaller group and it is working. Why not celebrate yourself? Great questions.

To answer this, I turn your attention to the purpose for which I used the oil industry as an analogous imagery for *Dream Octane*. This metaphor symbolizes that what we have inside of us may often be buried deep and that we may need to drill into our experiences to *Discover* it. Once uncovered—just as wildcatters like Pattillo Higgins of the early 1800s unearthed oil—that crude resource will need to be taken into the refinery and distilled. The refinery is used to *Develop* different forms of resources, such as gasoline, which can then be brought to gas stations. The gas station is the conduit that is used to *Deliver* the once hidden resource into a form that is used to power an engine inside of a vehicle that takes people to various destinations. This is where the mantra of *Dream Octane* was born: "*If innovative change is an engine, your unique dream and ability could be its fuel.*"

I used to believe that gifts were privileges provided to fortunate people who happened to come across opportunities that helped to expose them. I am sure many of us have heard it said, "that person was at the right place at the right time." It is true that good fortune in life may not be equally distributed. However, as we put good effort behind the resources we have buried within us, it could become good fortune to others if your niche meets a need they have.

Our giftings become gifts not when we acknowledge receipt of them, but when we intentionally give them away. When speaking to the elder leadership in Ephesus, the Apostle Paul shares a saying of Jesus not found in the gospels.[52] Paul notes He said: *It is more blessed to give than to receive.* Our gifts are designed to be given away, so once we discover them it then gives us a responsibility to develop and deliver them. Our niches manifest themselves in our gifts and foreshadow themselves in our dreams. An effective way of developing that value is to refine it with the awareness that *it's not about you.*

So, think about this experience that you have as being potential for service. The journey that you have already gone through—the life lessons that you have learned; what has inspired you to find your niche— should be the tool that's going to help someone else move or accelerate in his/her own life. Finding our niche and delivering it in ways that others believe is meaningful will help us develop what we offer.

As we work towards becoming an expert, it is important to note that what adds value to someone else is about how we help to meet a need. So, the challenge is to identify the audience in which you want to speak to, ask them questions around areas you can be helpful with, and apply your niche to accelerate a valuable portion of their journey. As you begin this reciprocating process of adding value to others with the content you have developed, your content itself will develop if you refine it by applying what you have learned while sharing it with others. Starting out on this journey is going to feel a bit like a dance. As you take a step forward to offer your content as a service to your audience, the information that you receive from them may cause you to take two steps back before you can step forward again. Don't worry, this is all a part of the process.

I learned this process when I began serving a group of individuals at Christ church who were endeavoring to become first time authors. Aside from the heavy lifting of working in the hospital during the pandemic, I had several things happening at that time that included creating content that complemented the niche finding process that I learned from Clickfunnel's training, building the funnel for my coaching platform, and finishing the edits for the content of this book.

The church was looking for leaders for a new virtual platform that was intended to connect people through common interest. The goal of the virtual *Connect Groups* was to provide individuals access to community while half of the nation—and world for that matter—was on lockdown. There was a large part of me that did not want to take on another responsibility, but my wife encouraged me to consider it. She thought it would be good for me to get back to helping others, so I filled out the application. After attaching the application to the email, there was an opportunity to back out. All I had to do was not hit the send button. But I felt I had more to give. I quickly hit send and it was there that the thought came to mind right in the middle of my hesitation: '*Look, it's not about you, Cliff.*' I soon found while helping to Free Koko that serving was more than an exercise in kindness—when you are developing—it is necessary.

The key difference between being a *go-getter* versus *going to give*

Before I introduce you to Dr. Ohmslaw and KoKo, I would like to take a quick commercial break. I know at this point you may be thinking to yourself; how many commercial breaks is this guy going to take? All I can say to that is I make no apologies, as I am an 80s kid who may have watched entirely too much television growing up. Anyhow, imagine being at that same Christie's New York event—mentioned earlier in the Change your Frame section—on May 8th, 2018 where *Nymphéas en fleur* (Water Lilies in Bloom), 1914-1917 sold for 84.6 million dollars. Now insert this next scene, which I completely made up.

Imagine the auctioneer walks up to the podium and unveils a violin as the next item to be auctioned. "This is a one-of-a-kind violin," the svelte built auctioneer says standing at the podium in a nicely tailored Italian navy-blue pinstriped suit. As he points everyone's attention to a perfectly perched violin on display he continues, "It was made famous by renown violinist Wilford Capecchi. He was known for traveling the world and playing beautiful ensembles for four distinct groups: prison inmates, widows, orphans, and dignitaries. As the story goes, whenever this violinist was asked why he played for only these groups his reply was always the same:

"I play for inmates because my father died as one.

"I play for widows because I saw the impact of my Father's death on my mother.

"I play for orphans because when my mother died, I know what it feels like to be one.

"I play for dignitaries because their financial support allows me to do what I love to do for the other three groups."

As the auctioneer continued his description of the violinist and his instrument, he stated that this was the only violin that Capecchi played. As a matter of fact, Capecchi chose at least one fortunate individual to sign the back of his violin each time he played in front of an audience. Capecchi's violin was handed over to family when it was inadvertently left on the dock as Capecchi headed off as one of the passengers of the first voyage of the Titanic.

Okay, maybe the Titanic is a bit much but work with me here. The point of the story, however, is back in the auction where we find the violin being sold for 2 million dollars. The winner of the bid took the violin back to his estate and placed it in his secure trophy room where he liked to show off his seven decimal point taste in luxury items.

This is where we find the distinction between being strictly a *go-getter* versus *going to give*. Both groups may have some level of achievement associated with either. However, there is an added layer of fulfillment with the latter. In the example mentioned above, the winner of the bid for Capecchi's violin derived value from the satisfaction received from the flattering of his associates who shared his taste in luxury items. Essentially, he—the *go-getter*—received value from what he achieved. Capecchi, on the other hand, received fulfillment from what he *gave* away. The violin became like a conduit for his gift to flow through and into the hearts of his audiences.

Capecchi's story may be rooted in make-believe, but the point is true to life: to obtain fulfillment in what you do for others requires offering important aspects of who you are. As you refine your niche it is vital to understand that success is not the only measuring stick. If it were, we would shorten the seven steps on the Life *Cycle* of *Excavation* down to four; *change* the title of Step #4 to *Find Your Perch* and then create a way to perfectly place your niche on display. The coaching session I had with Dr. Ohmslaw helped to reveal how damaging it can be if those we are closest to influence us to follow the erroneous *find your perch* mindset. Her story of Free Koko not only uncovered how Koko obtained freedom, but it also helped to liberate my perception around the value of pursuing fulfillment through serving others as well.

Free Koko

Before we begin our story, I am going to mention that there are underlined phrases in this section. When we get to Step # 5 *Neutralize Barriers Blocking you from Fulfilling your Dream,* we cover how one method of problem-solving is recognizing that the solution is often hidden inside of the problem. The underlined words/phrases could be clues to potential solutions. It is a way of not only showing you the problem but also including you in the thought process in potentially finding the solution as well. Okay, now let's meet Dr. Ohmslaw.

"I'm going to record now, and I'll send you the video," I said to Dr. Ohmslaw as we started our one-on-one session that I used for those whom I was helping to become a first-time author. There were thirteen members and although that was a small number, it was difficult at times to parcel out individual needs. We met over the course of three months and had six

Connect Group sessions. The one-on-one sessions that I was doing with a few members of the group were getting positive feedback from those who participated. Dr. Ohmslaw was one of the members who signed up for a session. Her initial email to me prior to this meeting expressed interest in learning how to start a podcast, and she also disclosed that her greatest struggle with writing her book was narrowing down the several book ideas she had in mind. She wrote, "I suffer big time from analysis paralysis. It's pretty terrible!"

I sent Dr. Ohmslaw the 5P Framework to review in advance of the session and let her know that it's been helpful with others whom I was coaching. I asked her to try to complete it with a family member, a close personal friend and/or mentor. "Don't stress about the answers," I wrote in the email. "I have seen it work best when we write the first thing that comes to mind. Answers can repeat and each category can have more than one item with an identical score. Have fun with it. We will discuss more on the 16th. I'm a geek with this kind of stuff so looking forward to the conversation."

Dr. Ohmslaw received her doctoral degree in business with a minor in education. At the start of our session, I began walking her through the *Life Cycle of Excavation* to help frame our conversation. I shared with her the seven steps and provided many of the same examples offered thus far in this book. I was encouraged by how engaged she was with the material, but it was her response to my question of *what did you write down for what your passions are* on the 5P Framework worksheet that caught my attention. We now pick up at the interview where we finish up with steps one through three and tie off our discussion on opportunity cost relative to one's comparative advantage.

"Yes," I said. "In this terminology, the neighbor would have high opportunity costs when trying to take that on, because the neighbor would have to do so much to get up to speed of what Farrokh has immediately accessed in this cache of knowledge."

"[It would be a] high barrier to entry," Dr. Ohmslaw replied.

"Somewhat," I responded. "Barriers to entry have more to do with competitive not comparative advantage. It is close though. So that is steps one through three. Now, before we go to Step #4, I want to go back to that 5P Framework form that you have. That form is really Step #1 on the Life Cycle of Excavation. The podcast idea that you have is actually Step #4, but I want to go through steps one through three quickly, okay? So, when you look at what you have down on your paper, and this is going to tie into your book, what do you have under passions?"

To my surprise she replied, "I have nothing. Now, I think it might be helpful to just say, [that] I come from a very conservative, Caribbean family. [I had a] very strict upbringing—almost soul crushing. I don't know if that's your background or not, but you know, it was very abusive for me. So, everything I've ever tried in my life, there has been much more criticism than I could have handled at any given moment in my life. For example, learning the piano, or wanting to do [creative] things, I would always start those things and then I would just be so discouraged because my father typically would just rip it all to shreds. My confidence growing up was almost non-existent. It's important to know that, because it [was] on going when I went to college, [and] I wanted to be a psychologist.

"When I first went into school, my mom said, [I had] to become a nurse or something in the healthcare industry. I didn't want to do that. So, I majored in psychology. I didn't tell her, but I wanted to be a psychologist, and I had this dream about working for the FBI as a profiler. The internet was just starting out…[and] there wasn't enough information there for me to be able to gather what to do, and I didn't have any influencers. There's no one in my life that could actually tell me how to do this impossible thing in my mind. But when I graduated and I got accepted into grad school for psychology, I asked my mom if she would help me pay.

"She said, 'No, because how many black psychologists do you know? I'm not paying for it.'"

"Wow!" I murmured, surprisingly.

She continued, "So, at every point where I've tried to figure out who I am, or I've had an idea of what I wanted to do, there's been so many roadblocks and [they] have done so much damage. It's only now as I've gotten older, [after] I lost my job three years ago, [that I realized that this] was the trigger that God used really [to get my attention]. The first email [I sent] was to pastor David Ireland. I didn't even know if he would respond to me because it's not like he really knew me. My husband's a musician at the church, but I emailed him. He responded and called me back within an hour. I said to him, I'm losing my job and I don't think that I'm going to make it through, because that was the very last thing that I had, that said to me: 'You have some sort of value in this world. You're in this job, you're doing well.'

"My doctorate was part of that. I'm not dumb like they said that I am. I'm much smarter. I'm much more capable. 'God didn't make a mistake with me' kind of thing. A lot of these things that I've done [were] sort of like "proof of life," if you want to call it that. I've never really taken time until now to try and figure out who I am, to work through all of those things that were layered on me. So, as I'm going through [the Niche Finder form], and it's one step at a time, I don't really know. When you ask *what excites you?* <u>I'm like, okay, well, my kids do, you</u>

know? I'm excited, but that's not the kind of thing you're talking about.

"*What are you passionate about?* I don't know. I really, really don't know."

At this point I began feeling both motivated at helping Dr. Ohmslaw and giddy about the ideas that were flying through my mind.

"First off I appreciate you sharing," I said in response. "I want to encourage you from the onset is that what you want to fulfill—simply put—*is possible*. The second statement I want to give you—which goes alongside the first one—is that *it's in you*. Although we may not have identified it yet, rest assure: God does not leave vacuums in people. He dropped something inside of each of us that makes us unique and sometimes—as I say in my book—we are the landscape that seems to be barren on the surface, but we have to drill. We have to drill beneath the surface to find a reservoir that is inside of us. For some it is deeper than others, but it doesn't matter whether it's deep or shallow. Whatever it takes at the end of the day, when we strike oil, it's designed to benefit more than the landscape.

"The landscape gives this [uniqueness] off, but really the natural resource that gushes from this geyser is designed to be developed, distilled, and delivered into something that's useful to somebody else, whether it be warming a house or fueling a car. So, that really is the framework for going through this process. Let us find what is inside of you that we can help identify and then distill into a form that can become fuel for some other engine of change.

"When it comes down to identifying your abundant factor the profession may not be the abundant factor. I've had this conversation multiple times, and when I talk to people, the first thing that comes to mind is like, 'Okay, what can I do?' but that may not be the abundant factor. Here's a quick example about that. My sister was a teenage mom, and she was judged for being one. People told her to drop out of school based on their limiting belief that statistically, the probability of success was pretty low. Over time she said these external voices started to become her internal voice. She shared this story when I interviewed her on my podcast as she was making the point of her struggles with imposter syndrome. So, here is my sister, who because she felt judged, now wanted to help people who felt judged. She also considered herself to be a very good listener. She went on to be a psychologist who works in the juvenile penile system. So, when I ask people, 'What do you think my sister's abundant factor is?' I find the responses interesting.

"Now, let me ask you…what do you think her abundant factor would be?"

Without skipping a beat, Dr. Ohmslaw quickly responded, "I would say empathy."

"Excellent!" I said. "That's exactly right. Now, what makes empathy the correct reason is that empathy can be used in psychology. She could have gone off to become a teacher…a career mentor, a coach, or whatever. She chose the field of psychology because that's the space that has the environment that would use what she has inside of her intensely.

"That describes Step #2, which looks for the environment that uses what you have in abundance. Now, you said something I thought was interesting and I'll shut up after this because I want to hear what you have to share. When you said, 'I feel passionate about my kids,' I would look at that. I mean, there may be something there. I would not want to stop with just saying, "Oh, it's just my kids." No, there is something there I would love to talk about a little bit more. But first tell me more about what you wanted to share."

Like the rumbling of the ground just before an oil gusher reveals itself, so did the excitement in her voice increase as she continued. "You're 100%, right," she said. "Your profession or your career is not necessarily the abundant factor. It could be—maybe in some, very unique situations, right? But it's not.

"I've learned that. I mean, I went into HR, which for the entire time I was there about eighteen years I hated it. Now, what I did love about it was like the employee relations, sitting down with folks and kind of drilling down in terms of, what are the issues we're talking about? What sort of interpersonal challenges [do] we have and helping them to understand [what they are]. If you want to approach your boss about this promotion or whatever the case is or discipline those kinds of things like <u>coming alongside people and helping them to be better employees, to sort of grow</u>, that's what I loved.

"The part that I hated was, you know, the fact that HR is sometimes weaponized, they fire people and do other things that [can] crush people's souls, and I did not like that. It was directly opposed to who I am. Not that I think everything is always rosy. It's just that, that wasn't part of what I wanted to do."

"Writing came about," Dr. Ohmslaw continued, "when I was thinking and thinking and thinking, and finally, I just remembered way back, when I was like in the <u>seventh grade</u> I had this English teacher who was a beautiful black woman. I can't really remember her name, but I remember what she looked like. <u>She had given us a writing assignment.</u> I remember when she gave us the writing assignment, I looked at this thing. What she did was she gave us a scene and told us to finish the story. I was thinking it was the first time I ever had to do that, that there was no way I was going to do well on this. I didn't know what I was going to write. I thought I was the least creative, imaginative person.

"Then I went home, I wrote the story out, and I remember being very detailed, even down to the sounds the floor panels made—all those things. It was like this little mystery thing that I wrote. Then I handed it in. I didn't think about it. But [when] she came back to me she said, 'You did such an amazing job. You should really consider being a writer'. Now imagine me telling my mom that—it was so out of left field. I thought to myself that she would say 'You can write for a living? Is that even such a thing for a young black girl…?' I don't know how many black folks in my junior high school or in my circle would have ever thought about writing or journalism as a career or anything like that.

"But my point is she was the first person that *ever* built me up, and that is what she used, and I latched on to that. Then for the last seven, eight years I've been sitting on these book ideas because there's this crippling fear that just continues to fester, and that's what I'm battling. I'm like, 'God, please deliver me' because I've spent the better part of my life hearing all the things that I can't do, kind of like your sister and what she walked through. I'm still trying to deal with those issues, and that's through prayer and Christ church helping me with the counseling, but that's the one thing I can remember as a positive growing up; there aren't very many positives."

I was encouraged by Dr. Ohmslaw and had a few thoughts that came to mind as she shared. Although it wasn't totally clear as of yet, I felt a picture forming.

"I appreciate you sharing those two analogies," I said. "As you were speaking, I began seeing a bulldozer that we could use to get through a few of these barriers you've mentioned. As I'm listening to you—it seems for every 'yes' that came up in your spirit around an activity that ignited you, there has been a 'no' that countered it. I would say, as we finish, just put down your 'yeses' on this form. Let's not have any 'buts' in here, any transition or contrasting statement that finishes your sentence. Let's keep the sentence incomplete and go with what comes initially into your heart. As we go through the Niche Finder form whatever activity from your past that causes you to think of an answer like 'yes' at that moment, put that down on your paper. What you just mentioned for example can go under patterns."

"Yeah," Dr. Ohmslaw said in response. "I did put that as number one under patterns."

"Okay, good," I replied. "I think things are lining up because that's exactly right. It would be a pattern. Now, when you speak about your passion, I hear in what you said about HR—before the but—that you liked helping people, right?"

"Mmm hmm," she said in agreement.

It always fascinates me how engaged people are when they speak about their niche. Once our insecurities are set aside, the energy level of the conversation instantly goes up. This part of the discussion with Dr. Ohmslaw was no different.

"You really enjoy it," I said. "I heard your voice lighting up. I'm sure if our cameras were on, I would probably see you smiling from ear to ear as you answered that part of the question. It is clear by your tone that <u>you really like helping people</u>, which is great! Let's put that down as one of the answers under the category of *passion*, because it sounds like this is something that ignites you.

"Now, let's look at the areas where you have experienced moments that felt purposeful. [However,] before you answer that, you can repeat answers. The category is not being measured against itself. So, you don't have to have one score to an answer higher than another answer in that same category. They can all be fives. They can all be ones. They can all be different numbers. Does that make sense?"

"Okay, I got that," she replied.

"Okay, good," I said. "Now under purposeful, what do you do—or have done—that makes you feel like: Wow, I was made for this moment?"

"Well," she said, "I do think that <u>one of the gifts that I know I have is encouragement</u>. My kids seem to think that I can talk people into almost, well, I won't say almost anything, but I can really encourage people to sort of step out on faith and I can do that for others. I just need to get to the place where I can do that for me. But, you know, physicians can't heal themselves either. …A lot of people come to me for writing, I will say, now that I'm thinking of it.

"I had a girlfriend who needed gastric bypass surgery but [when] she had asked her insurance, they turned her down, and she came to me and she said, '<u>Would you help me? Would you write a letter for me</u>?' This is a while ago—I'm talking about maybe fifteen years ago or something like that. We wrote that letter and she was able to have them reverse that decision.

"Most recently—and I'm talking about early 2020—one of my friends from my doctoral program reached out to me and she said, 'You know, my son-in-law was trying out for the police Academy in New York state, and he went for his test. He finally was given an appointment for his physical exam—which was like a bootcamp.'

"She said, he wasn't feeling himself, but he did it anyway, and he failed. He got the letter from them saying that he didn't pass. But he later found out that he was positive for COVID-19. So, this was at the beginning of COVID when tests were not available as quickly, and then when you did take a test, it was taking like two, three weeks for you to get the results. He kind of suspected that he hadn't done well, but then once he got the letter, she said, 'Would you mind writing an appeal for us? Because if anybody can do it, I think you can help us'.

"We went through the same doctoral program, in the sense that she and I are alike. The skills are there for both of us. So, I was kind of surprised, but I was also honored. So, I told her I would do it—and I did.

"I wrote it and I prayed over it," Dr. Ohmslaw continued. I then heard a faint **thud** against a table. Although the thud was subtle, it reminded me of an impassioned Pentecostal preacher tapping the top of a podium at specific points of emphasis in the message. Dr. Ohmslaw continued, "I prayed over it." Then I heard the thud again. It didn't come across as loud and obnoxious. As a matter of fact, I did not even notice it when we had the conversation initially. It wasn't until I played the recorded audio of our session back that I picked up on it. As I listened, the sound seemed to be unintentional. It was almost unconscious, as if it were reverberating her conviction.

"I said," Dr. Ohmslaw continued, "Lord, these are words." Then the thud happened again.

"But if you "bless these words," she said as the last thud landed like a songbird descending on a branch to release the music it had churning within itself, "...then it becomes more like a weapon of sorts. In terms of whatever it is that's preventing [my friend's son] from moving forward [in the police academy because] this was his last year to qualify age wise.

"I prayed over it.

"I wrote it for them. [The academy] accepted it and granted him an appeal. I have lots of emails of recent, where I even showed my husband the other day, there's <u>this little common thing</u>, where I've written something to encourage someone, and they would write back and say this brought tears to my eyes.

"Again, please don't take this the wrong way, it's just when I'm thinking about it, I feel like God sometimes will answer the unprayed requests that are in my heart where he knows how small I'm feeling, and then he'll allow a message to come through to say, 'No, no. This is something that you really should pursue.' So, I want to pursue it, *but I'm telling you*, every time I sit in front of a computer, *I feel like the least qualified*. I don't know if you felt that way, writing in your book."

"I'm going to answer that after we finish the exercise," I said jumping in with a lighthearted response, "because part of the rules we established is to *not put "the but"* in the conversation." We both laughed.

"Oops," Dr. Ohmslaw acknowledged.

"So, here's the thing," I continued, "I think it's really interesting, and I notice with this exercise, that we at times overlook our abundant factor. We may diminish our abundant factor because it comes easy to us. Or that aspect of our abundant factor on display may seem to be just random chance. It's never random chance. God has put something inside of you that is unique. It's uniquely crafted for a specific time and a specific audience. You can see this exampled in scripture where multiple prophets shared a message that was able to catch the attention of the groups they were reaching out to.

Ezekiel shaved off half his beard,[53] Isaiah had the coals of fire on his lips,[54] Jeremiah used the Potter and the potter's wheel[55]. These object lessons were all different approaches. Apart from Jesus—who was more than a prophet and communicated to all—each servant communicated in a way through the inspiration of God to a *particular* group who were receptive to the message they conveyed.

"Now, here's the point. Your message *resonates* with a particular group of individuals just like a tuning fork's tune. That tune was heard when you stated how your kids admired how you could convince or influence others with your words. That's, a gift!" I didn't tap the podium at this point but in hindsight I think I wanted to. "Think about it," I said, "people from different walks of life, at different moments in time have come to you and asked you to write something because they believe that you could help them.

"Whether it is the friend with the appeal letter to the insurance company or your former classmate who you felt was just as qualified as you are, they sought help from your gift. The thing that is inside of you appears occasionally, as a *glimpse*."

"That's exactly right," Dr. Ohmslaw responded. "It's only a *glimpse*, and then, it just disappears. That's exactly right."

Glimpse

I am going to take another quick commercial break here to talk about the word *"glimpse"* that Dr. Ohmslaw mentioned above. So far, Dr. Ohmslaw's story helps to uncover the opportunity that we all have in discovering what our niche is. Some may argue if finding our niche was this easy everyone would have awareness of what it is. However, offering what is helpful to others but unique to you may not be that transparent. This would make the goal of specializing even more challenging. To overcome that, pull out the list we summarized in Step # 3. Select the highest quality score—closest to 15— and lowest opportunity grade of "A" or the closest to it. The optimal selection off the summarized list from Step #3 would be a 15A. This would highlight the area that you have identified as being what you do well and is the easiest for you to implement.

One indication that you have drilled down on a helpful quality is that there will be moments when you glimpse that it has been helpful before. These *glimpse* examples are valuable as they point to groups and/ or industries that could benefit from your unique service.

In Step # 4, these small groups are referred to as your *microcosm*. We discuss later on in this step why endeavoring to *master your microcosm* is so important. Again, what we have that is helpful to others, but unique to us, is not always easily recognizable as things that we do well (our niche). It may only reveal itself as a glimpse. If we tie this back to the quote from one of the intellects of our modern times—Albert Einstein—this truism is at the core of the statement, we referenced in the Steve Harvey's section.

Einstein said, "Your imagination is everything. It is the *preview* of life's coming attractions." I added emphasis to the word preview as we've already covered imagination, but this preview is equally important. In the movie industry, previews help to build the anticipation of the movie with snippets of the film that catch our attention. It is not until we go to see the movie that we are either satisfied by the expectation that the preview set or disappointed because the movie didn't measure up. We will address some of these deterrents in Step # 5 *Neutralize Barriers Blocking You From Fulfilling Your Dream*.

We want to recognize the glimpse of these moments when our gift provides support, significance, or success for others. Once identified, we will then create content to serve more. Give away what you create that is helpful. Tweak it to make the resource you are offering more effective, then give it out again. Give, tweak, and repeat. Where the discovery section encouraged you to *keep drilling*, the development section admonishes us to *keep giving*. The portion of the 5P exercise above with Dr. Ohmslaw is an example of how the *glimpse* may appear.

Back to Free Koko:

As our session continued, we were able to uncover that Dr. Ohmslaw had several books she felt compelled to write. The first was a series of children's books, which incorporated her love for her kids and provided life lessons as encouragement.

She remarked, "So, we have a cat named Koko. The characters would be animals and Koko [would] get into all kinds of shenanigans and trouble. I mean, she really does in the house, and so we safely lock her up in the bathroom when she gets out of hand. So, that's why the whole idea of free Koko comes up, but she's really just such a sweet, beautiful cat. The idea was really about creating cat characters. Both my boys love cats, we have two of them, but my little one especially is just a cat kid. So, that's where it all came from."

The second book for Dr. Ohmslaw had deeper conviction. The book was entitled, *White Card,* and after our session she described it beautifully in a correspondence that she later sent me after having a transparent conversation with a friend who was white.

"...Now this conversation is important," she wrote, "because during our first Connect Group when I described my book, I believe I expressed that it was an answer to our white allies who are asking for help in understanding. What *White Card* offers is only a small part in a larger, complex dialogue. However, it is a dialogue that cannot be had without grace. People simply don't know how to wade into the conversation without fear of being hurt or of offending Black people. So, hearing her confess this informed me that I am on the right track. That perhaps there is something different we can say or consider. And of course [Cliff], episode 5 of your podcast with Dr. Smith stating that we need to go from 'allies to advocates' blew me away. God *is* doing something different, and I want to be obedient to that."

The initial thought here was why not just do both, however the slow but steady approach has a greater return. Tony Schwartz is the president and CEO of The Energy Project and the author of, *The Way We're Working Isn't Working.* He also wrote an article published in the *Harvard Business Review* entitled "The Magic of Doing One Thing at a Time" in which he stated "…when you switch away from a primary task to do something else, you're increasing the time it takes to finish that task by an average of 25 percent"[56]

The *Lifecycle of Excavation* is designed to help us uncover the one major thing we have in abundance (steps 1-3), refine it through serving others (steps 4 and 5) and eventually bring it to a wider audience (steps 6 and 7). Dr. Ohmslaw was experiencing what Tony Schwartz stated above; by thinking about too many projects at once, she was taking her time away from developing her abundance factor by starting out with one book. Eventually, and I am sure to what would be Tony Schwartz's delight, she decided to focus her attention on *White Card* and she began plans to create a podcast she could use as a platform to serve her audience. Steps 1-3 helped Dr. Ohmslaw place an importance on the glimpses we get of our abundant factor. However, this only covers the *Unique to You* aspect of Step # 4 *Specialize in Offering What is Helpful to Others but Unique to You.* As you pursue this aspect of giving, keep in mind: *Offering What is Helpful to Others* can be at times a bit of a paradox.

The Paradox of Value

If we think back to Pattillo Higgins, his story is an analogous comparison to how our abundant factor is often exposed as merely glimpses. He was a salt miner who believed that oil and gas resided beneath the salt domes of Spindletop Texas, despite the conventional wisdom of that day.[57] As a self-taught geologist, Pattillo may have made a correlation between salt domes and potential oil reservoir.[58] Scientists now know that oil reservoirs can be found trapped in salt domes.[59] However, back then the Gulf Coast region was regarded as not having oil—or petroleum—potential.[60] It is unclear what he saw that led him to believe there was oil there but whatever the glimpse, it left him with a dogged determination to bring it to the surface.

What he believed to be inherent worth was not exposed, so there was a struggle to convince the oil industry of that time that it was worth investing in long-term as the early sites kept coming up dry. The value that he believed that location had to offer was not fully exposed, so it was difficult to validate for others its intrinsic worth. If we step back in time even further than Pattillo Higgins, we will find another ripple in time in macroeconomics.

Referring back to Farrokh's *International Trade and Global Macropolicy,* David Ricardo was step number four on the *Six Steps to Increase the Overall Welfare of a Country.*[61]

However, before Ricardo's theory of specialization in 1817—based on comparative advantage—there was Adam Smith's absolute advantage. According to Farrokh, Adam Smith was the first to articulate that "international trade is not a zero-sum game and that, in fact, a single-minded reliance on exports is counterproductive.[62] In the book, *The Wealth of Nations,* there was a dilemma that the author Adam Smith was unable to answer as it relates to value. He was perplexed by the paradox of value or what has also been called the diamond–water paradox.

Educator Akshita Agarwal describes Adam Smith's dilemma in a TED Ed video I found on YouTube. It brilliantly describes how the diamond-water paradox works in the video entitled, *The Paradox of Value.*[63] She begins the video with having you pretend that you are the winning contestant on a game show and can select either a diamond or a bottle of water as a prize. In this situation, most would choose the diamond over the water.

However, if you place that same contestant in a desert and tell them they are dehydrated, which do you think they would choose: a diamond or a bottle of water? The obvious selection in this scenario would be the water. She remarks that the game show describes the *exchange value* of the prize options meaning "what you could obtain for them at a later time." The desert scenario she refers to is the *use value* "how helpful they are in your current situation." When you can only choose one out of the two options in a given situation, it creates the paradox of value.

In 1871, Carl Menger published a theory where he described value as being subjective. Menger, along with William Stanley Jevons and Léon Walras, helped to solve the diamond-water paradox that Adam Smith left undone in *The Wealth of Nations.*[64] They did so by founding *marginal utility* in which "the concept implies that the utility or benefit to a consumer of an additional unit of a product is inversely related to the number of units of that product he already owns."[65] If we go back to Akshita Agarwal's desert *use value* description, the first few bottles of water will be enough to satiate the contestant's dehydration. However, if there is a good chance of survival and there is enough water to get out of the desert and back to society, the diamonds would become valuable again. This is where Akshita Agarwal references opportunity cost. If you recall in Step # 3, opportunity cost is the amount we will lose if we choose the alternate option. The use value of the water when it related to sustaining life had a *high opportunity cost* because without it the contestant could die with pockets full of diamonds.

We all have something to offer, which steps one through three helped to uncover. Step# 4, however, is about how we take that idea and create content that is helpful to others but unique to us. The paradox that we encounter is in making sure that what we have to offer matches the environment—or audience—it is supplied in.

Now, connecting an individual's inherent value with the prospect of that worth being offered to a given environment can open the door for other principles that I would like us to steer clear of. We could easily fall down the rabbit hole of utilitarianism, Marxism and/or communism. At this point, I will kindly ask you to take a large step around these narratives so as not to fall into these socialistic points of view. This step is less about what society has to get from you and more of what do you have of value that you would be willing to serve others with. However, in order to do this, take the abundant factor that has already been flushed through the environment that has used it intensely and the comparative advantage that makes you unique and think to yourself in Step # 4: How can I better express this *one thing*? I hasten to add that the abundance we have to offer may take us being humble enough to ask for help.

The benefits of synergy and why others are necessary

I have to admit that I take both pride and pleasure in landscaping my lawn in Pennsylvania. It isn't an extremely large property, but it is enough to keep me busy with lawn maintenance for a few hours every other week. On one such occasion, I had to remove a tree shrub at the top of a hill that began dying and needed to be replaced. I had experience removing these types of shrubs and although it was only 2 1/2 feet in diameter and maybe about four and a half feet tall, I knew that the roots to these trees ran deep and that it could be a challenge to pull it out of the ground. So, I draped my face with focus and determination as I grabbed my shovel and began to dig.

As the shovel hit the mulch that surrounded the tree, I felt a sensation of being watched. My next door neighbor Steve, who also took pride in his lawn, was looking at me. The thought did cross my mind as to why he was peering in my direction, but it did not linger long as I refocused on getting this tree up. As my shovel hit the ground again, I didn't notice that he began heading in my direction with a 6-foot spear like metal rod in his right hand and a pair of branch cutters in his left.

He came over to me and said, "Here, Cliff, try these 'cause I know how much of a pain moving these shrubs can be. If you use this metal rod to expose the roots and then use these branch cutters to clip them it may be helpful."

I thanked him and grabbed the tools that he gave me. He then turned and headed back into his house. I took his advice, stuck the metal rod into the ground, twisted it around a few times, saw the roots, and then cut them. The entire exercise took about ten to fifteen minutes, which was a record for me. If you recall E.A.S.Y in Step # 3, this was an "E" moment for me. You may be thinking at this point, okay I know what I have that could be helpful to others but getting it done is going to be hard. It will take effort, yes, but with helpful guidance it could save you time and become more effective. I want to give you an "E" *Exposure to information* by showing you how my journey into content creation happened with the hope that it would be helpful in your journey and eventually afford you the opportunity of experiencing the "A" of *Accelerated change.*

Lights, Prisms and Apple

We creative people are like the light spectrum of a rainbow. Every color could be used in one way or another. All the colors are collectively and individually purposeful. However, whenever you see a rainbow in the sky, although the colors appear to come out of nowhere, they are merely exposing what is inherent within visible light. In other words, visible light that can be seen by the human eye is made up of several different colors: red, orange, yellow, green, blue, indigo, violet. Shortly after rainfall, if both water droplets and sunlight are in the sky, a rainbow can emerge from the sunlight being refracted / reflected through the water droplets.[66] The water droplets act like a prism and convert that white light to display the multiple colors of the rainbow that it is made of.

There is a synergy that develops when your content has harmony between products, quality, and consistency. Momentum develops and your content becomes a message expressed in different forms versus several unrelated great ideas. As an example, let's look at the spectrum of products that Apple has included in their press releases since 2012:

> "Apple designs Macs, the best personal computers in the world, along with OS X, iLife, iWork and professional software. Apple leads the digital music revolution with its iPods and iTunes online store. Apple has reinvented the mobile phone with its revolutionary iPhone and App store and is defining the future of mobile media and computing devices with iPad."[67]

Although these products are different, they are not disparate. They are all different expressions of the same mission Steve Jobs instituted in the 1980s. Steve Jobs had this as the mission statement for Apple: "To make a contribution to the world by making tools for the mind that advance humankind."[68]

There is a stark similarity between the light bulb like ideas of visionary Steve Jobs and the principle behind the spectrum of colors found in visible light. Steve Jobs took a single idea and made variations of it. His light—or bright idea—once reflected through the prism of Apple, has formed into the rainbow of products that currently stretches around the world. Now we can't all be Steve Jobs, but guest what: We do not have to be. Each of us has a light—or abundant factor—that we have to share. But it is important for us to focus that idea so that we form variations from it as opposed to being unfocused and run the risk of not having a clear message. Having great ideas are special but it can hinder the ultimate goal of getting to *Step # 7 of Maximizing Your Abundant Factor* if your focus changes frequently. Now that you have identified your niche using steps 1-3, focus on taking that single idea through all seven steps before you start to move on to any other item from your summarized list. *Dream Octane* is a single idea, but I learned that using this idea in different forms assisted me in serving audiences that saw my niche as being helpful.

Master your microcosm

If you recall, Step #2 described identifying environments where your niche is used intensely. We referenced Steve Harvey in this example and used the talent and comedy show stage as the right environment for the niche he has. Step #2 uncovers compatible environments where your abundant factor is used intensely, but Step #4 refines your offer to the audience that makes up that environment. Another way of looking at this would be that Step #2 is the comedy club stage and Step #4 is tailoring your content to John or Jane Doe seated in the audience. Who are you looking to serve? What are their needs and how does your niche help them to overcome something in particular? Now that you have identified what your niche is, find the group that it could be most helpful to and give it away.

I learned this principle as I was helping individuals to become first time authors in the Connect Group at Christ Church. It filled me with joy to offer advice on overcoming many of the hurdles of writing a first book. Some of the guidance shared was covered in the session mentioned before with Dr. Ohmslaw who was a part of that Connect Group. This wasn't the first time that I helped someone become a first-time self-published author, but it was rewarding to do so with a slightly larger group.

It took time to put together PowerPoints and clarify my thoughts around what I wanted to share; however, the conversations came E.A.S.Y I provided the group hurdles I was *exposed* to; shared where change was *accelerated*; gave them links to best practice I *studied* and offered frameworks that *yielded* results in the process.

The connect groups were designed for a three-month duration and were comprised of six separate hour-long sessions. To break up the teaching, I brought in a special guest for the second to last session. I introduced him to the group as Bishop

Stanford Senior Jr. with the cover of his book on the screen as a backdrop. He was someone I knew for over thirty-five years, and we were Godbrothers who treated each other at times as brothers. My intent was to provide these aspiring authors with a glimpse of what was possible, by hearing an example from someone who was where they currently were in the process.

In Proverbs chapter 11 versus 25, the New King James Version shares, "The generous soul will be made rich, and he who waters will also be watered himself." What caught me by surprise was how this selfless act of support used to water the group with inspiration provided splashes of motivation that encouraged my heart as well. We pick up at this point of Stan's conversation with the group as he shared the process he went through to self-publish his first book.

Master your microcosm: Fuel for Life

"About fifteen years ago or more," Stan said, "I became a youth pastor at a local church Cliff and I attended at the time." Stan has an uncanny ability of making his listeners feel as though they are hearing a story around a campfire. I'm not sure if it was the years in ministry, his personality, or a mixture of both, but his delivery causes listeners to lean into the conversation.

"I had this responsibility," he continued, "of trying to encourage the lives of teenagers. If any of you are parents on the line, you know, that is not an easy task. The Lord kind of dropped this thought in my spirit to just touch base with them on a weekly basis through a devotional." One note here for those not familiar with Christianese, the term "dropped in my spirit" is another way of saying *I was inspired.* This inspiration that Stan received motivated him to create short emails that he sent to a group of teenagers and college students. In the emails, he shared an illustration, provided a meaning to the story, and then wrote a few words of encouragement. We will unpack the importance of inspiration when we cover the I.D.R.E.A.M principles in Step # 6 *Organize the Delivery of Your Niche to a Wider Audience.* However, until then, let's get back to the campfire.

"And so, I started sending out emails to everybody," Stan said. "You know, a quick devotional that wasn't extremely long—just something to encourage them. I sent it out at the start of the week and that practice went on for few years. So, I had all these email devotionals and for years, people would say to me, you know you're a great writer. To be honest with you, I heard them, but I didn't really see that in myself. I guess a part of it was fear.

"It's one thing when you get encouragement coming from fellow believers in church: you could be the most mediocre singer, [for example] and one of the elder mothers in the congregation could still walk up to you afterwards and say, 'oh, baby, you know you bless my heart.'" Those from the *Connect Group* who were on the call smiled and nodded in agreement.

"But it's another thing," Stan continued, "when you talk about bringing something to the public: people aren't as cordial, and people aren't as patient. Constructive criticism is not as kind in the public arena as those who are familiar with you.

"And so, for approximately about ten years or so—it may have even been like twelve years—I was sitting on this potential book. Throughout the entire twelve years God had been pressing me and impressing upon me to do this book. I also had conversations with a number of people including Mr. Manning," he said pointing at the Zoom call in my direction. "And he would constantly get on me," Stan continued. "He would say 'Stan when are you going to do the book?' I would reply, 'Yeah, Cliff I'm going to do the book.' Then one day— and I'll never forget it—I was on my way home when Cliff called me. It was at the beginning of this year, and we hadn't spoken for a couple of months. When I picked up the phone— and after we exchanged our pleasantries—he said you know I haven't talked to you in a while. I know we need to do another IHOP meet up.'

"Cliff and I every so often like to go to IHOP and catch up over pancakes. So, I said yeah 'we need to set that up.' Cliff then said, 'but that's not really why I called you.'

"So, I'm like, okay, what's up? And he said, I just felt pressed by the Lord to call you and ask, 'what's going on with the book?'

"You know I'm used to this. I'm used to him saying this to me and I'm almost conditioned to giving the same old answer.

"But this conversation was a little different 'cause he was in his mode. I realized—from knowing him—the same old answer wasn't going to pacify him this time around. He was real firm with me and said, 'Stan, listen man, you have content. You have everything you need; you just need to put it to work. Start somewhere and get it done.' He then said, 'by the way you know what? After you get off this phone, I'm giving you an assignment.' At this point, I'm saying to myself 'okay this dude is really passionate right now and being assertive so I need to pay attention.' He said, 'All I want you to do is to go onto Amazon's Kindle Direct Publishing and create a profile for yourself. You know it will never happen if you don't start somewhere—you gotta start somewhere.'

"I'm like, 'yeah I guess I could take it slow.' But then I realized that he stirred up a fire in me."

I pause here to share with you an epiphany. Considering the pace of your audience's ability to assimilate the information that you are sharing with them is their call not yours. Yes, it is important to provide some sort of realistic time frames but there are those like Stan who will take what is helpful to them and add an accelerant to it.

The epiphany that I took from this exchange is this: What we have to offer that is helpful to others but unique to us is *just fuel*. The recipient is the one behind the wheel and they are the one who gets to decide how much to throttle the engine and how fast they want to go. Steps 4 and 5 are about refining that fuel from the resource you have within you; steps 6 and 7 are how you get the fuel to wider audiences and into the engine of change. With that being said, let's head back to where Stan throws another log into the campfire.

"Well, you know by the next time I spoke to Cliff," Stan continued, "within a couple weeks, I called to tell him where I was in the process. I told him that I had uploaded the manuscript.

"Cliff was like 'you, uploaded the manuscript already?'

"I said, yeah, I just went and got all the emails then switched them from email to a book layout format. Whatever was lacking, I updated, added more written material, and uploaded it."

Stan then said with enthusiasm and excitement in his eyes, "I'm ready!" He tapped the temple on the left side of his face. "I got ideas for the second, third, and fourth book already in mind."

Stan then said mockingly while both of us laughed, "Cliff's like Stan, hold up...hold on—wait a minute you are moving too fast.

"I actually remember saying to him, 'Listen, Bro, you started something in me that has turned into a monster. I can't eat or sleep without thinking about this book now.'

"I guess I'll use this point just to encourage you who are on the line. I realized in that moment that the whole thing about writing a book and sharing my thoughts is really just an opportunity to be a steward of what God put in me. What I had was seed. God gave me a seed and I sat on it for twelve years. If you remember the story of the talents, one received five talents, another got two bags, and the other one bag."

I'll jump in here to note that you may recall that this is the same story that Dr. David Ireland shared in his sermon about the three servants in Step # 1 *Recognize Your Abundant Factor*. It is the same story; however, Stan is describing Matthew chapter 25 versus 14-30 from the King James Version of the Bible. In this version, the bags of gold Dr. David Ireland mentioned are referred to as *talents*.

"One guy had five talents," Stan continued, "another had two talents and the last had one. I was the one with the one. Now it wasn't to the extent of the servant in the story where he accused the Master of being a hard person to deal with. But I think it was more to do with fear—I guess. I think I was underestimating that I had a voice that was worthy of the public hearing. I was underestimating the gift that was inside of me. And the time that I spent underestimating my gift and sat on it, it appeared dead.

"And the minute that my brother came in and sparked life into me about it, suddenly I had to do something with that seed. I needed to see it come to fruition and I couldn't do anything else. I had to spend hours and sacrifice you know, not going to bed, rereading the manuscript. Saying, oh, I don't like that, I gotta, you know, change that, erase that and so on.

"Throughout this time of getting to the point of publishing [Cliff and I] would speak. He would give me tips and pointers. He would say things like, 'Look Stan you're not gonna like the first edition, but you just gotta print it out.' I recall Cliff saying, 'print it out so you [can] see what it's going to look like.'

"And I remember printing it out and walking around with this ragtag manuscript in my bag. If I ever showed you the first manuscript, it had so much red on it you wouldn't even be able to read the content of it. I would go back and reread and change this and change that until eventually—it was ready.

"It's funny 'cause we would talk about this: what should have possibly taken over a year, took about two months. The next time we talked, I'm like, 'Bro, I need you to do the foreword for me because if anybody is going to do it, it's gonna be you. If it hadn't been for you getting on me, I wouldn't be at this point. [Cliff] was like, 'Sure, I got you. When do you need it by?'

"I said bro, I'm ready to publish in a couple of weeks. I want to get it out by March and he's looking at me like what— really?

"I said bro, I've been living, breathing and eating this thing—I need to get it out. I sent it out to be edited and did the cover graphics myself for the cover."

"Anyway, by this time it was around the middle of February as we were speaking through the process, and I felt led to bring the book out in the beginning of March. I wanted to wait, but then it was like the Lord was prodding me to put it out. So, I put it out the Sunday in March on my father's birthday. A part of the motivation behind this was I wanted to share the experience with my dad. I wanted him to know that I could not have achieved this milestone of putting out this 30-day devotional if not for the example and investment that he poured into my life. I needed to give back to him by publishing the book on his birthday so people could see, and I could make his name great."

"The ironic thing was, I put it out on that Sunday and then the same week we were hit with COVID-19 and the whole state locked down. I had all these great plans, but I rushed to do the book signing at Church on that Sunday. People were saying why don't you wait?

"And I replied, 'no, I just feel like God had a plan for me to do this right there and then. So, I dropped the book on Sunday and that Tuesday the state shut down.

"The amazing thing is that I was able to sell several hundred copies in spite of COVID-19, as they say*: out the trunk of my car.* I was able to get orders online and get deliveries out during this time. This did not include the additional downstream sales on Amazon. These sales were all happening by me bootstrapping the process and benefiting from word of mouth. So, I really wasn't doing a whole lot of advertising.

"The point that I'm making is had I just kept the seed in my pocket, I would not have had the achievement of publishing my first 30-Day Devotional book, *Fuel for Life.*

"Right now, I have five to six ideas in my brain, you know and [have] started to lay the groundwork for those going forward. I've also been in conversations with people who have purchased my book and then now they like, can we partner to do a book together?

"I'm like, 'okay.'

"And all of that started from a conversation that I had with my God brother Cliff who lit a fire under me and guided me along the way.

"I found a lot of times we as authors have the capacity:

"We have the content already in us...

"We have the idea already in us, but we lack the vision and roadmap to get our dream from point A to point B.

"We see what we see from our perspective. However, we need those inner circle people who see us outside of our perspective. They not only see us down the road but can help us to get there.

"People who have the time and the concern and the passion to help guide us from seed to germination, to development and eventually a matured tree.

"I was walking around with the seed for twelve years and my brother came into my life and caused me to plant it. So, people are now seeing it sprout.

"I had to get over my own fear...get over underestimating myself and my voice.

"As I close, I want to encourage you to not underestimate the impact of your voice. If you don't put that seed in the ground, you won't ever have the tree that it is designed to be. I could be looking at some bestsellers yet to happen, but you gotta put that seed in the ground, water it with effort and see that investment through.

"You've got to see it to the very end and the whole process is as simple as that. It can be at times overwhelming, but you got to push forward, you know and look at and start seeing things from the end, not from the beginning. If you see it from the beginning, you'll always be frustrated with what you feel *could be*. But if you see it from the end—where you are signing copies in front of a crowd or holding up your book and reading the words bestseller across the top of it—put your effort behind that.

"Seeing this work from the end, you will keep pushing forward even when the frustration is there, and you have setbacks because you're seeing the end of the thing. This principle is still churning in me as I just heard a preacher say this on Sunday. He said 'God sees the end of the thing before it gets there, and he pushes us to see the end of the thing that it can motivate us to get to that ending.' But I'm praying for you and asking God that as you put effort behind what you are doing God will bless all of your endeavors. So, with that I could say more, but I'm gonna shut up now.

"I'm gonna let my brother—the man of the hour— teach," Stan said as he turned the session back over to me.

"C'mon teacher," Stan said lightheartedly, "teach us now."

I laughed as I unmuted my microphone on Zoom and said, "Stan, you know I love you like a brother, man."

"Of course, my brother," Stan replied.

"I appreciate you sharing this encouragement," I continued. "There are so many nuggets in what you have to say the I literally have several follow-up questions, but I do have some content that I want to get to with the authors on the line."

"For sure," Stan said, "Naw, for sure…do your thing."

"I want to try to get through as much as we can," I said, "and then if we can, do some questions and answers. What I'll do is try to cut it short and have you come back to field questions from the group. If that's okay with everybody?" I asked turning my attention to those on the call, watching them respond in agreement. The rest of this content I will also share with you.

I was truly grateful for Stan's input to the group as a little encouragement goes a long way. We will stop here for me to be now firm with you and provide some encouragement by way of this quote from Zig Ziglar. He said, *You don't have to be great to start, but you have to start to be great.* At this point, if you have been actively participating in the process you would have recognized your abundant factor, identified where it is used intensely, and summarized your comparative advantage.

You would have pulled out the quality that has the highest quality score and was coupled with the lowest opportunity costs for serving others. This is where the two-step dance—of give, tweak, and repeat—we referred to at the start of this chapter happens. When you give away your abundant factor to serve others it affords you an opportunity to make that offer more refined. However, there is another dance that we can learn from honeybees that could mutually be beneficial for both you and those you are serving.

If you want to better serve your audience, learn the Waggle dance of the Honeybee

I'm sure many of us are familiar with the importance of honeybees, the role they play in cross pollination, and the benefits we humans gain from their involvement in the ecosystem. [69] If you are not, the short version is without honeybees, we humans would starve to death. The World Bee Day organization summarizes the honeybee's importance this way:

> *The greatest contribution of bees and other pollinators is the pollination of nearly three quarters of the plants that produce 90% of the world's food. A third of the world's food production depends on bees, i.e., every third spoonful of food depends on pollination.* [70]

So, the survival of our food source—and *us* for that matter—is strongly correlated to the survival of our friend the honeybee. However, this winged virtuoso is also highly sophisticated in how it finds and communicates where food sources are to its hive.

At the close of the 1920s, ethologist Karl von Frisch and colleagues, Konrad Lorenz and Nikolaas Tinbergen, won the Nobel Prize in Physiology for their study in insect communication.[71] Karl von Frisch uncovered that honeybees that find a food source of nectar not only share the converted nectar into honey with their fellow hive mates but also communicate where that food source is located.[72] When the honey-ladened bee arrives back in the hive, it moves in a careful pattern and performs a kind of dance that shows other bees the coordinates of the food source.

What researchers have uncovered by building on the work of Karl von Frisch is that bees communicate both distance and direction of the food source to other bees relative to the location of the hive, as well as the positioning of the sun. If the food is close to the hive the bee moves in a circular motion; if it is further away, they will walk in a figure eight pattern. In "bee talk" the duration of waggle indicates the distance of the flight. One second is approximately 750-1000 meters (about twice the height of the Empire State Building).[73] The bee will also walk in an angled direction that points out which direction their fellow hive mates will need to fly. When another bee leaves the hive, they will take that information and fly in the direction the waggling bee was pointing out for the distance that correlates to the duration of the dance.

Now, what does the honeybee's waggle dance have to do with you? We as humans have a much more sophisticated way of communicating because we can relay and receive information through various methods. Bees share their message with other honeybees by doing the waggle dance. We humans as content consumers share where the source of the content we consume *is* through word of mouth and/or sharing links within our networks. By learning the dance of the honeybee, it admonishes us to make content that is appealing enough that others who ingest it will bring it back to their network.

I learned this through podcasting and watching what worked for other content creators. The formula I use for selecting guests is to find people who are:

- *Interesting* to speak with.
- *Interested* in you and what you do.
- *Intriguing* and ask great questions that make you feel challenged and/or motivated.
- *Inspirational* in how they express themselves.

This method makes the podcast interview interesting to those who are a part of my audience. The guest now takes the episode after it is edited back to their network and members from their network may do a solo mission back to my content and join my audience as a follower. Each guest that we have on is a rinse and repeat of this method. Interviewing Char Newell not only exposed the *waggle dance* that drove part of her network to my podcast but also epitomized the benefits of mastering your microcosm.

Master your microcosm: *Char Newell*

At the time of this writing, one of the most listened to episodes on the Niche Finder's podcast was the one with guest, Char Newell. Now, as I was just starting out in the podcast space, my podcast plays were only in the hundreds. However, 34% of my audience consumed Newell's episode. I attributed this to the growth from the waggle dance she did with her network. She has such an infectious personality that we promoted the episode to other guests to be interviewed, which also boosted the listeners.

I like to review the profile of each guest as it adds to the layers of the overall conversation. Mrs. Newell has her Master's in Industrial and Labor Relations; she received certification as a strategic human resources business partner; is a certified corporate Life Coach, a certified relationship consultant, a certified Master Life Coach, and a certified Health and

Wellness practitioner, just to name a few. So, I think it is safe to say that this is a person who has something to give.

You would think, however, that such training would increase her ability to start her entrepreneurial journey into the coaching space commanding potential clients to pay her what she is worth. Eventually, she stated that she moved into that model but not at the start. Her secret to penetrating the market she was desiring to be in was to being less of a ***go-getter*** and focus more on what she was ***going to give***. Here is that part of the interview.

"In John Maxwell's book, *Failing Forward*," I said teeing up the next question for Mrs. Newell, "he actually has a great quote that reads, '*People change when they ... hurt enough that they have to, learn enough that they want to, and receive enough that they are able to.*'

"In that quote, I hear that there are times when we will struggle. What type of external struggles did you find yourself up against?"

Char's gregarious personality did not need anyone's permission to get put on display. This was part of the reason why we promoted her episode as a plug, however it also seemed to intimidate certain potential guests we pursued to be on the show. I wasn't pushing it as a standard, but it did have an endearing way of standing out. Her infectious laugh and positive demeanor seemed to possess the energy of two old friends embracing each other for the first time in years. That laugh is what punctuated her reply to my question.

"Wow, I mean which part?" Char said. "In corporate or when I started my business? There were so many struggles." She laughed again.

"Oh, you know what?" I said tickled. "Give me them in order: the corporate one first then the entrepreneur."

"Yeah," Char replied, "so corporate was a very tough struggle, especially being…an African American. For the most part, I was always the only female minority at the table. So that was the first thing and I always felt like—you know—it was always a fight for me, especially because I cared about my employees. I know I'm supposed to be for management, but I was never that human resources person. I felt like I was the liaison and I wanted to do what [was] best for the company as well as the people [who] work[ed] for the company because I do believe that *we are the asset*. You know, the people [who] actually show up every day and put in the work are the reasons why [a company is] even in business. So, why not invest in those folks?

"So that was a big struggle, always fighting for things; always trying to fight for my own growth as well. Trying to prove myself. I've always entered the organizations with the mindset of, I'm going to prove myself first and then go to the table and ask for what I'm worth, versus the other way around.

"Coming in with no, this is what I'm worth and then proving that I'm worth that. No, I was the opposite. I was like, okay, I'll take this for now, but when I get things started, I'll be able to prove that I'm worth more.

"So that was a big struggle and I felt like I didn't have control over my own career by working in corporate America. I felt like at any given moment, anything could have happened, and I've gone through that, where there were mergers, and the position was eliminated.

"Or the companies merged, and we had to let go of a lot of folks, which is also very hard. So, there were a lot of those struggles in corporate America, but you know I then said, I'm going to start my own business because this is what I want to do. I want to help people. I want to help professionals. I want to give them the knowledge that they need to be successful and actually give them a path to their own success. Because the truth is a lot of individuals that are working for someone have other dreams, aspirations, and goals. But they allow life to stop them from going after that.

"I started a business where I said, you know what, I'm going to help individuals find their purpose. I'm going to help them live the best professional life they could possibly live and show them that it's not about how much money you make; that's not where the happiness comes from.

"So, what were the external struggles at the start of my business? Woo," Char sounded exhausted. "I don't even know where to begin. It was coming out the gate, not really having a ton of contacts or a big rolodex of people where I could call to say, hey, I've started a business, let me tell you what I'm doing. Expecting the people that I did know to kind of help—that was mistake number one. I then said to myself, okay, what do I do now? The immediate referrals aren't going to come like I thought, so I said I'm going to start with one-on-one personal life coaching.

"So, believe it or not, when I started my one-on-one personal life coaching in the beginning, *I was doing a lot of coaching for free*. I was not getting paid because I wanted to also gain my experience. This was my first time even doing that on a personal note. I started with that, which was a big struggle in the beginning and then somehow, I managed to make a shift to organizations through the people that I coached.

"This is how life works and it's so funny—that's why you have to embrace every step of the way. Every aspect of it, because at least three of the people that I coached ended up getting amazing jobs—in amazing organizations—and they actually pulled me in.

"So, that's how I got my big break into making that switch from personal one-on-one coaching to now saying to myself, oh my goodness, I'm actually in a corporation coaching the leaders, coaching the staff, and doing what I actually love! It just happened."

"So, I love this," I said composed, doing my best to hold back the giddiness I felt welling up within me. "I want to take a commercial break on this real quick because I love the fact that you talk about coaching for free. I think a lot of people don't really realize the benefit of that.

"In my book, *Dream Octane, the Seven Steps to Discover, Develop, and Deliver Your Niche* this is Step # 4 where I refer to that as *mastering your microcosm*. This is the point in the process where you work on making sure that you have something that is worth bringing to a wider audience. You've got to pressure test that thing.

"I also love how the investment that you made of your own volition also expressed: I believe in you enough that I'm going to invest in this. You don't have to pay me*: reward me with progress*."

That moment was a synchronous crescendo for the both of us as Char responded, "Yes. Yes!"

"Reward me with progress," I repeated, "and that also had a downstream benefit for you as that is how your business was brought in. That's an amazing story."

"Yes," Char replied, "and I didn't expect that. I think it is just what you said, 'reward me with progress.'

"Still to this day, that's the thing that makes me happy. It's never just about getting paid; it is seeing people striving and doing well. That's what brings me joy when I could say that I played a role in your growth."

"I love it," I said as I brought that question to a close. I was grateful to Char for being a guest on the show as there was a great deal of insight that she shared with the audience. She helped to highlight the downstream benefits afforded to us as we master our microcosm. She could have stayed in her corporate role and celebrated the opportunity afforded to her to rise to such a position. However, she had a larger vision than the one she saw each day as she walked into her corporate office.

If she was simply a *go getter* this could have been one of the top rungs on the ladder of success for her, but her passion compelled her to find a way to *go* out and *give*. For Char, using her niche of helping to develop others in this space highlighted the company's asset: their people. *Specializing in offering what is helpful to others but unique to you*, as Char did, would not have been possible at that moment if she had not intended to be a giver initially. If you find giving away the uncovered value that you have difficult, there may be external and/or internal barriers standing in your way. However, as we transition into Step # 5 *Neutralize Barriers Blocking you from Fulfilling your Dream,* we will cover three keys to bringing our dream to fruition. As we delve into *energy, effort,* and *execution* we will find how a sixteen-year-old up against a gargantuan situation overcame the largest barrier of his day.

Chapter 7

Step # 5: Neutralize Barriers Blocking You From Fulfilling Your Dream

Barrier Neutralizer 1 of 3 *Energy: 5 Smooth Stones*

You don't have to be a Bible scholar, get dressed in your Sunday's best, and step foot into an early morning Sunday school session to have heard of the story of David and Goliath. The story has transcended cultural morays, permeated various religious circles, and has encapsulated what it means to have the unqualified underdog come out on top. After all, this sixteen-year-old teenager named David was no match for a man—let alone this *giant* of a person—who embodied both terror and destruction to the nation of Israel. But as fate had it, there David stood over his defeated foe, Goliath, who lay lifeless on the ground with a smooth stone lodged into the forehead and David was the one who had skillfully hurled it in his direction. However, if we back up to the scene before David finished the job by decapitating this Philistine champion with Goliath's own sword, we will find that David put his energy behind remembering that what qualified him for this moment wasn't the traditional tactical methods used in battle at that time, but what worked for him in times past.

From the outset, David wasn't sent there to fight anyone. His dad, Jesse, sent him to this area in Bible days known as Ephes Dammim to bring lunch for his three older brothers who were enlisted in Israel's army. This area was known as the boundary of blood for the historic battles that were waged between Israel and the Philistine armies. However, this meeting between the two adversaries was different. [74]

As David entered the encampment, he stumbled upon a strange negotiation. With the Philistine army to one side and Israel to the other, Goliath offered an interesting proposition to the army of Israel. Instead of having both armies fight against each other and add more blood to this area poised to receive it, why not send just one Israeli soldier to fight against Goliath as the deciding factor of who would be the victor? If Goliath defeated the Israeli soldier, then Israel's army would become the slaves of the Philistines. However, if the Israelite soldier defeated Goliath, then the Philistines would become Israel's slaves. Sounds like a reasonable enough proposition until you look at what the Israelite soldier would be up against.

Depending on the source that you are referencing, Goliath stood around 6 feet 9 inches according to the oldest surviving Greek translation of the Book of Samuel known as the Septuagint or nearly ten feet tall if you reference the Message version of the Bible.[75]

Now, I'm 6 feet 4 inches and I can see over most people I come in contact with. So even if he was 6 feet 9 inches, he would be towering over an Israeli soldier considering the average height of an Israeli man is 5 feet 9 inches. The armor that Goliath wore weighed 126 pounds and to add insult to injury, he spent 40 days (about 1 and a half months) in this area, pacing back and forth pushing his proposition for Israel to pick a champion to fight him. The short description of Goliath—in the eyes of the Israeli soldiers—was that he was big, strong, and hurled intimidating words. However, this shepherd boy named David stepped onto the scene with a different mindset. His courage emanated out of his faith in God, and he saw his previous victories as a microcosm that he already mastered.

> "David said, "I've been a shepherd, tending sheep for my father. Whenever a lion or bear came and took a lamb from the flock, I'd go after it, knock it down, and rescue the lamb. If it turned on me, I'd grab it by the throat, wring its neck, and kill it. Lion or bear, it made no difference—I killed it. And I'll do the same to this Philistine pig who is taunting the troops of God-Alive. God, who delivered me from the teeth of the lion and

the claws of the bear, will deliver me from this Philistine"[76]

This was David's response to King Saul who discouraged him from fighting Goliath as he was merely a child, but Goliath had been fighting since he himself was a child. Seeing David's determination and hearing his unwavering faith in his God, King Saul wanted David to at least have a fighting chance, so he offered David armor to wear.[77]

There was one problem, though, the helmet and protective outfit did not fit. On top of that, David wasn't familiar with wearing such things so he could barely move. He instead chose to trust in what he was familiar with: his faith and his experience. So, he went down to the brook and picked up five smooth stones. Although David believed that the outcome would ultimately be delivered by his faith in God, he still prepared for the moment. He used a sling fighting method that he was most familiar with, but he also picked up five smooth stones. These stones had to be small enough to fit into his sling, yet large enough to make an impact. They were also smooth enough to improve the release of it from the pouch of the sling with just the right timing and angle. The victory came from only one stone—the first and now infamous one—but David was prepared for that moment.

This shepherd boy named David believed that God was with him when he was up against a bear and guided his blade as he defended his sheep against the ferocious desires of a hungry lion. Yet—and still—God used him in such a unique way when Israel's army stood paralyzed before Goliath. Although being victorious was a desired goal, the entire army found themselves cowering in fear from the optics and vitriol coming from this gargantuan *barrier* that stood in the way of that *dream*. However, David had a counterculture approach to the same problem. His niche *was* his faith. It permeated how he took care of his sheep, saw life, and how he was to contend against the enormity of this problem. Roman's 12:3 states that "…God has dealt to each one a measure of faith."[78]

In Dr. David Stoop's book, *You Are What You Think*, he states to this point "it is not a question of whether we possess faith or not. It is rather a question of where we place our faith. And our thoughts are the best barometer of the object of our faith." Hebrews 11, which is the chapter of the Bible known as the Hall of Faith, references David's victories against kingdoms such as the Philistine armies as being conquered by faith. However, David's faith was rooted in one other quality: a heart that was willing to put faith in action. David expressed this activation of faith through his courage. As a result, his convictions not only revealed that he was up against a large obstacle but more importantly, David believed that God was bigger than the problem that was bigger than him. This is important as Goliath was not only up against the army of Israel, but he also stood in the way of David fulfilling a dream.

Could we pause here for a moment to reference something we've already covered? Remember the *Like Mike* section from Step # 2? If you recall Michael Jordan's and Mike Tyson's entry into environments that utilized their abundant factor intensely were both different. Michael Jordan pursued mastery of his own volition once he was motivated to make his varsity team; Bobby Stewart, on the other hand, saw something special in Mike Tyson, which led him to connect Tyson with renowned boxing trainer Cus D' Mato.

At first glance, we see that David's path into utilizing his abundant factor was closer to that of Michael Jordan's as he did so of his own choice. However, David's niche made him distinct and caused him to stand out like Tyson did to Bobby Stewart. We see this unfold in the chapter right before David meets Goliath in the valley of Ephes Dammim.

It was in Bethlehem at his father's house where David's dream was imparted to him. Without falling too deep into the story, the short version is in Chapter 16 of first Samuel, David at sixteen years old was told by the prophet Samuel that one day he would be king over all of Israel. Samuel the prophet then anointed David, which was a way of sealing the prophecy over his life. Shortly thereafter, David went back to tending his sheep.

However, that moment resonated with David as in Biblical times, a prophet acted as an agent who expressed what was to come. Similar to Einstein's quote, prophets gave voice to "...previews to coming attractions." As a result, David neutralized what was blocking him at that moment. As we transition into the next section, we will highlight how neutralizing what's blocking you from fulfilling your dream begins with putting energy behind what you have done well in times past. However, to overcome the immediate barriers blocking you it will also take effort and execution as well.

Effort: *Neutralizing may not eliminate what's opposing you*

As you begin to master your microcosm there will be opportunities for you to refine—and challenge—the message that you are crafting for your audience. If you recall, Steps 4 and 5 are like the oil refinery for the crude resource we discovered from drilling down on steps 1-3. It is here where you will pressure test what you have to offer. If we take a closer look at the term *neutralizing*, it could make for interesting conversation. At the time of this writing, when you Googled the word neutralize its definition means *to render something ineffective or harmless by applying an opposite force or effect.* Although neutralizing may not eliminate the barriers that are blocking you from fulfilling your dream, it is an important step in the refinement process.

On the *Life Cycle of Excavation*, Step # 4 is to *Specialize in Offering What's Helpful to Others, but Unique to You.* Step # 5 is *Neutralizing Barriers Blocking You From Fulfilling Your Dream.* Just to be clear, when I say neutralize them, I don't mean that you will eliminate or make the barriers less potent. They may still be in existence, but they will no longer stop your movement in the direction of your dream. Before we close out this chapter, we will cover two other barrier neutralizing techniques to overcome internal deterrents that can detour us from our dream. This is an internal barrier that gives us excuses to stop bringing our dream to a wider audience or terminate forward progress all together.

I've had coaching sessions with individuals who thought *neutralizing* sounded like a soft term. Trust me, I get it: If you have suffered from limiting beliefs, eliminating these barriers should not only get you to your goal but also remove this opposing force for good. Unfortunately, opposing forces are rudimentary principles in life: for every positive there is a negative; light contends with darkness, our endeavors by default get confronted by complacency. One student that I was coaching saw one of her barriers as making excuses. She defined that excuse as, "…nothing more than a past hindrance that projects itself into your current decision making and paralyzes what you do for your future." Although I can appreciate that point, I hasten to add that barriers may take counseling, perceptive coaching, or some other constituent to help to get you unstuck. However, the investments made in finding the right person/team to help you in this area will be worth the effort.

The point is this, what we are up against may not be fully eliminated or even substantially minimized. However, with the right support it can be neutralized. Neutralizing these barriers embraces the process, not perfection. Michael Jordan said in one of his Gatorade commercials:

I've missed more than 9,000 shots in my career. I've lost almost 300 games. Twenty-six times I've been trusted to take the game-winning shot and missed. I've failed over and over and over again in my life. And that is why I succeed.[79]

What stops us from fulfilling our dreams quite often is ourselves. We lack some aspect of energy, effort, or execution that would help to refine what we have to offer. In Dr. David Stoop's book, *You are What You Think,* he speaks to these impediments:

"Knowledge is never enough either. Lots of people have all kinds of impressive credentials and have accumulated volumes of important knowledge and skills, but they never really been able to get their lives moving in any direction. We look at them and shake our heads thinking of all that wasted potential and wonder why they put all that effort into "getting ready" when it appears to everyone watching that they don't intend to ever "get started."[80]

If we tie these principles back to the story of David and Goliath, it helps to refine the point. David, to a certain extent, minimized the threat of Goliath when he compared the danger he was up against with the power he believed his God had to make him victorious. However, David's minimization supplied courage and confidence to *neutralize* the threat posed against him. David did not fully eliminate the threat of the Philistines by killing Goliath. Goliath was merely a representation of the bigger issue—the Philistine army—but that army was still there even after Goliath lay lifeless at the feet of David. As a matter of fact, David fought against the Philistine army several times afterward as a newly minted member of the Israelite army and battled them even after becoming King.

Now, let's go back to where we discuss what we are doing to neutralize some of these barriers and how that may be fortifying us for the future. This, however, may entail you to having to eat some scorpions.

Eat your scorpions: The tail of the Honey badger

Neutralizing the barriers is also telling the story of the little things that we at times have to overcome. We may have events that happen in our life that feel negative, and we can't understand why they are there. It is like the diet of the honey badger.

By this I mean the honey badger is an interesting animal. Growing up, my dad was a big nature buff. I remember watching everything from National Geographic to Nova and various other public television programming. One episode started with a honey badger that went up against a cobra. As the two began to fight each other, the snake lashed out at the honey badger and the snake landed direct strikes as the badger bit and clawed the cobra. The honey badger eventually subdued the snake but then, it seemed the honey badger also succumbed to the cobra's venom. What happened next was the honey badger slowly curled up next to the lifeless cobra and it looked as though it had died. However, when they time lapped the footage, you could see the honey badger begin to move again. He got up and devoured the snake.

The narrator explained that as cubs, honey badgers primarily eat scorpions. As the honey badger cubs try to consume these scorpions, they get stung by the scorpion tails. Consuming the venom of scorpions allows the badger's body to grow accustomed to venom. The sting of the scorpions prepares the badgers for snakes' venom. So, when the cobra becomes a part of their primary diet as full-grown badgers, they are ready for them. But it all started from having to eat those scorpions.

If we think back to the Dr. Legaspi interview I had mentioned earlier, I actually saw the value of these *venom moments*. I learned from his episode that neutralizing what is blocking us from fulfilling our dream at times involves —as Dr. Legaspi put it—having to: 'Think big but start small.' Now, understand that when starting small, you develop through the micro failures you encounter at that level. However, those mini failures are developing antivenom in you for situations that could potentially kill your dream. If not for the incremental failures, the immunity needed to withstand bigger situations may not exist when antivenom is needed against the cobra-like conditions that will come our way.

This is why you want to neutralize those barriers. In steps 4 and 5, you actively help your audience and understand that you're going to have failures. As you begin to master your microcosm in Step #4, there will be people who will not understand what you are telling them or be helped by you initially. That's okay—it's part of the process.

I learned from coaching others that even those with a great blend of intellect and childlike curiosity as time goes on may not amount to a success story. This happens at times where people start on the journey towards their dream and then without reason, they pull over and—as Les Brown says— put it in park.

Now, someone's decision to do that could be solely their doing. However, whenever these situations happen, I have found a tremendous amount of value in taking a good look at the parts of my messaging I could refine or make clearer. As I started teaching the principles on the *Lifecycle of Excavation*, I had my share of these failures. I would at times walk away from the conversation wanting a certain result for the person who was engaged in the lesson but felt as though some aspect had fallen short. Other times, I felt like I wasn't getting my point across in a way that was helpful.

So, that caused me to reflect and ask myself: How can I make this point clearer? How can I make this understandable to a broader audience? A few ideas that came out of those self-reflective exercises were the E.A.S.Y method, 5P Framework, and I.D.R.E.A.M principles—which we will cover in Step #6.

Once you find your audience and begin serving them, you may not feel like much of a success. While you are in the refinery no matter how helpful you try to be, what you are offering may need more work. It's okay, hang in there. Make the necessary adjustments to your material and use it to serve again. You will neutralize the barriers that are blocking you from fulfilling your dream by serving and refining what you are offering.

At this point, it is important to understand that success, although often depicted as a pinnacle, is a process.

By that I mean, if you only look at the result, it could drive you to the wrong conclusions. Bill Gates states, "Success is a lousy teacher. It seduces smart people into thinking they can't lose." Sounds like an oxymoron but what he's saying is true; if we only look at the successful outcome and miss the process that got the individual to that point, it could lead us down a fantasy that the path was easy for that individual. When, in fact, they overcame obstacles and finally arrived at a point of fulfilling their dream.

When Michael Jordan said that he failed time and time again and that's why he succeeds, he was describing the value of failure in the process that leads to the end result of success. Each time that Michael Jordan failed—if I were to put it in *Dream Octane* terms—he ate a scorpion. This part in the process is not easy. At times it will be painful. When you watch the footage of the honey badger versus the scorpion it is obvious that the stings of the scorpion's tail hurt. But I would argue that pain is necessary.

The same could be said for what you may feel as you begin to serve others with your niche. Some things will be well received as you serve your core group and other things may not. When—not if—this happens, it's fine: Soothe the pain from the sting by eating that scorpion. For some, eating their scorpion may mean getting to a job before everyone else does to get an edge against the opposition. Others may have to stay late after everyone else has left the gym to shoot hundreds of shots because the one that was missed could have won them the game. Again, whatever it is, step on it and eat it; you are being prepared for a more challenging situation.

On the *Life Cycle of Excavation,* steps 1- 3 are defined as putting energy behind what comes easy. Steps #4 and #5, however, have more to do with giving that niche away as a service and receiving feedback than making the necessary adjustments before giving it out again. Step #5 is understanding that the niche that you are using to serve others will place you in the refinery and it may be difficult. There are bitter pills in life we will have to ingest. There will also be times when we mess up and will have to—as it is said—*eat crow* as we humbly render a needed apology. These moments aren't sweet, but they are opportunities that can refine us. Pain that is experienced on the path of progress is an acquired taste, yes, but make no mistake: It is a scorpion in camouflage—eat it!

The other guy with the bright ideas

Thomas Edison was an inventor in the late 1800s whose bright ideas seemed to constantly get eclipsed by some deficiency. When he invented the automatic vote recorder, it functioned in a helpful way of tabulating votes, but it didn't have a market with politicians.[81] Although his talking doll had a market, it shattered easily once played with and one mother who returned the doll referred to its voice recording as "ghastly."[82] The electric pen was too messy and although the tinfoil phonograph made him a household name, the parts used to make it work were fragile and easily broken.[83]

However, this guy with the bright ideas also possessed a lighthearted perspective. Just think, at the time of his death in 1931, Edison had nearly 1,100 patents to his name but even his successful inventions had their share of challenges. When it came to inventing the lightbulb, he and his associates had to test thousands of possible carbon filament materials to find the right material that was both durable and inexpensive. [84] Additionally, when he invented the alkaline storage battery, Edison and his associates conducted ten thousand tests to find the right combination of materials.[85]

Around the nine thousandth test, Edison's close friend, Walter S. Mallory, expressed his feelings about the experiments that—as he puts it—got the better of his sympathies. His remarks helped to shed light on Thomas Edison's mindset. In the authorized biography by *Frank Dyer and T. C. Martin, Edison: His Life and Inventions* (the first edition of the book is 1910) Mallory remarked, "Isn't it a shame that with the tremendous amount of work you have done you haven't been able to get any results?" Edison immediately turned, looked at him with a smile, and said, 'Results! Why, man, I have gotten lots of results! I know several thousand of things that won't work!'"

Edison's response was the sound of him neutralizing the barriers that would block most from fulfilling their dream. Discovering what we have in abundance, or our niche, takes *energy* to focus on what we do well. On the other hand, developing—as in Thomas Edison's example—takes *effort* to *execute* our pursuits despite the naysayers that surround us. Edison's test lasted for a finite period. He learned from his mistakes and continued to iterate to the fulfillment of his dream. As a result, his final iteration of the household lightbulb came from him eating his scorpions, thereby illuminating the world against the venom of darkness.

Again, eating your scorpions means preparing your heart for pain as you serve. You will undoubtedly have to endure some hurtful situations to refine the best version of what you have to offer and shape it into its most generous state. Keep going, you are being fortified. Doctor Marc Urquhart epitomized benefits of persisting through the challenges we will face in an interview that I did with him for the Niche Finder podcast. He spoke about his journey and the value of doing hard things as being a part of the process that led him to success. Let's take a step now into the mindset that he referred to as being *indomitable*.

Barrier Neutralizer 2 of 3 *Effort*: Becoming Indomitable

I met Dr. Marc Urquhart at a level two trauma center some twenty years ago in the heart of Jersey City. Yes, it is the same hospital where Mama J and I worked together. However, the interaction between Marc and I had nothing to do with potlucks or plated delicacies. No, we both were at the start of our careers. He was an orthopedic surgeon in need of diagnostic imaging on the patients he was treating, and I was the diagnostic imaging technologist who prided myself on obtaining the best images possible for the physicians to better treat their patients. He was one of the young, energetic—yet approachable—orthopedic surgeons who had recently been brought on to help meet the clinical demand that had reached its capacity at this location. There are some people in life who you meet and instantly click with, as if you had a longstanding kinship connection. That is how it was for Marc and me.

Additionally, because we started around the same time, and were both about 6 feet 4 inches in height, of comparable skin complexion, and of similar build, people often confused me for him while in the perioperative area. I appreciated the title elevation from technologist to physician if only for a moment until I corrected the compliment. However, aside from that fun fact, during the surgical procedures that I provided X-ray support for, I gained a deep appreciation for his steady handed approach to helping people with a slew of bone abnormalities become better overtime. His resilience came through as a self-effacing blend of patience and determination, which I came to admire. Having him on The Niche Finder Podcast was a bit of a treat for me as it gave me an opportunity to learn more about the ancestral influencers that helped to steady his surgical hands.

"Did you have any mentors along your way?" I asked Marc, mid-way through the interview.

"Oh, so many mentors…. Growing up…my grandfather was my rock and was someone who when you look at his career, he sold insurance for the first portion of it. Then he was a mail carrier the remainder of his career…. It didn't even matter what his profession was. He was a citizen of the world.

"I told my children—and Cliff, I know you'll appreciate this—because we've been going through a challenging time with this pandemic.... [that] your great grandfather, my grandfather....was your age when the pandemic of 1918 struck.

"And you know my grandfather was never one to complain about anything. And I was like, why did he never say anything about it? He never made mention of it. It's one of those things. I think he's just such a rock and had such a mindset."

I could sense that this portion of the conversation was dear to Marc as the cadence of his speech began to slow as if to ensure this moment paid homage to his ancestry.

"Strong-willed, stubborn—yes—but [he was] just relentless. Indomitable.... He was the rock of the family, the pillar of the family. History will bring to light the challenges he had to go through on a day-to-day basis. Your life wasn't safe even without a pandemic for people of color at that time.

"He went on to do his job, survive the pandemic, World Wars, the Great Depression.... [It's like] David—or King David—from the Bible, after he defeated Goliath, he didn't say: 'Oh yeah, I just whipped such and such.'"

"I'm done," I added, in anticipation of where he was going with his point.

We then both laughed as he responded, "You don't start dropping names about your victories or battles, you just keep doing. You do what you do. You hang in there. Persevere. You survive…So my grandfather was just a pillar of strength…and that's just from a moral character standpoint. He was the rock of the family always there—always there providing the necessities."

Dr. Urquhart shared several stories that I thought added many practical tips that expressed the values of putting effort behind fulfilling your dream. The hidden virtue in being indomitable is that it speaks to the value that develops within us in environments that give us many reasons to just give up. As you put effort behind refining your niche, understand that the only true competition for those who pursue mastery is themselves. I like the way Dr. Martin Luther King spoke about this area:

> "If a man is called to be a street sweeper, he should sweep streets even as Michelangelo painted, or Beethoven composed music, or Shakespeare wrote poetry. He should sweep streets so well that all the hosts of Heaven and Earth will pause to say, here lived a great street sweeper who did his job well."

As we close out this section, let's shift our attention from *energy* and *effort* to the importance of *execution* in neutralizing barriers that are blocking you from fulfilling your dream.

Barrier Neutralizer 3 of 3 *Execution*: What x When = How.

My journey into getting this book into your hands, starting with my first online funnel and coaching people from the material of this book, were all confronted with this big question: How? I would like to clue you in that I have discovered that *how* really is not the problem. If put into the right equation, *how* can become the solution. With that said let's take a closer look at *The How Equation*.

Understanding The How Equation

Truth be told, *The Niche Finder Framework* would not have gotten started as soon as it did if not for a friend from Business School named, Jerome Bridgman. He was one of the top performers in our class who remained humble and generous with the level of understanding that he had around the material. He was also a master project manager who had the highest level of certification in project management. As I was formulating the ideas around the *How Equation*, I wanted to bounce the Framework off of him and get his thoughts on how well these principles could possibly help others execute and neutralize the barriers that are blocking them from fulfilling their dreams. I asked him if I could do a Zoom call with him to go over the principles and he agreed. This is a snippet that explains the how equations and his response to how he believes they tie into the project management framework he had expertise with.

"You know, I appreciate you doing this with me," I said as we began our call. "I'll just tell you that my primary goal...comes down to these things; I feel I do better when I can flush thoughts out with people. But one of the things that happened is, as I'm flushing these thoughts out, things come out the way I want them to, but then, I can't remember the finer details of the conversation, even when it's a great conversation around a topic that I want to put inside the book, so this is one of them. This how equation is definitely one of those topics, but I want to measure it against not just this concept that I have, but against best practice, and also learn a little bit about, as a project manager, how you see things.

"There are six questions that one asks when it comes down to solving a problem with the *How Equation*. Those interrogative questions are the *why*, the *who*, *where*, *what*, *when*, and *how*...

"*Why* is your *reason* for what you're looking to do. *Who* is the *resources* you need to tap into; have you designated the resources that you're going to use to solve that problem?

"*Where* is formulating your *region of interests*. *What* is delineating your action. *When* is what I believe to be how you iterate your *intentions* over time; and *how* then puts a frame around your *resolution*.

"Out of all these six areas…the biggest problem that I find that tends to happen in solving a problem, is how…How am I going to do that? How am I going to find time? How am I going to find the money?

"Well, in this framework of…solving the how equation, I put how as a solution …and the reason for that is when you look at things that you have already accomplished retrospectively, you start to see that you are describing how you did it and you start to describe two things. You start to describe your what and your when. And so, the how equation is basically…take what you need to do…multiply by when you need to do it, then it will give you HOW you do it. Therefore, **WHAT** *times* **WHEN**, *equals* **HOW**. So, in this formula, how is no longer the problem; **HOW** becomes your solution.

"The next question then turns out to be, how do you derive your WHAT? This is the second segment in the *How Equation*: WHAT times WHEN equals HOW.

"Here's one example, and then I just want to get your thoughts…. I had a nurse manager who had no leadership experience and she had a major project that she had just stepped into and was in a new leadership role as a nurse manager. She was in a department that—although she knew the doctors—was incredibly demanding and she was tasked with putting a new inventory system in place.... She showed me that they didn't have proper par levels. So, I showed her how to do a par level sheet, but we started out with WHY. Why do we need to solve this problem?

"And some of which I just kind of gave you the answer to the reason WHY we were doing this. We didn't want to run out of supplies, and we didn't want to have a bunch of expirations. So that was our WHY. Then we had to figure out WHO were our resources in solving this problem. So, we'd go to the radiologist who she's working with; we'd go to the nurses who need inventory, and the technologists.... Then, we start to look at our region of interest. Where are we looking to target?

"We had to decide on our region of interest and that was our WHERE. And once we defined all of that, we then had what we needed to do. We knew we needed to design a par level or inventory sheet to effectuate change. Once we designed that sheet, we then started to iterate. So that's the WHEN. So, WHEN is where you talk about initiation. We initiate with WHY, but once we had the WHAT, we delineated what our action was going to be.

"We then also reviewed the plan with the team again.

"Therefore, you go back and you say, this plan that I have, is it lining up with my WHY?

"Does it solve the reason for which we're going into this?

"Do our resources agree with this plan?

"Do we have the proper scope?

"Did we meet the target with this plan we came up with?

"Once all of that is confirmed, then we iterate. We iterate our action steps then work towards assimilating it into the working environment.

"And then we test it. At the very end, the HOW that we're now looking at is that we frame how we do it, or how we've done it rather with reward and recognition. So, this is the *How Equation* that I want to get your thoughts on."

"It's very interesting," Jerome responded. "The HOW, the WHAT and WHEN; WHAT times WHEN equals HOW. I liked that a lot. And you said the WHAT equal to WHY, WHO, and WHEN, I liked the way you played around with these words. These are the keywords that you need to use in order, from my experience in project management. The **WHY**, the **WHO,** the, **WHERE, WHAT, WHEN, HOW**, even especially when you communicate, is also very important, because communication is about 90% of a project manager's time. If you always consider those words you use here, WHY are we meeting; WHO needs to be there; WHERE it's going to be done; WHAT topics we need to address; WHEN are the deliverables due to be completed, or HOW the task is going to be executed.

"All these things sort of circulate when it comes to project management, and to me, it's also a different way of looking at the five phases to project management. When you talk about initiating, planning, executing, monitoring, controlling, and closing a project. So, as you go through this, you would realize some of these things really aligned the WHEN the HOW, et cetera, because when you initiate a project, that's when you're trying to define your project goal.

"Then, you need the right people to give you that authorization to start, because if you don't get that authorization, then you will not get support on the project at all. The second phase is the planning group. What is this all about? You establish it and you refine the objectives and define the course of action acquired to attain those objectives.

"Then after that, you jump into the execution phase that's the process performed to complete the work defined in your project management plan. You want to satisfy all your project requirements. Let's say you're building a house and you create a work breakdown structure. Then, in your work breakdown structure, you have three phases. You'll want to, number one: look at how many rooms you're going to need.

"What are the dimensions? Can you get in and out without parking the car in front of the house and get your wife or kids out before you get into it? So that's all the things that you will sort of look at.

"In executing, after you align all these things, you look at it and you say, okay, I'm going to execute this now. Is it really working towards my plan? The monitoring and controlling are the fourth phase of it. That's the way you track what's being done. You track, you review, you regulate the progress and the performance of the project, and you identify any areas in which there are changes to the plan.

"You know exactly by the end of it that everything you've done is completely well-thought of going towards the end.

"And the final one is the closing, that's when you ensure that everything that you've done so far is up-to-date. If you have any existing contracts, you have signed off on the contracts, all those things.

"The one thing that a lot of people forget about is the importance behind how you close the project. You must assemble your team at the end. So, you can ask interesting questions:

"What went right?

"What went wrong?

"How can you change things?

"Then you put this in a repository somewhere in your company's database.

"So, everything that you have listed here: the **WHY, WHO, WHERE, WHAT, WHEN and HOW**—to me—all ties into that initiating, planning, executing, monitoring, controlling, and closing a project."

Having this conversation with Jerome helped me to see that I may have been onto something. In hindsight, I saw that the hurdles I had overcome with finishing *Dream Octane* resulted from me taking *What* I needed to do and multiplying it by *When* it had to be done.

The diligence in prayer and fasting helped to clarify my thoughts and/or reinforce actions. Additionally, deriving my *What* with productive reasoning (*Why*), the right people resources (*Who*) and purposeful regions of interest (*Where*) made the activity being pursued more meaningful. I knew why I wanted to finish my book as I saw it as a tool that others could use to help them discover, develop, and deliver their niche into compatible environments. I even had my target audience in view from Step #4 as I crafted my message from *mastering my microcosms*—but the *Who*, needed to be developed. As a result, I took on the challenge of carefully crafting my team.

Self-made—Really: Did you forget the team?

It is mind boggling to me how many people still believe in this notion that people can become self-made. No matter how brilliant of an idea that you have, it is only as good as the problem that it solves.

However, even when your idea becomes the solution that solves the problem for someone else, it still takes a team to scale that idea to a larger audience. The solution that *Dream Octane* had to offer was stuck in this area. I didn't want to seek the traditional means of publishing my book, so I began taking various courses to help to give me perspective around the options that I had. One of the trainings that I did was with Clickfunnel One Funnel Away. It was a thirty-day challenge that helped me to see that content creation was needed but only if that content flowed into a funnel that converted for you. I had to start somewhere, so I went to Tim Ferris's book, *The 4-Hour Workweek*, where he referenced the company he used to start his online business and I signed up for them.

How I obtained my virtual assistant (VA) in India

The following is the email response to the initial welcome inquiry that came from the manager of the support team with GetFriday virtual assistants in India. This was the entry into starting my online business and I knew that I wanted to create an e-book that complemented the content of my book. So, from the very first interaction with the pre-sales manager, I began crafting the product. Here is the beginning of our first exchange:

Dear Fazzle,

Thank you for your timely response to my enquiry, it is appreciated. I anticipate that the requested work may amount to 5 hours a month. However, this may require adjustment higher or lower starting out.

I would need to vet three of your most qualified candidates to choose from. References should be included, however, new VA who are inexperienced will be considered on an individual basis. A test assignment I will use to decide fit for selecting one candidate will be for each to ghost write a 1,000 word paper on how to find your niche in life. Citations and references must be included.

These VA candidates will be given 1 hour to research and write this submission. The goal is to have it done in an hour so have each one stop and send what they have even if the 1000 words are not completed. As mentioned below, the

VA must be able to execute extremely well. Let me know if there is a cost associated with this service as I will be considering this in my decision as well.

Thank you again for getting back to me. It is hoped that this will be the beginning of something special between our companies.

Sincerely,

Clifton C. Manning, MBA, BSMIS, R.T.(R)(ARRT)
Principle
Quality First Imaging Consulting LLC.
https://www.linkedin.com/in/clifton-c-manning-mba-5a073671/

Although I initially didn't have the slightest idea of *how* I was going to make this venture into moving online work, I focused on the process steps (*What*) that Tim Ferris mentioned in his book. I also spent time outside of my 9-5 job (*When*) working with GetFriday's client services to get my virtual assistant up and running. I knew my reason (*Why*) for reaching out to them was to get assistance with developing an e-book. I also knew that the region of interest (*Where*) was to serve coaches, counselors, and corporate trainers by helping them avoid the dangers of moving online without having their niche included in what they had to offer. That was the base that I built on. So, this ask from GetFriday helped me to see who would rise to the occasion with a quality product despite the time crunch being imposed upon them this first week.

The following is the response that I got from the support team for my inquiry.

Dear Clifton,

Greetings!!!

Thank you for your patience.

In regard to your task requirements:

I have checked with the concerned team for a quick feasibility check and below are their thoughts on the same:

The task is doable from our end and we indeed can share three profiles of the assistants to work on the task.

To initially work with our service, we suggest you purchase 6 hours under Task Based Plan (Ad Hoc) to get started with the task. The 3 assistants will be working for 2 hours each. One hour to research and one hour for writing the article.

Based on the results of the article you can select one primary assistant for upcoming projects after trial.

Below are the pricing details:

Total hours: 6

Hourly rate: $14

Total cost: $84

Validity: 1 week

On confirmation from your end, I will send the payment link and assistant profiles who will be working on the task. On receipt of payment, we will send you the assistant details and can get this started at your earliest convenience.

I'm looking forward to hearing from you.

Warm Regards,

Fazzle,

Pre – Sales & Support Team GetFriday.

https://www.getfriday.com/

The support team sent me the invoice, and I immediately made the requested payment.

I then wrote:

"Sounds good thank you. I appreciate the thorough response....

"As far as the requested reports I will need the following:

Topic: 8-10 page report on the "Benefits of Finding and Monetizing Your Niche Online."

Length: A minimum of 1000 words.

Durations: 1hour research/ 1 hour writing.

References: These must be clearly cited with a copy of each article referenced sent with the report.

Let me know if you have any questions.

Cliff

I sent his request on the Monday and although the three candidates that he found had a week to complete the task, I received this response within two days:

Dear Clifton,

Greetings!!!

Thank you for your prompt response.

In regards to your requirements:

We would like to let you know that one of your assistant Joe has completed the task and I herewith have attached the document for the same. Please do review it and share your thoughts for the same.

We will update you with work of other assistants at the earliest.

Thank you for your understanding and patience in advance.

Warm Regards,

Fazzle,

Pre - Sales & Support Team GetFriday.
https://www.getfriday.com/

When I opened the document and reviewed it, I was shocked at how well done it was. To be completely honest, if I wasn't so specific with the assignment, I would have thought that Joe had plagiarized the article.

Two days after that, Fazzle sent me an email stating the other virtual assistances were still working on requested documents and within hours of the email he sent me the other two submissions. They were all excellent. I then combed through each and sent back this reply:

I took the time to review in detail each submission and was impressed with each virtual assistant. I don't believe that I would go wrong selecting any of them. However, I will be selecting Joe based on the key take aways that I outline below. This was a close decision but, I believe Joe has complimentary skillsets that can help me create content that I am looking to generate. I will send an outline of our first project this week for him.

Just so you know if you decide to go down the path of obtaining a VA you are under no obligation to write back such a thorough response. But I wanted to provide some form of feedback to the group for taking the time to do the exercise. These types of exercises help me to make objective decisions.

However, simply letting the recruiter know who you would like would suffice.

The first meeting with my new VA was through the Google hang out app. It was scheduled for 6:30pm EST. In hindsight, I was amazed at the level of responsiveness that I received as Bangalore India is 9 ½ hours ahead, so 6:30pm eastern standard time was 4am by them. This was my first time operating on the global stage and I was ready to get things going.

Joe and I hit the ground running with an initial call that was brokered by Fazzle. After the handoff, Joe and I continued our conversation on a separate call. It gave me an opportunity to convey the vision of creating content which would be provided as a resource for those I was looking to support. The first task that I gave Joe came from the initial assignment mentioned above. I anonymized the other two submissions from Delia and Mark, then asked Joe to consolidate all three submissions into one e-book that would be given out online. After his initial draft, I then signed up for Fiverr.com, which was a site I heard had a multitude of freelance workers ranging from editors, book formatters, and book editors for low to moderate prices. The e-book was one task that I needed to get polished up, so I found someone I felt comfortable working with based on their bio and had them refine the draft. This method worked well for the e-book, but I wasn't comfortable with using this method for revising the over one hundred-thousand-word barrier that stood in my way, which was finishing the edits of *Dream Octane*. I had to neutralize this barrier with help from a specialist. So, I began researching online for an editor. It was tedious work as editors come in so many different specialties, but my efforts were undeterred—some might even call them *indomitable*. As a result, this exercise not only connected me to someone who had the potential to be a great fit for my project but also reinforced the value of being tenacious.

Just Call Me Tenacious

The thing to try when all else fails is: again. —John Hagee

Just call me tenacious was the title of my LinkedIn inbox message to Elise Gallagher, a Freelance Editor who I found a few weeks before I signed up for virtual assistant support. *Dream Octane* was special to me, and I wanted to get it out to the masses with the most effective method possible. In the various trainings that I did, which spoke to delivering your book online as a hook or lead magnet, each one consistently encouraged teaching the material from your book even prior to it being completed. Signing up for my virtual assistant was a means of doing that. However, I still had over

100,000 words and a manuscript that I considered to be a hot mess. I then painstakingly researched online how to find a nonfiction editor, came across a highly informative blog that had Elise Gallagher's name at the very top and then signed up for the LinkedIn premium account so that I could direct message her a proposal request.

Elise Gallagher · 1st
Freelance Editor: Copy edits, proofreads, developmentally edits fiction and select non-fiction

AUG 2, 2020

Clifton C Manning, MBA · 10:08 AM

Just Call Me Tenacious

Good morning Mrs. Gallagher it is hoped that this message finds you in good health and doing well. I am a self-published author with more passion than skill. I am currently working on a book that helps people uncover their niche in life. It is a business book that uses analogous principles from history to bring about applicable steps someone could effectively use today.

I will be using an online funnel to offer my material but needed help turning my current manuscript mess into something fluent and meaningful. After researching online for an answer to my predicament, I came across a blog by Dave Chesson.[86] Your name rose to the top of my list because: (a) You specialize in the genre combination of business plus history (b) I learned a great deal from his article and (c) He made it easy because you were at the top of his list with his endorsement of you being his editor.

I attempted a few times to reach out to you on Reedsy but could not find your name. As a matter of fact, when I typed in your name someone else's profile came up. I then went back to search for you, found you on LinkedIn and signed up for the premium package so that I could InMail you this message. It is hoped that this melodrama affords us the opportunity to explore if there is mutual agreement between my work and your service.

Thank you for taking the time to read through my long-winded request for a quote and I look forward to hearing from you in the not-so-distant future.

God's choice blessings to you and yours,

Cliff

AUG 3, 2020

Elise Gallagher · 7:32 AM

Dear Cliff,

Thank you so much for reaching out to me. I am sorry it was so hard for you to find me. I am out of office on Reedsy so that's why my profile didn't come up. I am unable to take on new projects until the end of September, but your book sounds very interesting!

Do you have a specific deadline in mind? Have you written part of the book and are stuck on finishing the rest, or is it all written, and you need an editor?

Please feel free to email here so you can cancel Premium subscription if you would like. https://reedsy.com/elise-gallagher

Again, thank you for reaching out,

Elise

Clifton C Manning, MBA · 8:23 AM

    Good morning, Elise it is good to connect with you. Thank you. I'm glad that the Reedsy situation is one that is prompted by you and not some technical error which was my concern.

I currently have over 120,000 words written of the book with the quality of the information ranging from genius to gibberish. I am doing the chiseling a way of formatting and editing this information to make it a less confusing fit within the context of the overall theme as well as make it concise.

Strategically, I also plan to start a Podcast to interview influencers with questions that coincide with the material within my book. The goal would be to have them share with the audience how they found their niche and briefly describe the journey they took towards success.

    I will email you.

Thanks again,
Cliff

The hidden benefit of collaborating with people who are excellent in their respective fields is that it provides an opportunity for you to learn something new from their expertise. This was no different with working with Miss Gallagher as her clarifying questions helped to give me a glimpse into other dimensions of the writing process that I had not been previously exposed to. Completing *Dream Octane* was one of the most difficult assignments I ever had to do. However, it taught me that some hard tasks that we must execute on may need to be broken down into smaller segments that make up the larger whole. This exercise is likened to when I had to clean out my cluttered garage. Everything in the garage at one point was very important to me and became hard to let go of. However, as I removed and/or rearranged the bulk of the items, I realized that the moments that made up those things is what made them important—not the things themselves.

This perspective is what helped me to cut significant portions of *Dream Octane* out when Elise and I eventually began our editor agreement through Reedsy.com. I then brought up my 120,000-word manuscript, pulled out the proverbial trash bin, and removed 70,000 words out of the manuscript. This allowed Elise and I to start with a 50,000-word document that—if I'm completely transparent—was still a hot mess.

I believe God's providential hands helped my tenacious efforts to neutralize the barriers that were blocking my dream of getting this book into your hands. The team I eventually began working with—that ranged from GetFriday's Virtual Assistant Joe, Elise as my editor and even guest from the Niche Finder podcast—all helped to add a layer to the finished product that you are holding. So, if you ask me the question if I believe that I am *self-made:* I can truly say, no. These moments—in my opinion—have been brought to you by God's grace and the support of excellent resources. As a result, these provisions have not only come along side me but also helped to neutralize the various barriers that were blocking me from fulfilling my dream of finishing this project.

Now that *you* have found your niche in Steps 1-3 and refined it in Steps 4 and 5, lets enter the final two steps on the lifecycle of excavation that make up the Delivery section. Just one note before we go there: you may want to take a flight or step into the boxing ring with a man name *Rock.*

Deliver Section

Keep Believing....

Chapter 8

Step # 6: Organize The Delivery Of Your Niche To A Wider Audience

The boxing ring and black box recorder: How Chris Rock uses small stages for his big moments

S tep # 6 *Organize the Delivery of Your Niche to a Wider Audience* is just that: organizing to deliver. The original ideas that we have will not be perfect but that's okay, there is value in iterating. Comedian Chris Rock is a wonderful example of this principle. Biography.com highlights his noteworthy onstage accolades as being: "…*two Emmy award-winning HBO specials…and…twice hosted the Academy Awards.*"[87] Yet Chris Rock doesn't just naturally perform his deliveries with perfect precision; his polarizing perspectives and well-placed punchlines are not without practice. Chris Rock is one of the top comedians who understands that the big stage requires several small stages.

In preparing for his global comedy tour, Chris Rock made forty to fifty appearances at a small venue near his home in New Brunswick, New Jersey called the Stress Factory.[88] He would bring a yellow legal-size notepad to the stage and go into hundreds of different comedy bits to see what worked and what didn't. Many jokes would land well, but some of them would not.[89] It was as if each failed joke took off like an aircraft, stalled in the air, then crashed and burned.

Chris Rock, however, treated each fallen joke as if it had its own airplane black box recorder and sorted through the rubble—with pen in hand—looking for pieces of information that he could use for the next flight. The venue he performed at would have less than fifty people who would listen to the bits with giggles and awkward moments of silence as he retooled his routine on the yellow legal pad on the stage in real-time.[90]

A *Harvard Business Review* article quoted Rock as saying, "Rock told the Orange County Register, 'It's like boxing training camp. I always pick a comedy club to work out in.'"[91] Now, when Chris Rock was tapped to host the 88th Oscars® in 2016, he trained the same way. According to the *Washington Post*, two weeks prior to hosting the prestigious event, Rock practiced at the famed comedy club, Comedy Store, in West Hollywood.[92] The *training* Rock did at the club amounted up to roughly ten times in two weeks. He used this venue to get comedy reps in onstage as he floated new jokes he intended to use in his Oscar monologue.

Just like a boxer cutting weight and refining the pinpoint accuracy of his jab, Rock used fifteen-to-thirty-

minute sets to hone his comedic materials. The Comedy Store's booker Adam Eget stated, "He really trimmed the fat and made it real lean." "There were some," Eget continued, "even after day four, he'd [Chris Rock] say, 'I'm not going to be able to do this joke.' But then, you'd hear him do it again and he'd have tweaked a word or two."[93]

Bringing your niche to a wider audience requires public opinion for you to gain a deeper understanding of what works and what doesn't work. As we mastered our microcosms in Step #4, we gleaned understanding by serving friends, family, and those in our fellowship circle. By serving, we position our niche to be refined with the technique of *give, tweak,* and *repeat.* From there we distilled our niche even more in Step #5 as we learned how to neutralize barriers blocking the fulfillment of our dream by eating our scorpions. Those two refinery steps are what prepared us for Step #6 and Step #7, which now brings our niche into the public environment. Don't worry, if you have applied the principles in each step up to this point, even if you *don't feel ready* for your moment, you may very well be *made for it.* The previous steps that you have successfully completed are evidence of that.

By using the small stage, Chris Rock honed his niche into well-crafted material that he shared on the big stage with ease. That proactive style of training he did to prepare for hosting the 2016 Oscars made him ready for that moment. As a result, Insider.com placed him at number 7 in *The 18 best Oscar hosts of all time, ranked.*[94] When they compared how well he hosted in 2005 with his second appearance in 2016 they remarked, "Rock was invited back in 2016 and fared much better. His no-nonsense style of comedy was welcomed in the year of #Oscarssowhite. His willingness to take on the Academy of Motion Pictures when they deserved it felt just."[95]

2016 was the second year in a row that no Black actors were nominated in any category.[96] However, Rock handled this turbulent issue as if his monologue was set to autopilot. It was as if he turned on the speaker system in the *Oscar* aircraft and announced, …This is your captain speaking: "You realize, if they [Academy of Motion Pictures] nominated host, I wouldn't even get this job."[97]

The point is this, sharing your niche to a smaller public audience prepares you for a larger platform. I saw this truth while applying this principle in my own online launch. I found that although the entrance into the public arena may not feel good—if you learn and tweak your material each time—it will be worth it.

My Funnel Fiasco: *Mayday! Houston, we have a problem.*

There was something hidden in our salutations that seemed to lay the runway for our conversation. We were both pressed for time yet prioritized this moment as if cautiously pulling our aircraft from the gate and into its place in line on the tarmac. You may recognize his name from references made of some answers he provided in the classroom setting within my Executive MBA program at Rutgers University Business school. Bala Pitchandi is a friend I met in business school who—when I look back at our tenure there together—consistently supplied some form of support to our group. His approach always came across as thoughtful and the responses shared were thought provoking. He referred to himself in an article he published online as *"Indian American, Progressive, Dad, Husband, Technology Executive, Eternal Optimist. Not in that order."*[98] I refer to him as a genuine and low-key genius. I asked him to be a part of my initial launch of my online seminar as I knew I would get meaningful feedback. So, here we were like two aviators turning on the fasten seat belt sign to pilot this conversation into the air.

"Cliff?" Bala said cross-checking if I could hear him over our Zoom call. We had some connection issues but were finally able to work them out.

"How are you?" I asked.

"Good, how are you?" he replied.

"I'm good, man," I continued. "I hope you don't mind. I'm actually on the road driving so I'm gonna record this on Zoom so I can take notes after the fact."

"Yeah, yeah," Bala said, "of course no problem."

After we quickly exchanged snapshots as to where we were with life—me with the book and he with his engineering leadership / entrepreneurial coaching start-up—we pulled the nose of our conversation into the air and raised the landing gears.

"2020 has been really good for me," Bala said, "because I have more time to myself, which I invested in building my coaching business. I'm coaching one CEO and Chief Product Officer, advising a couple of companies, and building my own company and it's all going well."

"You know what?" I said. "I'm not surprised…one thing that I admire about the engineer's mindset is being able to tackle extremely difficult problems and find a way to make things better. I see your journey as no different. I have a friend who is a biomedical engineer and I asked him about that. Because I saw this trait while in school with engineers like yourself and I said to myself 'why is it that the engineers seem to rise to the top?' I'm sure we have people who were doing well, who were not engineers—don't get me wrong. But it's something about the top 20% being made up of majority—in

my opinion—engineers and my friend said, 'Well, I can't really speak to the phenomena that happened in your class, but I can tell you that in school as an engineer, they [the engineering professors] always taught us that you can make things better. But even when you make whatever you are working on improving better, eventually another engineer could come after you and better your best. It's just something about that mindset of continuous quality improvement that I find fascinating.'"

"Yeah, yeah, that is so true," Bala replied.
"I think it's just something like not being daunted by the complexity and the enormity of a challenge. It's something that is so ingrained....

"It's just like, oh *okay*, this is what the challenge is. How do you break it down and how do you make progress towards the goal; however large it may seem."

So here is the part of the conversation where I'm going to remove the fasten seat belt sign and allow your imagination to move freely around the cabin. At this point we will also be serving food for thought and a few samples of perspective that I found refreshing.

The reason why I called Bala was to gain insight into my short comings with the first presentation that I did to a wider audience. This was my first live online webinar that I had taken weeks to prepare. I was not finished with *Dream Octane* yet, but the various trainings I did around moving your business online all recommended that if you wanted to get into the online space you had to just get started. So, I did.

I learned that although imagination is helpful with constructing what you want to offer, you cannot conceptualize yourself into becoming a better presenter. You have to practice and as Chris Rock did, step in front of people to find what lands well and what crashes. I did my first presentation the day after Christmas with roughly 13 out of the 40 people who signed up in attendance. Many of them I knew from business school, or they were family. Either way it was a live event, and it gave me an opportunity to share the thoughts I had on my PowerPoint deck. It was exhilarating to finally hear myself in this way and the deeper I got into the presentation, the lighter it felt. If I were to put this first moment of bringing my niche to a wider audience it would be, 'Mmm, yes! *Houston*, we have lift off!'

The first and middle part of the presentation was like being on autopilot: the material flowed; the audience was attentive but the *close*—well let's just say—became like me sending mission control a 'mayday' for help. I was able to land the event without any injuries. Still, from a technical standpoint, I felt a good amount of turbulence at the end as I made my pitch, so the closing of the presentation felt clunky.

The comments afterwards were very encouraging from friends and family, which I was grateful for. However, I knew Bala— who was also on the call—could help me put a finger on the areas that I intuitively felt were off but could not put into words. As we go back to the discussion with him, I'm happy to report that he didn't disappoint.

"Yeah, so let me know your thoughts man," I continued, "and I'll let you know some of the things that I've already started getting feedback on after you finish sharing and then let's see how we can meet in the middle."

"Cool," Bala replied, "I took some notes and I'm happy to send this over to you by email as well.

"So let me start with things that I thought were really good. I think the thing that I really liked was that you were well prepared. You were able to clearly talk about the framework and connect with your own personal stories throughout. I felt it kept the audience engaged for the whole time. So overall I felt as I walked away that it was not a waste of time. I was able to identify a few things that I could go back and apply to my own business.

"And then I think some of your strengths came through: your delivery, your modulation, and your charming / engaging personality really came through during the webinar.

"Uhm, so that's on the positive front.

"On the things that could be improved—I'll start with the first one: the deck. I felt as I was watching the presentation, I wished that I was able to see you as opposed to the deck. Making that eye-to-eye connection is so important, especially when you're talking about those personal stories about your dad's time capsule of a briefcase from your childhood.

"You want to make that eye-to-eye connection with your audience in those moments and I felt that the slide deck was getting in the way.

"Maybe you could find a way to transition back and forth? When you talk about something very personal, that you want to connect with the audience on, you could toggle the screen back to you and make the eye contact, then transition back to the material when you are ready.

"So that's one.

"The second opportunity for improvement was you were more passionate and less process when you were talking about your personal stories. I could see that as you were sharing your frameworks like the E.A.S.Y method there were a lot of *ums* and *ahs* as you went through it. I think you just need to practice it more to deliver it clearer.

"That was something that I noticed.

"The third thing was around when you got to the end and started talking about the funnel, it felt a little bit abstract. I think you jumped into the funnel.

"I mean I knew what a funnel is so I could connect to the content.

"But I wondered if you would need to explain this more thoroughly as to what this is and why you feel it's something that can help.

"For people like you and I who are in the business world we may understand but someone else who is very green in that area may not quite understand what a funnel is and why it is something that they need to invest in.

"Does that make sense?"

"Oh absolutely!" I said in response. "First off, I appreciate you even doing this—and trust me—the next time that I share a presentation, 100% of your points will be incorporated.

"So, I will.

"I will un-share my screen and speak directly to the camera and my audience.

"I will rehearse more to ensure that I am delivering the content clearer. Ironically, my son Elijah said the same thing with regards to the last two points that you made.

"He said after the presentation, 'Dad I think you were saying: 'ahh and umm a lot.'

"I then said to him, 'Okay, thank you' and you picked up on that as well.

"So, I'm definitely going to rehearse that more.

"Then with regards to the funnel my son said, 'Dad that last slide that you were showing with the funnel I didn't understand it.' He then made the points of—because my son is fifteen—where his thought process was when he said: 'but I figured that you were talking to people who were older than me and knew what funnels were, so I'm sure they understand what you were saying.'

"But that's never the goal. I want a fifteen-year-old—or even a fifth grader—to understand what I am sharing.

"So, I'm definitely going to retool that, for sure.

"I appreciate you echoing those points.

"Well let me ask you this Bala: What did you think about the pitch at the end?"

"The pitch was good," Bala replied.

"I think if I'm being completely candid here: Although I wasn't completely sold on it, I was intrigued enough to want to hear more."

"Yes," I said nodding to myself in agreement even though our Zoom cameras were off.

"I think," Bala continued, "that's really the purpose of this first webinar. You want to get people intrigued enough so that they continue engaging with you and the subsequent parts of your package.

"What would have sold me more on the pitch would have been some testimonials. Like some case studies on how X, Y, and Z applied from your program had a particular benefit.

"Or you had this *cohort* from these people who used X and achieved results in this way.

"…Many people will listen to a presentation and say to themselves: 'Okay, this sounds good, but has anyone used this? What other people used this and how did this add value to them?

"Going back to the other point about passion and process: all you're trying to do in this first presentation is to get to the second date.

"You're trying to make sure that "A"—they first like you as a person, as coach and a guide—and "B"—they're intrigued: they can see what you are offering helping them get to an ultimate goal.

"Then the second date is them saying 'I like the framework; how can I apply this to myself?'

"Once they see the value and how they can apply it to themselves, then you can talk money and how much it's going to cost them.

"It's very similar to what I do with my coaching. I do an hour of free coaching on a one-on-one basis. You just talk to me, we'll go through where you are so that I understand your situation. After the first session, once we identify that our interests align, we talk about commitment. Because it will take commitment from both sides.

"[This is where] I'm like, 'I only take a select number of clients, if I want to put in the time, I want to make sure that you are actually also invested in this...I give them some time to think about it [my rates]."

"So, I do a second call where we go and talk about the expectations from both sides. Only after then do I send them my contract, which works out really well and I have like three clients right now…it has been incredible as it's all by word-of-mouth marketing.

"I don't have a website—it's all through word of mouth. They [current clients] just refer my service to their friends… I actually right now like have a waiting list of people who want to be in the coaching program."

"Nice man!" I said after taking all that Bala was saying in. From then we talked a little bit more about what he was exactly coaching his clients on, which was just as fascinating but without having a website I began to be curious as to how he was scaling his business model, which is what prompted my next question to him.

"You know, Bala," I said, "if you are able to take what you're sharing with people on a one-on-one and put it into a

program—that would be powerful. You could serve more people."

"Exactly, yeah," Bala said in response. "I'm also thinking of the same thing. [I've been saying to myself] how can I do this at scale, rather than doing it on a one-on-one? One-on-one takes a lot of time—right?

"…One thing that I've been thinking about is doing group coaching, which I know some of the coaches do.

"As well as do podcasts and more one way medium rather than an interactive medium. So those are things that I'm thinking about getting into in the future."

At this point I began to feel as though this conversation was becoming another ripple in time for me. I realized that the launch that I thought was a failure wasn't a fiasco at all. I gained a better understanding of how to close, which I deeply appreciated Bala for, but I also took away from our conversation the value a bringing my message to a larger group—with cohort coaching. I wanted to maximize not only the feedback but also the potential return. This is where the Dream Octane Coaching Cohort (DOCC) was formed.

DOCC

I decided to take the advice that Bala recommended and put together a small cohort of high-capacity individuals. It was a mixed multitude of people with varying degrees of expertise. Some emerge from the microcosm I was serving in Step #4, experts I interviewed previously on the Niche Finder podcast or individuals who have been supportive of the *Dream Octane* brand along the way. The Dream Octane Coaching Cohort (DOCC) became a 6-session webinar that I was able to be more assertive with. What made Step #6 different than Step #4 was that I wanted to make it more challenging for people. I created homework assignments to ensure the principles being shared with the group was actively being applied. This created an opportunity where I could use the instructional information being provided to uncover their hidden potential as the key to unlocking their access to the session. It became a *help-me-to-help-you* type of situation.

From the beginning of DOCC, I sent everyone an intake form and instructions on what to do. This gave me a *pulse check* of where each person was in their journey of discovering, developing, and delivering their niche as well as setting clear expectations from the start.

Here is a snapshot of what each member signed up for:

• There will be 6 coaching sessions with homework assignments due prior to the date of each Zoom coaching session.

• Each of the 6 Zoom meetings will have a different access login and passcode to participate. However, access to each session will only be granted once the homework for that

session is completed by 11:59 p.m. the day before the Zoom meeting coaching session.

• All participants' homework assignments that are submitted late will be sent to the Zoom coaching recording video after the meeting. You can expect to have it arrive within 24-48 hours after the coaching session is completed.

• If you are unable to attend a coaching session, to participate in any subsequent coaching sessions, all homework assignments must be submitted and up-to-date by 11:59 p.m. of the most recent session. In other words, if—for example—Session 1 is missed, before you can join Session 2 the homework assignments for session 1 and session 2 would need to be completed and handed in by 11:59 p.m.

To be honest, I wasn't sure if this approach was going to work as each high-capacity individual—in my estimation—already had their plate full. To name a few, the cohort was made up of a project manager from Columbia University/ life coach; a Neuroscientist turned executive coach; a Registered Nurse working on her first book; a marketing strategist in charge of a healthcare vertical at one of the largest radio stations in the greater New York area; a Finance leader who worked for local government and; a Registered Nurse growing a Caribbean based non-profit business that provided underserved high school students in urban communities access to college scholarships through marching bands.

At first glance, the target audience appeared disparate, but they all had the same interest in discovering, developing, and delivering their niche. Although I thought the approach wasn't going to work, Mickey T—the RN with the Caribbean based non-profit business—at the start of Session 3 convinced me otherwise as she noted a prompt I sent her for the assignments.

"I actually verbalized everything," Mickey T said as she began to express how the 5P Framework assignment we cover in Step #1 of this book brought about an epiphany for her.

"And I said to myself 'oh, you know, this thing could actually come alive.' I said for real: *Jesus take the wheel,*" she said through a laugh as if that moment tickled something in her heart. Knowing Mickey T for years I was familiar with her jovial demeanor, but this was one of the times that the group, who was getting to know her, became exposed to that aspect of her personality. On the Zoom call you could see the random flicker of individual cameras popping into profile as others giggled along with her.

"Cause you know sometimes," she continued, "when you're actually working on something… you want to breathe life into your vision there can be such anxiety and fear that this dream is not going to happen.

"And then Cliff sent me a text message, that said, were you kidnapped by responsibility or something like that.

"In other words: where are you and where's my homework?" And I sat there and said to myself, okay, Mickey T, if you are not going to do this thing you are going to be locked out: cause this man is not going to let you in.

"And I'm truly enjoying this whole coaching process because, you know, I had this vision for the past four years to launch a podcast and a videocast.

"Then last week someone called me from Jamaica, saying we're launching this online TV platform and we want you to bring some ideas to contribute to it.

"And then recently some well-known comedians from Jamaica coincidentally reached out to me. Yeah, it's crazy.

"I'm like, is this really happening? Things are aligning. "So, I have to say thank you, Cliff, for that little nudge, because sometimes it's all we need…But you know, I'm looking forward to seeing what the end result will be, so kudos to you as a coach and knowing when to *poke the bear*."

As a coach I just want to clarify what's happening here. I had no influence on the opportunity that was presented to Mickey T nor can I guarantee any outcome with 100% certainty. The latter is control by God's will, the efforts of the individual and alignment of fortunate situations. However, the former has to do with heightened situational awareness that is within the realm of our control. What I mean by that is after you have discovered what your abundant factor/niche is by looking at your past success (Steps 1-3) and refined it through faithful service to others (Step 4-5), it will clarify which public arenas is the best fit for what you have to give in abundance (Step 6 through 7). The epiphany that Mickey T was experiencing after going through the cycles up to Steps 1-5, was that she would now be able to recognize the opportunities being presented to her.

There was a Chief Operating Officer who I mentioned in my Introduction that I used to work for. He was a serial entrepreneur who in the five years that I knew him went on to establish over twenty plus businesses with his business partner in that short amount of time. I once asked him, how is it that you are always finding these opportunities? His response to me—in short—was '…opportunities happen all the time but not everyone can see them.' This is true. The efforts you put behind Steps 1-5 will better position you—once you reach your Step #6—to see the opportunities that align with your niche. This is where you will see that opportunities are happening all around you. After arriving to this awareness, the next important step is to find a platform where your niche can be *funneled* to this wider audience and help to bring value to this new group. One thing to keep in mind as you do this: remember to obtain from your audience the *three stones*.

Stone Soup

As a child I remember coming across a book by Marcia Brown entitled *Stone Soup*. The story begins with three soldiers in the late 1700s who were walking towards a village hungry and in need of rest. When the villagers saw the three red coated soldiers walking in their direction, they became very nervous and began to hide the food that they held so dear. By the time the soldiers got to the village, the people in a town were all outside pretending to need food. The soldiers reasoned amongst themselves then turned to the villagers and said, "'We have asked many of you for food and you have none so we will have to make stone soup.'"[99]

As it turns out, each of the villagers had food in their homes but concealed it once they saw the three soldiers approaching the village from a distance. The term *stone soup*, used by one of the soldiers, caught the attention of those villagers, which then opened the door for the soldier to provide the recipe. One of the soldiers asked to have a large iron pot brought to where they were in town. The peasants in response quickly bought the largest pot that they could find to the town's square and filled it with water per the soldier's request. The fire was lit and one of the other soldiers said, "Now we will need three stones. You can't have stone soup without stones."[100]

Three stones were fetched and as soon as they were thrown into the pot of boiling water the soldier who was stirring the pot began requesting for the rest of the ingredients: salt and pepper, carrots, cabbage, and beef bones. The soup was then topped off with milk and barley, which made it fit for a king. The villagers were so happy once the soup was finished that everyone enjoyed the stone soup in the square and then danced late into the night. They were so appreciative of the value that these soldiers brought to them that they gave them the finest places in the village to rest for the night. This was all accomplished by the witty inventions of these three soldiers with the help of three stones that ended up providing a moment in time that the villagers would speak about for years even after the soldiers were gone.[101]

One of the most important lessons that I find within this story is the power of ideas. However, the idea alone is nothing without the ability to *effectively disseminate, clearly communicate,* and *consistently demonstrate* the value that thought has to others. Hidden inside of this story of the three soldiers is the understanding that their power wasn't in their uniforms. Although the uniforms represented prestige, the soldier's initial appearance intimidated the villagers. For whatever reason, the army they represented wasn't welcomed, but the idea they *disseminated* as they *communicated* it throughout the town, peaked the villager's interest. As the

village fascination began to grow, the soldiers also *demonstrated* that the incremental investments the villagers were making helped to build something of substance everyone could enjoy.

Victor Hugo, the author of, *Man's Search for Meaning* has been attributed this quote that is applicable here: "[t]here is one thing stronger than all the armies of the world, and that is an idea whose time has come." The most powerful item that the soldiers had with them wasn't the army they represented but their ability to deliver their niche.

If we take a closer look at this story, we will find that their niche was in their ability to survive and overcome obstacles. At the start of the story the soldiers needed food and shelter; by the end of the story however, they had both. How did they do that you ask? The answer was in their ability to market their ideas. If we overlay this story on top of how funnels work, it could help us to flush out the steps for delivering your niche online.

The perspective value funnel traffic will place on your niche

First, let's begin by understanding how online Funnel traffic behaves and then we will tie in *Stone Soup* to highlight the key principles. There are three types of traffic that you will find online from a marketing aspect: cold, warm, and hot traffic. Understanding the behaviors of each aspect will help you to know what you need to offer someone in that category and what not to attempt.

Online marketing funnels, if designed correctly, are intended to attract and eventually convert prospects into paying customers.[102] The dance that happens on the delivery section is not like the waggle of the honeybee nor is it the one step forward and two steps back we did while mastering our microcosms. No, this dance is a toggle between patience and persistence. Initially, you must patiently establish a relationship with the prospect as they gain a deeper understanding around who you are and how your niche can add value to them. Then, as the relationship deepens through a series of value adds on your part, the funnel can tactfully— and persistently—move them towards a converted sale.

Cold Traffic

It doesn't matter how brilliant of an idea you have, the only thing the audience cares about is how this idea will impact them. I signed up for a training held by Myron Golden PhD entitled, Make More Offers, which helped me to understand the distinction between these three different types of traffic. When it came to cold traffic, he remarked that cold traffic is interested in how you will either "…move them *away from pain* or *provide a payoff.*" In short, no one cares about

your product if it doesn't first do one of these two things: move them *"away from pain* or *provide a payoff."* Cold traffic is that way because the prospect doesn't know who you are or what you are about. However, what grabs the attention of cold traffic is a hook or lead magnet.

The Hook

A hook in funnel terms is what grabs the audience's attention. It is not just words; it must be something of value that adds additional value as more of the content is shared. These are your attention getters and promises that help to establish the relationship. In the story of *Stone Soup*, the soldiers' hook was their uniform. When the villagers saw those red coated soldiers from a distance, it surprised them emotionally. In marketing, hooks can be announcing something interesting, surprising the prospect emotionally, inviting the prospect to partake in a payout and/or solving the source of some pain they have.[103]

Lead Magnet

The lead magnet is the promise of what the prospect will receive. In the story of *Stone Soup*, the redcoat uniforms were the *hooks* that got the villagers' attention. However, the lead magnet became the promise of making stone soup. "'We have asked many of you for food and you have none so we will have to make stone soup.'"[104] If you remember, the stones that made the soup came from the villagers. The interesting thing about lead magnets are that they provide you as the giver and indication of what the receiver is interested in. If the interest is strong enough, the receiver will be willing to exchange something they have to help get them to the promise that you as the giver is offering. "Now we will need three stones. You can't have stone soup without stones."[105] In funnel terms, the hook is the ad that you create on YouTube, Facebook or the like. This is what gets the prospects' attention. In the advertisement something would be offered, such as—for example—a free book, training, webinar etc.[106] These are lead magnets. However, to get access to these items the prospect would need to supply their email—also known as a lead—in order to get what is being offered. So, tying this back to *Stone Soup*, the villagers confirmed their interest for more information once they provided the soldiers with the stones.

Warm Traffic

Cold traffic adds interactive value by effectively disseminating information. However, prospects become warm traffic once they exchange what is being asked of them in order to get the payoff or pain avoidance promise being offered. In our soup story referenced above, the villagers had to give the stones to begin the process of making stone soup. Technically, the villagers initially gave the soldiers a pot filled with water and a flame to set it on. However, those items were secondary to the primary offer of providing stone soup. If you recall one of the soldiers remarked: "Now we will need three stones. You can't have stone soup without stones."[107] In the funnel space, the large pot and flame under it could be likened to a prospects time and attention. The soup symbolizes the area where the prospect's interest is, but the three stones add a layer of specificity to what's being desired. When a prospect arrives at your funnel site for your lead magnet and provides their email address to obtain the promised item, they are supplying the three stones. There are a variety of methods that could be used to package the desired offer such as providing: product demos, free online seminar, free e-book, or the like.[108] Although the soldiers had obtained the three stones as a goal, that was not their end game. To get to the final stage in the traffic process, the soldiers had to increase the flame of the prospects' attention to shift the traffic from warm to hot.

Hot Traffic

This traffic represents prospects that have seen some results and are open to exchanging more *with* you to receive more *from* you. The villagers converted to hot traffic when they started supplying more ingredients for the soup: salt and pepper, carrots, cabbage, beef bones, etc. In funnel terms, this is the prospect purchasing a low ticket offer or product from you. What has been provided up to this point has established trust by proving a payoff or has helped to avoid pain. The soldiers provided the villagers with enough value as they delivered on the soup that was being put together before them that they were willing to exchange the ingredients they had hidden in their cupboards.

Once that occurs, the prospect would be more inclined to offer more. In this story, the soldiers received food and the best lodging the villagers had to offer. From a funnel aspect this is likened to a prospect signing up to a high ticket offer for your coaching program. This, in essence, is a high-level description on how traffic can transition as value is added to them from you helping to fuel progress for them in one way or another. However, the value exchange—as we covered in the *Stone Soup* example—is primarily facilitated by your message being packaged in a way that best expresses your expertise.

7 tips for designing and expressing your expertise

I found it interesting that as I was searching for the background behind the problem-solving principle known as Occam's razor that's credited to logician and theologian, William of Ockham, that the information gathering portion of the process was not so simple.[109] The simplified version of what has come to be known as Occam's razor is: "The

simplest solution is almost always the best." I could not help but be overtaken by the irony in how this principle is often misquoted and at times, depending on whether or not you're using it in medicine relative to other things, can become very complex.[110]

Now, as you already know, I love jumping down rabbit holes when it comes to research, however as I pursued this answer to Occam's razor, I became deterred by the complexities of the responses.[111] My reason for bringing this up is less to do with educating you on the principle of Occam's razor and more to do with being discouraged by complexity. When it comes down to communicating our message to a wider audience, the simpler and more understandable we can make the message the more persuasive it then becomes. With that said, I would like to introduce you to seven tips that you could use to keep—and/or help to make—things simple for your audience.

At this stage of the Life Cycle of Excavation, you can now add layers to the "Y" in the E.A.S.Y Method. These seven tips will help you to *yield results from your expertise* by delivering what you offer through frameworks that *define* your expertise.

Remember how Michael Mauboussin paraphrased Gregory Northcraft's definition of expertise, "the difference between *experience* and *expertise* is that *expertise* is having a predictive model that works." I want you to know that creating frameworks for others to use will help them to remember the tools you are providing them. However, memorization is only one benefit. Putting your message in a form such as this also becomes an exercise on helping the mind to think. Arguably one of the greatest thinkers in our modern time, Albert Einstein, said, "Education is not the learning of facts, rather it's the training of the mind to think." As an expert, being able to convert your message into a form that helps people to think increases the resonance and persuasiveness of your delivery.

Here are seven tips to help convert your message into predictive model(s) that you can use in a live environment and tweak to iterate to its highest utility for others. If you are in the educational entrepreneurial space, find a way to craft your unique message into one or more of these seven methods. Once crafted, speak to an intellectual property lawyer on how to put a trademark or patent on the models you created.

1. Acrostics

Acrostics help to *structure learning*. Acrostics are *a composition usually in verse in which sets of letters (such as the initial or final letters of the lines) taken in order form a word or phrase or a regular sequence of letters of the alphabet.*[112] In short, acrostics are the first letter of multiple words that form the spelling of a new word. The E.A.S.Y method is an example of this. Acrostics are often used in poetry but can be used in prose as well.[113] They help to structure learning in a way that is easier for the student to remember detailed information. For example, if you take a grammar schoolteacher who is helping her math students to recall the *order of mathematical operations*, she could use the following acrostics to help drive their recollection: "'*Please Excuse My Dear Aunt Sally*' i.e.: *p*arenthesis, *e*xponents, *m*ultiply and *d*ivide before *a*dding and *s*ubtracting."[114]

Providing the delivery is clear, using acrostics as you share your message will help to draw people into your lesson structure. As an expert—if you package and distribute the message effectively—deploying acrostics on the internet could drive cold traffic exposed to it back to you. This creates an opportunity to capture that traffic into your funnel and provide them with more high-value content that could eventually lead them to wanting more of your services/products. Robert Kiyosaki has a great acrostic on FOCUS. He is noted for creating: *Follow One Course Until Successful.*[115] This principle was one of the five qualities that, when combined, gives an entrepreneur the *Midas Touch.*[116] Although this was the only acrostic he used, the statement

F.O.C.U.S says it all. Acrostics are important because they help to *structure learning.*

2. <u>Acronyms</u>

Acronyms help to *simplify labeling* things. Acronyms are like acrostics so when it comes to word phrases the two are at times used interchangeably. However, acronyms are not only created by other words, they are also abbreviated form of words. By definition it is: *a word (such as NATO, radar, or laser) formed from the initial letter or letters of each of the successive parts or major parts of a compound term.*[117] Acronyms are great to use when situational awareness needs to be applied. Think about it: how many of us learned about the branch of the government known as the Federal Emergency Management Agency (FEMA) if not for natural disasters, such as Hurricane Katrina? If we go back even further, the National Aeronautics and Space Administration (NASA) embodied the United States goal for achieving the *national objective of a human trip to the Moon by the end of the 1960s.*[118] Same can be said for the most recent COVID-19 pandemic terminologies like the World Health Organization (WHO) and Center for Disease Control (CDC).

How can an expert benefit from utilizing acronyms? One example of this is seen in healthcare with a man named, Quint Studer. I remember reading his book, *Hardwiring*

Excellence: Purpose, Worthwhile Work, Making a Difference several years ago. This book documented his journey as a healthcare Administrator working at a hospital where he helped them achieve award-winning service. The book outlines several models that were formed into evidence-based practices with *simplified labels* that helped healthcare workers perform best practice methods as a standard for operations. One such technique was referred to as AIDET, which was an acronym put together for initial patient interactions. It stood for *A*cknowledge, *I*ntroduce, *D*uration, *E*xclamation, *T*hank you. The healthcare workers had to apply these principles of acknowledging the patient, introducing themselves; providing the expected duration of a given procedure; explain the care associated with it, and thank them. This all led to increased patient satisfaction scores once these principles were *hardwired* consistently in each interaction.[119]

AIDET was just one of several different models that the Studer group designed. As they grew in affectedness, they caught the attention of a Chicago-based company that specialized in a broad array of clinical enhancements within healthcare organizations. Then, in January 2015, the Huron Consulting Group purchased the Studer Group and their best practice models for $325 million.[120] The Studer Community Institute noted on their website: "*Huron is sort of known as the expert on process improvement and streamlining costs; Studer Group is known as the expert in culture, employee engagement and patient experience."* Quint Studer added, *"Putting those two aspects together is great for both and great for health care."*

Acronyms provide *simplified labels* for your message. It can help to   package your content into models that others can easily remember in complex situations and quite possibly produce potential for future return.

3. <u>Analogies</u>

Analogies help to *synchronize lessons*. Merriam Webster defines an analogy as *a comparison of two things based on their being alike in some way.* [121] In business, communicating with analogies helps your audience better understand complex ideas by relating them to situations that they may already be familiar with. By synchronizing the larger point with the object lesson, the speaker is able to resonate with those they are communicating with.

In a *Forbes* article entitled, *This is the Best Way to Clarify Complex Ideas,* the contributor Esther Choy remarked, "[c]omparing the familiar with the unfamiliar is a leadership communication and storytelling tool that helps clarify the complex, giving audiences a way to quickly get the gist." They can also help to make your ideas actionable. In an article

entitled, *Analogies and Business: The Fastest Way to Get Your Point Across,* the author notes "[w]hen communicated properly, analogies can convey everything from the urgency of an idea, to the value of a deal, to even simplifying a business strategy."[122]

Analogies are another way of simplifying your message. If done correctly, it can bring intrigue to your communication as it resonates and afford your points to be remembered. Analogies help to *synchronize lessons.*

4. Allegories

Allegories help to add *storytelling layers* to your teachings. Allegories are similar to analogies as they both provide parallel context for the message you are conveying; however, allegories have a longer duration. Where an analogy is typically used within a statement or section of a story, an allegory is *a symbolic representation which can be interpreted to reveal a hidden meaning, usually a moral or political one.*[123] John Bunyan's *Pilgrim's Progress*, Dante Alighieri's *Dante's Inferno (The Divine Comedy: Volume I, Hell)*, and C.S. Lewis' *The Lion, the Witch, and the Wardrobe* are all examples of allegories. Each book has *story layers* that these authors build upon to draw the audience into deeper meanings of their lessons. As an expert you can use allegory to help your audience to follow a logical train of thought. It's sort of like having something valuable inside of you and likening it to crude oil in the ground. Once it is discovered, you then have to develop it before delivering it to a wider audience. Allegories help to add *storytelling layers* to your teachings.

5. Algorithms

Algorithms simplify complex processes by providing *step-by-step logistics*. We use algorithms all the time within healthcare. Clinicians use them for designing treatment plans for patients, frontline staff have them handy to organize the steps within a given workflow, and hospital administrators also use them to help recognize performance improvement activities. With the latter they help to make transparent the steps involved in a given process. If, for example, you have sixteen steps you may find that four of the steps could be consolidated or eliminated. Doing this could make things more efficient, safer and/or less cumbersome. Algorithms simplify complex processes by providing *step-by-step logistics*.

6. Alliterations

Alliterations create *similar sounding list*. The Merriam-Webster dictionary defines alliteration as *"the use of words that begin with the same sound near one another (as in wild and woolly or a babbling brook)"* Now, you may—or may not—pick up on this, but I love alliteration when it comes

to expressing your expertise. Alliterative expression brings poetry into a business arena where over utilized business proses have dominion. This creates a penetration point—and a stage—for alliteration to be put on display.

I mean, let's be honest, how many of you are only reading this section to see what the next "A" word will be— or whether the flow of these patterns will get derailed somewhere along the way? Stephanie Denning notes in an article she penned for *Forbes* entitled, *"Does Poetry Have A Place In Business? One Unsung Success Secret"*. The value in adding eloquence to business communication, "Business language is boringly uniform, with all executives latching onto the same business jargon...When you happen upon someone who can communicate the same idea clearly, without using the clunky worn-out words and phrases, it acts like a magnetic pull."[124]

Alliteration is powerful because it brings the conversation into the minds of others in a package that has simplified and/or conveniently collated an idea. In a *Harvard Business Review* article entitled, *The Benefits of Poetry for Professionals* by John Coleman, he pulled a quote from Harman Industries founder Sidney Harman that he made to *The New York Times*, [125] "I used to tell my senior staff to get me poets as managers. Poets are our original systems thinkers.

They look at our most complex environments and they reduce the complexity to something they begin to understand."[126]

If we basketweave the allegory contained within *Dream Octane* we find a series of alliterations that are designed to express the journey and the attributes that help to make finding your niche possible: **discovery** requires **determination**; **development** needs **discipline**; and **delivery** necessitates **diligence**. Alliterations help to express your expertise by providing *similar sounding list.*

7. Archetypes

The last tip for expressing your expertise is archetypes. Archetypes have importance because they help to provide *symbolic links.* Where stereotypes have a negative connotation and are based on *generalized assumptions,* archetypes are more aspirational and are an *idealized version.* The Merriam Webster dictionary defines archetypes as "*the original pattern or model of which all things of the same type are representations or copies.*"[127] In the psychology arena the same source notes archetypes as being "*an inherited idea or mode of thought in the psychology of C. G. Jung that is derived from the experience of the race and is present in the unconscious of the individual.*"

Psychotherapist Carl Jung created frameworks that he used to describe the different personalities and what he

believed to be the *collective unconscious*. Jung noted that this *collective unconscious* possessed universal characteristics which are shared between all humanity. Now the point of raising this as an example is not intended to compel you to subscribe to this philosophy or not. No, the primary focus is really to highlight the method that Carl Jung used to express his understanding that he had when coining the term archetype, which became a symbolic link for different personality types and human behaviors. Archetypes help to express your expertise as they provide *symbolic links*.

Remember, as you attempt to mold your message into one or more of these tips for expressing your expertise, keep on the forefront what Einstein noted, *"Education is not the learning of facts, rather it's the training of the mind to think."* This process of tailoring, tightening up and/or retooling your message into a simplified manner is training your mind to think, and as you do so, you are positioning your material to do the same for others. For some of us, the fulfilment of that dream may need a spark.

Every Dream Needs a Spark: Terry Fox

On March 9th 1977, an eighteen-year-old named Terry Fox had his right leg amputated 15 centimeters above his knee. The goal was to stave off an aggressive bone scan cancer discovered less than ten days earlier. Most people would rightly believe that this first year Canadian kinesiology student at Simon Fraser University would have every right to give up all aspirations of ever running again. But for Terry there was a spark the night before his amputation. His former basketball coach brought in some inspiration from a magazine that depicted another amputee who ran in the New York marathon.

From that moment Terry resolved, "It was then I decided to meet this new challenge head on and not only overcome my disability but conquer it in such a way that I could never look back and say it disabled me." [128] That commitment would be immediately tested over the course of the next sixteen months as Terry contended with rounds of physical and chemotherapy. However, what immediately began after this ordeal would be known as the Marathon of Hope.

The sixteen months of rehabilitation did more than just adjust him to his new body frame. Seeing the number of children stricken by various cancers since his diagnosis ignited a desire to raise 1 million dollars by running 5,000 miles (about twice the width of the United States) across Canada. On April 12, 1980, Terry started his journey at 4am covering twelve miles before resting and finishing the remainder of the day with fourteen miles. Twenty-six miles is

a full marathon, but he would do that amount every day on average for one hundred and twenty days.

On September 1, 1980, 3,339 miles (about the width of the United States) into his 5,000 miles goal Terry discovered that the cancer had spread to his lungs and required him to stop the run and receive treatment. Terry Fox died June 28, 1981, one month before his twenty-third birthday. Although his race ended for him that day, his inspiration became the fuel for a movement. His initial goal of raising $1 million dollars for cancer research, which would be $4,415,360.82 at the time of this writing, was exceeded. To date, over $750 million has been raised worldwide for cancer research.[129] What ignites you?

As we begin to round out the close of the *Life Cycle of Excavation,* I would like to give you one other tool to put into your toolbox. Similar to the E.A.S.Y method that you would pull out to affirm that you are *made* for those moments when you are feeling unqualified, I want to offer you the I.D.R.E.A.M principles when you feel a loss of power in pursuing your dream. Where the E.A.S.Y method helps to reinforce the elements within you that make you qualified for particular moments, the I.D.R.E.A.M principles are what provides the sparks you need to deliver your niche to others. It is what ignites the spark within you.

So, what are the I.D.R.E.A.M Principles anyway?

Just as you would pull out the E.A.S.Y method to help validate that your preparation helps qualify you for those moments you were made for, pull out these I.D.R.E.A.M principles in those instances you feel out of power. So, if you cannot find the power to put behind delivering your dream, consider incorporating one or more of these principles in your daily routine:

Inspiration: *What ignites you?*

In an article entitled, *The Scientific Study of Inspiration in the Creative Process: Challenges and Opportunities,* the authors defined inspiration as being "...a motivational state that compels individuals to bring ideas into fruition".[130] They also shared the definition from musical virtuoso Wolfgangus Theophilus Mozart where he refers to inspirations as what "fires my soul".[131] Inspiration is like an ignition switch.

Among the multitude of items, the researchers unpack, the scientific relevance inspiration houses within itself caught my attention. Todd M. Thrash and Andrew Elliot note that "...inspiration involves two distinct processes—a relatively passive process that they called being inspired by, and a relatively active process that they called being inspired to."[132]

I was intrigued how inspiration gives rise to being *inspired by* and/or *inspired to*. For now, let's focus on the value of the passive form of the inspired state: to be *inspired by*. This is where I find it so important to take the time to refuel yourself as you begin delivering your niche to others. This is not Step 5. When it comes to being *inspired by*, we are not neutralizing a barrier; we are energizing who we are.

So, how are you being charged up? When it comes to your niche—now that you discovered and developed it—what are you doing to ensure that it gets delivered? In short, this is placing an importance on being refueled: at the end of a long workday; in the middle of a challenging time; when you felt like you've had to contend with so much adversity. It doesn't matter what low energy level you find yourself on, you need to be able to refuel.

What are you doing in those moments?

Are you the type that gets refueled waking up early in the morning to write? That's one thing that I like to do because that fuels me but what is it for you? Is it getting up to exercise—getting that adrenaline and those endorphins going in your body early in the morning? What about prayer and daily devotional time? For me the latter is the catalyst that helps to keep me in the proper perspective. Without this I end up on the wrong side of things, which is another book in and of itself.

The point is this: get yourself ready for your next moment and prepare yourself for what needs to be done. The importance of the "I" in the I.D.R.E.A.M principles is making time to fuel up, so you are ignited and become productive in the *engine of change*.

In a 4- stroke engine within a vehicle, there are four phases or strokes: intake, compression, power and exhaust.[133] In the power phase, *Your spark plugs are what supply the spark that ignites the air/fuel mixture, creating the explosion which makes your engine produce power.*[134] This controlled explosion within an engine is what helps the engine components to go. As those components begin to shift, it provides power for the vehicle to move.

So, if not for the spark—or the inspiration—the fuel sitting in the engine would just be a wet substance, beaming with potential. The spark is then necessary to get things going. My encouragement to you with the "I" in the I.D.R.E.A.M principles is to make time to focus on the things that ignite you. These are the things that will help to ignite your niche as the fuel in the *engine of change*. Inspiration will help to produce the power that you need. However, as John Wooten put it, "Don't mistake activity for accomplishment." Inspiration is important but we also need to ensure that we are

heading in the right direction. The "I" in I.D.R.E.A.M is inspiration: *What ignites you?*

Direction *What guides you?*

In 2014, there was an article written in the *Huffington Post* by contributor Sheldon D. Newton, best-selling author, International Speaker & Pastor.[135] The article was entitled, *Wisdom Is The Principal Thing.* The title captured my interest as it is taken from the book of Proverbs chapter 4 verse 7. This article goes on to say that *"success still evades many"* because they pursue knowledge but lack wisdom.[136] Pastor Newton notes that wisdom is the principal thing, which he breaks down into the three key learning components in the book of proverbs: knowledge, understanding, and wisdom. Knowledge is *information*, understanding is *comprehension of information,* but wisdom is *application of the information.*[137] I also like to see wisdom as the application of truth. When you take information (knowledge) and gain some comprehension (understanding) around it, you can then move to application (wisdom).

The article encourages the use of wisdom to guide our actions by first putting goals around what you enjoy doing— or in *Dream Octane* terms: Discover your niche.

Secondly, fortify yourself with information from great books on the subject that you engaged with: Develop your niche. Lastly, he admonishes us to pray and ask God for wisdom to apply that knowledge: Deliver your niche.

Wisdom therefore is the pursuit of excelling at best practices that are lawful and true. It is making time for the things that are in line with fulfilling our God given purposes and actively adding value for others. These are all principles that are rooted in wisdom and so the "D" in I.D.R.E.A.M is Direction: *What guides you?*

Recognition: *What rewards you?*

Where do you feel treasured? Albert Einstein said, "Try to become not a [person] of success but try rather to become a [person] of value." When we focus on serving others with the things that make us valuable, that exposure highlights our worth especially when it helps to solve a recipient's problem. Have you ever found yourself in a situation where support is needed or even times when you find yourself in a circumstance where you say to yourself: Somebody's gotta do something about this_____ thing—fill in the blank? Often when we feel those frustrations, inner gnawing's, or urgings for change, it is typically tied to something that we're equipped to do. We may be fearful of it, but Mark Twain said, "Courage is not the absence of fear, but the mastery of it."

When we look at those moments in time that we were made for, these are the same moments that are waiting for us

to step into. These moments often hide the recognition that we were designed to receive. As we start doing the things that are helpful to others but unique to us, we will find what rewards us. Being the go-giver versus the go-getter mentioned in Step #4 creates the muscle memory that we now call upon in Step #6. In Proverbs 11:25 NLT notes, "The generous will prosper; those who refresh others will themselves be refreshed."[138] What rewards us is often tied to a larger purpose for us. The "R" in I.D.R.E.A.M is recognition: *What rewards you?*

Education: *What equips you?*

John Wooden said, "It's the things you learn after you, 'know it all' that counts." Not too long ago I was watching a reel on YouTube and randomly came across a video with basketball player Giannis Antetokounmpo. He was being interviewed by a reporter who asked this question: "So, Kobe Bryant, you worked out with him what did you learn from him?"

"Yes," Giannis replied, "You've got to be simple; you've got to work on your craft; think outside the box and you always got to be a kid. That's what he told me."

Giannis then folded his arms while shrugging his shoulders and wrinkled his face as he looked confused. "Be a kid?" he asked, "What do you mean by be a kid? You've got to mature you've got to be a man..." Giannis said in response to Kobe's advice.

Kobe replied, 'No, what I mean by being a kid, is a kid use their fantasies. You can see a kid being creative [taking] two rocks and playing around with them.' He said when you were a kid you always want to learn—you ask questions." Giannis took this advice and applied it. Then in a few years he won the Most Valuable Player Award in the NBA and a few years after that, he won his first NBA Championship for the Milwaukee Bucks.[139]

I heard it said—by a source I can no longer recall or find—that to get to the next level in life, you must stay in a learning posture. I believe this is a stance that positions you to receive. No one knows everything, which is a good thing. This gives us an opportunity to humble ourselves and ask questions which keeps us learning. Zig Ziglar said it this way, "In times of change, the learners shall inherit the earth while the learned find themselves beautifully equipped to deal with a world that no longer exists." The E in I.D.R.E.A.M is education: *What equips you?*

Action: *What develops you?*

What helps you to become better? How many things can you think about getting better at that doesn't involve some form of action or effort? Few—if any—things. Why? Because just conceptualizing greatness is not enough, it takes tenacious effort to achieve. Take the brilliant thoughts that you have, best practices that you've already seen, and put them into *action*. Mya Angelo said it best, "There is no greater agony than bearing an untold story inside of you."

Are you a writer? Then write.

Are you a speaker? Find a platform where you're welcomed and speak.

If you're a dancer, then move: Find your beat and dance to it.

If you are an athlete: Find your sport, do it to the best of your ability, then *be like a kid* as you hone your skills to better your best. It is just that simple. Now that you have discovered and developed your niche, that gnawing desire to do it is your spark: Do it. God gave us these things as gifts to give away, but we need to continue to develop them.

We develop our niche through action. There are four C.A.F.I keys to development. If you remember changing your frame, the C.A.F.I keys would be like a shadowbox in artwork, or a frame within a frame.

Consistency

The first one is you need consistency. Whatever it is that you're looking to do, and bring into the world, you need to be consistent with it. This means that you need to have some repetitiveness about the actions that you're doing. The Niche Finder podcast is a weekly show that has been consistent since we started releasing a new episode every weekend. Russell Brunson shared a nugget of truth around the importance of being consistent when he remarked that many of us have a favorite program that we started watching in the middle of the season but once we found we liked it, we went back to the beginning to catch up. In short, don't give up in the middle of what you are doing. If you give up in the middle, people may never find you in the middle and go back to your beginning.

Accuracy

Accuracy is also necessary in development. It's just like exercising. If you're exercising in the gym for two hours and your body mechanics and form are all wrong, then you are not going to develop properly. You may *develop* an injury, but you will not develop the muscle goals you are looking to achieve.

I experienced this firsthand when I tore the meniscus in my right knee. According to the orthopedic surgeon that I went to, I had two options to either repair my meniscus surgically or go through physical therapy to address the problem. I opted to do the latter and the therapy lasted for several months. However, one day as I was exercising on my own, I caught myself arching my back too far forward as I was doing my lunges. Then, the inevitable happened: My back

went out on me. This led me to a new physical therapist that specialized in difficult cases such as my own. It was at Dr. Owen Legaspi's office that I fully healed my knee and newly acquired back injury. Additionally, the physical therapists at his practice taught body awareness and proper body mechanics and muscle building techniques. By practicing these techniques *accurately,* I became stronger than I have ever been.

Frequency

This aspect is like consistency. Consistency is the manner in which we do a thing, but frequency is intervals in between what we are being consistent with. Consistency has you wanting to work out and frequency provides the defined times in which you fulfill that desire. We need both in combination with each other. So, if you want to work out consistently every month, you then will need to layer a frequency of 3-4 times a week to have gains on your development .[140]

Intensity

Let's stay in the gym theme. Most of the time I like to work out in the house with calisthenics: pushups, pullups, sit-ups and the like. However—not judging at all—I find it interesting on the occasions that when I do go to the gym there is always someone there shooting the breeze—just hanging out. They haven't broken a sweat, their workout outfit looks like it was just taken out of the dryer and there is more conversation than action going on. You need to have some intensity if you want to develop.[141] Your body must be continually subjected to a range of stimuli to consistently improve.[142] Get it done as you put these C.A.F.I keys into *action*.

Meaningful development can occur when we apply the right amount of action behind the C.A.F.I action keys: consistency, accuracy, frequency, and intensity. These are the four keys that make up the essence of action. As a result, the "A" in I.D.R.E.A.M is action: *What develops you?*

Motivation: *What drives you?*

The last portion of the I.D.R.E.A.M principles is motivation. Oswald Chambers said, "Perseverance is more than endurance. It is endurance combined with absolute assurance and certainty that what we are looking for is going to happen." Motivation can breed perseverance if administered proactively at the low points of our delivery journey. Where inspiration is the *spark,* motivation is the *drivetrain* that gets us going. If we tie this back to the "I" in the I.D.R.E.A.M we will gain a better understanding of motivation. We mentioned earlier that Psychologists Todd M. Thrash and Andrew Elliot noted being *inspired by* and *inspired to*. Inspired by is the uplifting aspect of inspiration. But being *inspired to* is the motivation. The research notes, "The process of being inspired by involves appreciation of the perceived intrinsic value of a stimulus object, whereas the process of being inspired to involves motivation to actualize or extend the valued qualities to a new object."[143]

Being *inspired to* is where you get engaged to do something. It gives rise to the characteristics the researchers refer to as *approach motivation*. What is approach motivation? In short: this is where you start to create. You've been inspired, now this aspect of inspiration motivates you to create or solve something.

What drives you?

What gets you out of your seat and into your moment? Whatever it is put some intentionality or strategy behind it. Whenever you feel de-energized, demotivated or disenchanted around an unfulfilled dream get motivated by applying any of the principles mentioned above. Be strategic; as an example, the moment you leave work, tell yourself that the first thing you're going to listen to isn't going to be the news. There is a high probability that much of what's being reported may have already been covered in the news cycle heard earlier in the day. In it's place make it something that's going to uplift, inspire or engage you. Make it an activity that can motivate you to be better, greater than where you are and help you to move in a direction of where you need to be. The "M" in the I.D.R.E.A.M principles is motivation: *What drives you?*

There is more that could be covered as it relates to delivering your niche to a wider audience. However, it's important to give room to you as the reader to apply these principles and discover the value your own journey has to offer. As we transition to the 7th and final step in the *Life Cycle of Excavation*, the question I charge you to take with you is: *Do you have more to give?*

Chapter 9

Step # 7: Maximize Your Abundant Factor: Do You Have More To Give?

Oscar is better than Chips: *Kobe Bryant*

> *"The meaning of life is to find your gift; the purpose of life is to give it away."* —Pablo Picasso

On March 4th 2018 at the 90th Academy awards, basketball legend Kobe Bryant was nominated for and then won an Academy Award for best animated short film entitled, Dear Basketball. He was the first professional athlete to ever win an Oscar but that wasn't the only thing that made this feat so special. The greatest surprise was in Kobe's response to a reporter's question he received backstage immediately following receiving the award. The reporter asked, "After winning 5 NBA championships now holding an Oscar, how do you feel?"

Kobe inhaled and exhaled quickly, looking up as if the reporter morphed into a basketball hoop that he was about to sink a game winning free throw into. "I feel better than winning a championship, to be honest with you," Kobe replied. "I swear I do.

"You know growing up as a kid," Kobe continued, "I dreamt of winning championships and working really hard to make that dream come true—but then to have something like this..."[144] he said while pointing his hand at the Oscar he was holding, "[it] seemingly came out of left field."

What appeared to sweeten the victory for him was what happened as he was nearing the end of his career. People would ask what his plans were after retirement. When Kobe told them that he wanted to be a writer he said people would give him an almost patronizing response, like 'aw that's cute' or imply that life for him going forward would be depressing.[145] There was only a handful of supporters for his dream of being a writer, who included his wife and three daughters at the time.

Nevertheless, he built a studio inside his house and began writing. Most people thought that he would end up coaching or having some role behind the scenes with basketball, but Kobe was intent on bringing his dream of writing to others and he put effort behind it. He discovered writing served a purpose outside of himself. From there, Kobe developed that raw talent with others who helped to refine his gift and eventually delivered it within various arenas.

In his response to a question from another reporter, Kobe encapsulated the potential in having more to give even after being successful in your first environment. "Obviously you've won championships, Olympic gold medals, and now this.... You talk about this meaning more to you but at the same time, can you talk about the struggles that you may understand now that someone who has achieved fame may have trying to find a new outlet?"

"The hardest thing for athletes to do," Kobe said "when you start over you really have to quiet the ego.

"You have to begin again.

"You have to be a learner all over again.

"You have to learn the basics of things. That's really the hardest part. So, my advice to athletes is—first and foremost—find the thing that you love to do. I wake up in the morning and I can't wait to write—I can't wait to get to the studio. So, when you find the thing that you love to do, everything else tends to make sense."[146]

This serves as a great example that even if we are wildly successful in one arena, we may still have more to *give* in other areas. From a creative standpoint, we are not all equal. Our differences make us unique, and that uniqueness then gives us a responsibility. The dream for Kobe of pursuing his writing career was far-fetched to some, but winning an Oscar validated for him his move towards writing. This made him the first professional athlete to be nominated for and win an Academy Award.[147] It is for this very reason that we cannot just *discover*, we must also *develop* and *deliver* value into the engines of change we are here to fuel.

Maximizing your abundant factor begins & ends with *one thing*

Can we pause to take stock of the amount of progress we've made thus far? Although a lot has been covered, the *Life Cycle of Excavation* is designed to focus on finding, refining, and distributing your *one thing*. By one thing I mean the niche that you prioritized from your 5P Framework and ushered through steps 1 to 6. This is in *Dream Octane* terms, your *first iteration*. I want to tease this out to ensure that you are clear on the purpose of Step # 7 *Maximize your Abundant Factor*. In short, it is intended to be a transition back to the 5P Framework you pulled your initial *one thing* from and use that list to extract your *next thing*.

Remember we covered that your abundant factor is not in competition with others, and if you recall, nor do the qualities on your list compete against each other. However, before you can change and go on to your *next thing* as Kobe Bryant did, you must first yield fruit from your first iteration. This will involve taking time to water the seed for your *one thing*.

Focus on one thing: Tyler Perry

Perry stated in a video posting on Youtube.com that many people ask him the age-old question: "How did you make it?" To this he replies, "There's only one answer to that…truth be told it was nothing but the grace of God."[148] His journey—like Steve Harvey's—spent several years struggling to bring his *one thing* to the stage. Although Perry has a comedic edge to his creativity, his *one thing* was writing, producing, and performing in his theatrical plays .[149] To do that he worked odd and end jobs, saved up tax return money to rent out the 14th Street Playhouse in Atlanta so he could put on a production of his autobiographical play *I Know I've Been Changed.*[150] In the video posting he likened putting effort behind working on your *one thing* to be like watering seeds in the ground. "You can plant seeds all day long," Perry said, "You can go around giving your business card to people..., knocking on doors and auditioning…you can do all of that every day of your life, and nothing happens." He then looked into the camera with a look of sincerity that seemed to combine both resolve and conviction, then said: "When a seed is planted in the ground all you can do is water it.

"You cannot control the sunshine.

"You cannot control the weather and you cannot control whether the locust will come and try to destroy it. All you can do is plant your seed in the ground, water it and *believe.* That is what allowed me to be in this position right now."

Let me quickly highlight what Perry's *position* amounted to at the time of this writing. His accomplishments included the following creations:

- Two television sitcom series, one of which—*House Of Payne*—became the recipient of the NAACP Image Award for outstanding comedy series.
- Author of two books with his first—*Don't Make a Black Woman Take off Her Earrings: Madea's Uninhibited Commentaries on Love and Life*—becoming a *New York Times* bestseller.
- Originator of seventeen feature films.[151]
- The genius who conceived more than twenty stage plays[152].
- Developer of nine television shows.[153]
- The mastermind behind the 330-acre Tyler Perry Studios home base in Atlanta, Georgia.[154]

With that said let's get back to Perry's *one*—and initial—*thing*.

"I would not stop believing," Perry continued. "I planted my seed; I worked really hard." The seed that was securely planted in Perry's mind was getting the first play that he wrote in front of a captive audience. He then resolved to line up all his efforts early on to water that one idea.

"I had one idea," Perry continued, "that was to do a play. My only idea, my only focus was to do my one play. And I knew if I could get that to work, everything else would come to past. There are so many people going in so many directions: this week they're doing this; next week they're doing that...I usually try to get them to focus: focus on *one thing—one area.* [To] put all of your energy into one area. If you spread the water across many seeds, you don't have as much water [as] you would have for one seed. So, focus on *one thing,* make it your priority and stick with it no matter what."

I was tickled to find that as I began laying out this portion of the book, that it provided another organic called back to a previous point made in the *7 tips for designing and expressing your expertise* section. The connection was in the name of Perry's video which bared the title of Robert Kiyosaki's quote F.O.C.U.S: Follow ONE Course Until Successful. Maximizing your abundant factor takes the focus you have placed on your one thing and charges you to *Follow ONE Course Until Successful.*[155]

"I remember when I did my very first show;" Perry said, "I work my butt off to save $12,000 in tax returns...rented the 14th Street Playhouse, put that show up and thought that 1200 people would come over the weekend and 30 [people] showed up—and I knew every one of them.

"But I didn't stop.

"That didn't deter me."

This cycle of disappointment for Perry continued for six years ranging from 1992-1998.[156] However, in 1998 his play was moved to House of Blues in Atlanta. It was ramping up to be his last attempt at launching his play, but instead of it failing as it did in previous years—this time—all eight shows sold out. [157] That play was then moved to the famed Fox Theatre, where upwards of 9,000 people were in attendance.[158]

When we find our *one thing*—which the 5P framework is designed to help you to uncover—we must stick with it, until successful. It may not be immediately apparent that the niche that we have validated by taking it through steps 1-6 is bearing fruit, but we have to keep watering the seed.

TD Jakes said "If at first you don't succeed, try-try again. And if you don't succeed that time, try-try again. And if you don't succeed that time, try-try again. And if you don't succeed that time, write a book about what you learned from how you failed. There is always something to do with what you have experienced."[159] As you maximize your step seven, keep in mind that although iterating your *one thing* until successful is important, there is value in the process.

The value in iterating towards your dream: *Art and Fear*

In David Baylis' and Todd Ortolans' book, *Art and Fear,* they tell a story of a ceramic's teacher who, on the first day of class, divided his students into two different groups.

The class was told that the grades at the end of the semester would be as follows: the grades for the left side of the class would be on *quantity* while the right side of the class would get a grade based on *quality*.[160]

On the final day of class, the grading would be different for both as well. The quantities group would receive an A if, when he placed the pounds of pottery they created on a scale, it weighed 50 pounds. If it weighed 40 pounds, then they would earn a B and so on.

Those being graded on quality would receive a grade for the one perfect pot. The book goes on to say that when it came time to receive grades the group that had the highest quality was the quantity side of the class because as they were busy producing pot after pot, they inadvertently perfected their craft. Whereas those who focused on perfection ended their efforts with nothing more than theories and a pile of useless clay.

For many of us when failure occurs, we stop forward progress instead of working towards retooling our efforts. In other words, we stop doing the things that we believed we failed at, but there is value in iteration. It is easy to give up on moving forward because failure provides evidence that what we are doing has not worked. However, failure doesn't have to be the end of the story for it to be a part of it. The Merriam Webster dictionary defines failure as a *lack of success in some effort; a situation or occurrence in which something does not work as it should.*[161] This is not the same as being flawed, which is *having a defect or imperfection.*[162] In other words, your pot may not be perfect, but that's ok—keep working on it. There is value in iterating.

To flush this point out, I highlight a quote by Zig Ziglar that further counters the definition of failure with Zig's definition of success: *"Success is the maximum utilization of the ability that you have."* Maximizing your abundant factor is pursuing your one thing until successful; as well as understanding that delivering your niche is a process that is about incrementally moving forward. In speaking with Dr. Erica Urquhart MD, Ph.D., she helped to clarify that as you incrementally move towards maximizing your abundant factor—or niche—it may not require a high degree of intensity, when what you are rendering is in your *DNA.*

What level of intensity is needed to stay consistent: *Erica Urquhart, MD, PhD, MBT, MBA*

I feel fortunate having had a longstanding connection to the Urquhart family over the years. After I interviewed Marc—the husband—on the Niche Finder podcast, he recommended that I interview his wife, Erica. She and I were able to carve out time and eventually made it happen. I had elevated expectations for the interview. However, Dr. Erica Urquhart's insight during the recording still exceeded them. If you need an example of what it means to pursue various dreams by using the process of iteration, Erica is a great reference. Here is an abridged rundown of her academic iterations from adolescence to present day:[163]

- Distinguished high school student: "America's Top Student Leader" by the National Association of Secondary School Principals.

- Science Student of the Year at the California State Science Fair.

- Harvard National Scholar, graduating with a degree in biomedical engineering.

- Graduate of Johns Hopkins University School of Medicine with her M.D.

- Obtained a PhD in molecular and cellular neuroscience.

- Chief Resident upon graduating Cornell University-affiliated Hospital for Special Surgery.

- Acquired a Master's in Biblical and Theological Studies (MBTS) from Dallas Theological Seminary.

- At the time of this writing Erica was at the tail end of iterating her way through an Executive MBA from The University of Oxford, UK. Her goals included expanding her network, increasing her business acumen, and creating sustainable as well as equitable transformation in healthcare.

As you can see, here is a person who found her one thing in medicine, then iterated her way through to excellence in other areas she had interest in. During her interview on the Niche Finder podcast, she shared her secret for being consistent. Like many of us who are creative, she spoke to calling upon the energy to stay a defined course when the inspiration—or initial spark—that motivates one to begin, feels absent during the journey.

"I tend not to be satisfied with just enough," Erica, remarked. She considered herself to be a person who *thrives on inspiration and imagination*—as do I—so I found myself leaning into her response for this shared struggle.

"I wanted to be inspired," she continued, "I want *it* to be great. But consistency really comes from being able to break the bigger project or task into smaller elements that can be pursued over time, in the absence of that spark of imagination, or that flow, that one might seek."

"Mmm" I muttered in response as if that insight was a morsel of truth that exploded on the pallet of my understanding. But as I chewed on that moment it also nourished a parallel theme for me. Maximizing your abundant factor, is a mixture of two things: the first is completing the first iteration that started with the quality you prioritized from your 5P framework. However, the second and equally important portion of Step #7 is to bring that quality through to completion. By completion I mean yield success from it before moving on to your next iteration. It's like programming a destination that you've never been to into your navigation app on your phone so that you drive in the correct direction. For example, with the mountainous area I live in Pennsylvania, there have been times when my phone lost signal while using the navigation but the course, I had programed in remained on my phone. Once I got back into an area where I had cell phone service, the route either updated or if there were no changes in my course the driving directions remained the same. Erica's initial spark of inspiration was like putting a destination into her navigation. When the inspiration that started her on her course was no longer apparent—or there was signal loss—she incrementally continued the defined course until what she sought was obtained over time.

In brief, if you have not obtained success with your first iteration, stay the course. However, does this mean that as you pursue this course that you should go after it with reckless abandonment? The short answer is no. As we pull away from this pitstop we veered on to, lets head back on our journey to *Maximizing your Abundant Factor* with Erica elaborating on this point.

"So," I said to Erica as I segued from our conversation around consistency and moved to my next question. "What level of intensity do you believe someone needs to have to pursue and maintain the course towards finding and developing their niche?

"That's a powerful one," Erica replied. "You know, I think that question belies a philosophical perspective that you can manufacture—the niche. But I would say that the niche is: God given, inspired, and it's in your DNA. If you are really in your niche, it's in your DNA—it's a part of you. There's a congruence there. And so, with that, then it's a matter of allowing what is within to manifest without—or externally.

"And so, the intensity at times can be a barrier to that flow or that expression. There are occasions where you just have to let go and let what's inside come out. And when you do that, sometimes you find that what is produced is far beyond whatever you could have imagined if you had pushed, so it's a balance between…these terms: the *organic* and the *muscular*. By that I mean, how *muscular* do you have to be in order to let this *organic* quality manifest into something that is that God given niche?

"There are times when you have to push through, but I would say the intensity? Hmm," she said reflectively, "…maybe it's just because of my life experience—I shy away from intensity, and I gravitate toward that expression or the natural flow of letting what's inside come out."

Let us pull over for a moment to close this section out as I also want to switch seats with you—as the reader—and put you into the driver seat for the next section. Before we pull off again, have you lost your initial inspiration that started you in the trajectory of your dream? As, you adjust yourself in your seat remember Steps 1-6 provided a map: stick to the plan. Your niche is God-given and by staying consistent with the fruitful course you have been on, your abundant factor will be maximized overtime. However, as you move purposefully towards this destination, let us place in view the value of legacy.

From Merchant of Death to prized possession.

Let's pull off on a more somber note and as we do, picture this scene happening to you. I am curious to know how you would respond to picking up the morning's paper only to find an obituary of your untimely death steering back at you. I would imagine that one would be puzzled or concerned to see such a thing. However, would seeing that, cause you to be motivated to do something different in your life? History helps to answer this question with a story about Alfred Nobel. In 1888 Alfred's brother Ludwig died and a French newspaper in error published Alfred's obituary.[164] If that wasn't enough, the paper renamed the inventor of dynamite with the nickname of *Le marchand de la mort est mort* which translates in English *The merchant of death is dead*. Is it true that Alfred invented a more innovative way of handling nitroglycerin that made it more stable and easier to handle?[165] Yes, it is. Did Alfred hold 355 patents that also comprised designs for "nitroglycerin detonators, blasting caps and a smokeless gunpowder called ballistite?[166] Absolutely. Was there a generous amount of money made from his explosive ideas that were manufactured in nearly 100 factories?[167] You better believe it. However, his thought process when he made dynamite was to prevent war, not cause it. Alfred Nobel was even noted as saying: "My dynamite will sooner lead to peace than a thousand world conventions. As soon as men will find that in one instant, whole armies can be utterly destroyed, they surely will abide by golden peace."

Some may argue that Alfred Nobel's motivation for designing dynamite may have been a bit naive. However, I shared this example to be less of a critique of his reasoning for inventing dynamite, and more of what he did after this epiphany. For the inventor of dynamite, reading his obituary in that French newspaper, which depicted his legacy in such a negative light, was like having a bomb go off in his hands. From there he secretly modified his last will and testament to establishing prizes that would bear his name.[168] At the top of his death, he had 355 patents.[169] The rough estimate of Nobel's fortune was two hundred million dollars when he died, and he instructed in his will that the interest accrued was to be used annually to award Nobel prizes.[170] This resulted in the bulk of his fortune being divided up into these five categories: physics, chemistry, physiology/medicine, literature, and peace. Nobel wanted to reward "those who, during the preceding year, shall have conferred the greatest benefit to humankind."[171] To date over 943 individuals and 25 organizations have been awarded the Nobel prize.[172]

So, do you have more to give? A few of the Nobel Prize laureates mentioned in this book did. Mother Teresa left behind her 17-year career as a schoolteacher in place of serving impoverished souls in India and providing other humanitarian efforts around the globe; economist Bertil Ohlin[173] was a professor as well as a politician but provided international economy trade theory that led to his Nobel recognition; and ethologist Karl von Frisch had a passion for studying the behavior of fish, but it was his work with honeybees that captured the world's attention.[174].

Now that you are in the driver seat, where to? Are we *stopping* the journey with your past successes or are we *starting* there? Knowing what you know now, if I were to give you Alfred Nobel's name and ask you to plug in a destination of his legacy where would you end up: The merchant of death or the founder of a prized possession? If you have been successful in one area, that's great. However, what's the next item on your 5P Framework list? Although there is no guarantee that our niche will receive noteworthy recognition—like Alfred Nobel—we possess the ability to alter the trajectory of our legacy. With that said, do *you* have more to give? I don't have to know you personally to answer this question. Being that the niche/gift/abundant factor/value that you have to offer is God-given, so long as there is life in your body you will always have more to give. You are not too old, too young, too poor, too messed up to leave behind a legacy that will benefit those who will travel the road behind you. As we bring our time together to a close, I'll move both you and I from behind the wheel of this journey and into a more appropriate position. It is my belief that the last aspect of *Maximizing your abundant factor* is going to need us to be—less drivers—and more like fuel in the engines of change.

Fuel, Facts and Faith

Fuel: Find your engine and end with the beginning in mind

Many modern-day engines that require premium fuel can adapt to regular 87 octane rating gas by adjusting the timing and performance to work with the lower-octane fuel.[175] However, in the old days if premium fuel was required and lower octane fuel was used, the engine would begin knocking before leaving the gas station. Inversely proportional to that is a phenomenon that happens when lower grade octane is placed in vehicles that are located at higher elevations, that fuel will perform at a higher-octane rating simply because it is at an elevated environment.[176] I share these two examples to emphasize the point that having the right fuel within compatible engines is important.

The same can be said for you as you deliver your niche. Have you ever come across someone who was working in an area and all they have were complaints? Some of it could be personality or it could also be an indication that the fuel that that individual has to offer is incompatible with the engine that it is being offered in. As a result, there is a steady knock throughout the day. Now whether this is due to the individual's perspective, a high pressure (high octane) setting or poor work (low octane) environment, these situations create opportunities to rise.

We rise when we utilize what we have in abundance to help fuel the change for the better in our given environment. This could be starting your own business that helps to deliver your niche effectively or it may mean leaving a given situation, which at times may be a practical solution. However, rising incorporates perspective in the process. Applying our niche with elements of gratitude, faith, and hope—to name a few— can help to raise our perspective as we work towards influencing value adding change. Again, see what you have done in times past that could be retooled in your current situation. As you do this, you will iterate your way to a more robust outcome and simultaneously raise your octane level.

End with the beginning in mind

In his book, the *7 Habits of Highly Effective People,* Steven Covey popularized the statement *begin with the end in mind.*[177] This speaks to knowing where you want to be at the end from the start of your journey. I believe that as you find your niche, work your way through the cycles, and end up delivering it, you will know that you found success when you do the inverse: *End with the beginning in mind.* What am I saying here? You are not done with your one thing until the engine of change you begin fueling with your niche reflects the 5P Framework quality you prioritized at the start of your iteration.

This success could culminate with you enhancing a passion, pattern, proficiency, problem-solving ability, or purposeful activity for you. Maybe that is a promotion as you share your qualities that you have in abundance in areas or assignments that can appreciate them. Of course, we want to use wisdom in the delivery if putting your niche on display is not compatible with the environment you are in, then find your engine. It could be your current work environment or taking your experience and packaging it in another form—like a podcast, social media channel, funnel and/or book. Once you package your message your engine—or environment—will look like a mixture of Step #2, Step #4, and Step # 6. Stay diligent and keep retooling your content like we covered with Chris Rock tweaking his material in Step #6. Your dream is worth it.

Facts: At what point does a U.S. dollar lose its value?

Let's say as you were walking in an empty field, you stumbled upon a $100 bill with no owner or point of origin in sight. Is the value of that bill still worth the amount that is printed on the face of it? Considering that it is dirty, slightly warn, and obviously lost, would it be as valuable as a newly minted $100 note? What if on the same field you spotted in the distance another $100 bill? This one, however, is half torn with less than fifty percent still showing, or even worse, it is unrecognizable, destroyed by insect, fire, time or the like. Is it still worth $100?

Well in the United States of America, the answer to all three of these questions would be *yes*. According to the office of engraving and printing, a damaged note that has more than fifty percent missing can be brought to the local bank and the location can replace it.[178] If more than fifty percent of the note is destroyed and/or not clearly identifiable, it would need to be sent to the office of Engraving and Printing where they have individuals who specialize in mutilated currency. So long as the owner follows a certain process, the note could be replaced.

I would contend that the value you have to offer through your niche is comprised of a similar allowance. The value we have as individuals may not be backed by a federal reserve, but God has a support system that transcends man's institutional arrangements. By this I mean, the one who created us has not left the assessment of our worth strictly to the opinions of others. Jeremiah 29:11 states "*...For I know the plans I have for you," declares the Lord, "plans to prosper you and not to harm you, plans to give you hope and a future....*".[179] Factually speaking, our value has value because—like currency—it is backed by greater worth. However, although this fact remains true, maximizing that value you have in abundance takes faith.

Faith: Our value is designed to have different backing

As human beings we are incapable of separating ourselves from the image in which God has created us in. However, we do have the ability to distance ourselves from the purpose he placed within us to give away to others. That distancing can come by way of being a victim of misuse, misguidance, or missed opportunities. It is in these moments that the quote by Rick Warren comes alive, "[y]ou never know God is all you need until God is all you have." For me, maximizing my abundant factor took me falling to a low point where I *backed* away from God, even though I believed his desire was to get me *back* to where he needed me to be. I felt the pressure of *shamers*. You know the ones who don't know enough to be considered informed but possess *just enough* information to sound like they are. It is here that I learned the true value of being grateful for God's grace that he extends to us through his son Jesus Christ; thankful for the gifts (niches) afforded to me that are now resourceful, refined tools that I can share with others. Les Brown has a quote, "[i]n life you will always be faced with a series of God ordained opportunities, brilliantly disguised as problems and challenges." There is much more to be said on this subject, but it is best kept as another book I started entitled: *UProoted*. Until then, if you have a similar situation, my encouragement to you is instead of *backing away* from God, get *back* to him and allow him to be the *backing* of the value you have to offer.

Your story could be a failed business that left your potential unrecognizable or your dream disintegrated. I want you to know that the footsteps that have trampled you don't define you. Those who trust in God will tell you that he has a way to restore you. Whether the trampling of your worth is from others or your own doing, God specializes in identifying your value.

There is more in you. Consequently, the value you possess that is worth maximizing can die if it gets confined to an environment that minimizes it. TD Jakes remarked in an interview "...don't let people describe you, because if they do they will incarcerate you..." and I could not agree more.[180]

TD Jakes continues, "if you put a period where—I believe—God put a comma you limit me down to how you understand me...a person has more than one gift.

"More than one talent.

"More than one pursuit.

"And if you've got a great job, that's good but there is more in you than what you do...don't let people limit you to what they think is appropriate for you. Do everything that you are gifted enough to do."[181]

We have been designed with elements of value buried within us that make us who we are. Some of us may get glimpses of these buried qualities through different situations but most times it takes faith to see these invisible traits. Our value is discovered in step 1-3 and developed through steps 4-5. The reason we have it to develop, however, is because it's in our inventory. TD Jakes further illuminates this point as he continues: "Whatever is in your inventory is all you can produce. Your responsibility is to take what you have been given and turn it into something that it was not when it was originally handed to you."[182]

Okay, you can queue the Boys 2 Men, *It's So Hard To Say Goodbye,* **ringtone as you read these last few pages…**

So, to my fellow niche finders, I want you to know that we are not all equal. Our niche is what makes us unique, but that uniqueness then gives us a responsibility to discover, develop, and deliver the value we have to offer. However, no matter where you find yourself on the *Life Cycle of Excavations*, I am with you applauding your efforts. To those of you who are on Step # 1: *Recognize your Abundant Factor,* giving concentrated efforts to completing your 5P Framework will be an investment that will help to undergird the rest of your movement on the cycle. If Step # 2 *Optimize Where Your Niche is Used Intensely* is where you have landed—no worries—think about the environments where your niche typically receives its greatest recognition. Opportunity cost is the tool to help whittle down your 5P Framework from multiple qualities down to your one thing on *Step # 3 Summarize Your Comparative Advantage.* Keep in mind as you transition into the Develop section on Step # 4 *Specialize in Offering What is Helpful to Others but Unique to You,* that it's not about you: Develop your niche through service. When—*not if*—barriers confront you and you feel like giving up, use what we covered in Step # 5 *Neutralize Barriers Blocking You From Fulfilling Your Dream* to overcome them. Almost there now, for those of you on Step # 6 *Organize the Delivery of Your Niche to a Wider Audience,* open your niche to the public and take careful notes on where you can retool your message to make it a better expression of your expertise. Don't stop there, as Step # 6 is only the beginning of the delivery section. Use what you have learned to bring your first iteration of your niche through Step # 7 *Maximize Your Abundant Factor* and onto success. Once there, go back to Step #1, select the next highest quality on your 5P Framework form, rinse, and repeat.

I appreciate you taking the time to allow me to walk alongside you with this information. Helping you to discover, develop and deliver your niche with this book has also helped me to complete my first iteration. So, if there are any lingering skepticisms of whether the steps work, the evidence is now in your hands.

As we bring our time together to a close, I would like to further encourage you. The same way that reservoir of crude oil was hidden beneath the surface—in Spindletop Texas with Pattillo Higgins—so does a reservoir of crude resources reside within you. With that said, we then have a responsibility to put the drill bit to the ground of our hearts and excavate our value. That discovery, however, is only the starting point. For the need also exists for us to develop and deliver the value that lies within us.

But how do we develop our true value? The short answer begins with focusing on the contributions that makes us different. That God-given ability that gives us the capacity to make a difference. We start here because quite often our greatest value is intimately connected to our greatest offerings.

This starting point is not today: your completion of this book. No, your value has been exposed long before these pages were written. However, I designed this for you to find, refine, and redesign how you offer your niche. Maybe the oil for you on day 1 was a desire to overcome some major hurdle in your work environment but your tenacious way of using your niche helped you to solve that problem and simultaneously ignite an entrepreneurial fervor within you. Maybe the geyser of your imagination brought you into a classroom with a heart to help ailing individuals, but the mastery of the curriculum turned you into a high-octane health care professional. Refining the niche within will help you convert your untapped reserves into a valuable commodity. The more you refine, the higher your octane.

Finally, today is not the end of the refinement process, but the beginning of the delivery of your value. The next progressive step moves you from where you are to the fulfillment of your dream. This is less about what drives you, and more about what you are here to drive. Anyone holding this book is one example of the type of energy that can help to convert the potential of some future engine into power for progress.

My prayer is that you continue to refine the reservoir within you. May you find engines that will ignite more ideas, insight, and influence that are still undiscovered inside of you.

I'd like to pause to thank friends and family for supporting my dream of finishing this work.

And I thank you—the reader—for this opportunity and pray that God blesses you in the great things you're about to do. If you're in the discovery phase keep drilling; at the development stage, keep giving, and if you are ready to deliver your niche, keep believing. The goal is to have you *end with the beginning in mind*. I look forward to hearing how you begin to embody the mantra known as the Dream Octane Movement: "*If innovative change is an engine, your unique dreams and abilities could be its fuel.*"

Thank you again and let's connect on the below mentioned social media links or interface as a V.I.P on the next www.launchmyniche.org challenge.

Interested in hearing more?

- Learn how to avoid the *3 Biggest Mistakes Consultants, Coaches, and Counselors* make when attempting to move their niche online!!! Join the next www.launchmyniche.org challenge.

If you found any of the steps helpful, share a video testimonial on any of the below mentioned social media sites as encouragement for others:

- Instagram: https://www.instagram.com/cliftoncmanning/
- Facebook: https://www.facebook.com/profile.php?id=100063308682089
- LinkedIn:https://www.linkedin.com/mwlite/in/clifton-c-manning-mba-5a073671

Or let's talk about it on:

- Clubhouse: https://www.clubhouse.com/@dreamoctane.org

End Notes

Chapter 1

[1] The Editors of Encyclopaedia Britannica. (2021, March 27). *Mother Teresa*. Retrieved from britannica.com: https://www.britannica.com/biography/Mother-Teresa

[2] Biema, D. V. (2007, August 23). *Mother Teresa's Crisis of Faith*. Retrieved from www.time.com: https://time.com/4126238/mother-teresas-crisis-of-faith/#

[3] Forbes.com. (2021). *Richard Williams*. Retrieved from Forbes.com: www.forbes.com/profile/richard-williams/?sh=30f2d146a078

[4] Kane, B. (2018, October 9). *One Million Follows, Updated Edition*. Dallas, TX: Ben Bella Books, Inc. Retrieved from "Used with permission.": https://www.amazon.com/One-Million-Followers-Massive-Following/dp/1946885371

[5] Forbes.com. (2021). *Richard Williams*. Retrieved from Forbes.com: www.forbes.com/profile/richard-williams/?sh=30f2d146a078

[6] Kannan, Shilpa. (2013, September 3). *Bangalore: India's Silicon valley*. Retrieved from www.bbc.com: https://www.bbc.com/news/av/technology-23943861

Chapter 2

[7] Twin, A. (2020, July 7). *Competitive Advantage*. Retrieved from www.investopedia.com: https://www.investopedia.com/terms/c/competitive_advantage.asp

[8] Twin, A. (2020, July 7). *Competitive Advantage*. Retrieved from www.investopedia.com: https://www.investopedia.com/terms/c/competitive_advantage.asp

[9] Chin, K. (2020). *Competitive Advantage vs. Comparative Advantage*. Retrieved from https://mkainsights.com: https://mkainsights.com/insights/strategy-and-business-planning/competitive-advantage-vs-comparative-advantage/

[10] Brunson, R. (2015,2020). *Dotcom Secrets*. New York City: Hay House, INC.

[11] Dictionary.com. (2021). *Niche*. Retrieved from www.dictionary.com: https://www.dictionary.com/browse/niche

Discover Section

Chapter 3

Step # 1: Recognize your abundant factor

[12] Chin, C. (2019, November 06). *The Difference Between Experience and Expertise*. Retrieved from Commonplace: https://commoncog.com/blog/the-difference-between-experience-and-expertise/

[13] Proverbs 13:22. (2021). *The Holy Bible New International Version (NIV)*. Retrieved from www.biblegateway.com: https://www.biblegateway.com/passage/?search=Proverbs%2013%3A22&version=NIV

[14] Tracé Etienne-Gray. (2020, September 16). *Higgins, Pattillo (1863–1955)*. Retrieved from Texas State Historical Association: https://www.tshaonline.org/handbook/entries/higgins-pattillo

[15] Lukasz R. (2021). *History of Oil, History of the Modern Oil Industry*. Retrieved from ektinteractive.com: https://www.ektinteractive.com/history-of-oil/

[16] Texas State Historical Association. (2018). *History Of Oil Discovery In Texas*. Retrieved from texasalmanac.com: https://texasalmanac.com/topics/business/history-oil-discoveries-texas

[17] History.com Staff. (2010). *Spindletop: Black Gold*. Retrieved from History.com: http://www.history.com/topics/spindletop

[18] History.com Staff. (2010). *Spindletop: Black Gold*. Retrieved from History.com: http://www.history.com/topics/spindletop

[19] The Underdog. (2019, July 20). *The dyslexic Les Brown: I was identified as mentally retarded*. Retrieved from www.youtube.com: https://www.youtube.com/watch?v=OG1Arib4UsY

[20] Dr. Owen Legaspi, P. D. (2015). *Staff*. Retrieved from www.aplusrehab.com: http://www.aplusrehab.com/staff/

Chapter 4

Step # 2: Optimize Where Your Niche Is Used Intensely

[21] Target Brands, Inc. (2021, February 20). *Water Lilies, 1916 by Claude Monet Canvas Print*. Retrieved from www.target.com: https://www.target.com/p/water-lilies-1916-by-claude-monet-canvas-print/-/A-52174559

[22] Rogers, M. (2021, February 21). *Frame Destination*. Retrieved from www.framedestination.com: https://www.framedestination.com/blog/picture-frames/the-most-expensive-picture-frames

[23] Invaluable. (2019, July 29). *In Good Taste*. Retrieved from www.invaluable.com: https://www.invaluable.com/blog/most-expensive-painting/#:~:text=The%20world's%20most%20expensive%20painting,November%2015%2C%202017%20at%20Christie's.

[24] *Arius*. (2021, February 27). Retrieved from shop.ariustechnology.com: https://shop.ariustechnology.com/blogs/news/top-5-most-expensive-claude-monet-paintings-ever-sold

[25] Target Brands, Inc. (2021, February 27). *Water Lilies, 1916 by Claude Monet Canvas Print*. Retrieved from www.target.com: https://www.target.com/p/water-lilies-1916-by-claude-monet-canvas-print/-/A-52174559?preselect=52087886#lnk=sametab

[26] Cain, A. (2017, November 3). *How to Frame a $100 Million Painting by Leonardo da Vinci*. Retrieved from www.artsy.net: https://www.artsy.net/article/artsy-editorial-frame-100-million-painting-leonardo-da-vinci

[27] The Outcome. (2019, June 27). *When Life Breaks You | Steve Harvey Motivational Speech On Success*. Retrieved from www.youtube.com: https://www.youtube.com/watch?v=Un-gNbNwwsQ

[28] Triggs, C. (2013, October 03). *Steve Harvey: I Was Homeless for Three Years*. Retrieved from People.com: https://people.com/celebrity/steve-harvey-i-was-homeless-for-three-years/

[29] Triggs, C. (2013, October 03). *Steve Harvey: I Was Homeless for Three Years*. Retrieved from People.com: https://people.com/celebrity/steve-harvey-i-was-homeless-for-three-years/

[30] Motivational Instinct. (2020, October 18). *Don't Lose Faith - "I Almost Gave Up" | Steve Harvey Heartbreaking Story*. Retrieved from Youtube.com: https://youtu.be/oi1IhajNJxc

[31] JeffIsOld. (2009, December 22). *Sympathetic Resonance*. Retrieved from Youtube.com: https://youtu.be/hNKiFGvigrQ

[32] McPeck, M. (2014, May 01). *Sympathetic Resonance*. Retrieved from www.youtube.com: https://www.youtube.com/watch?v=sxRkOQmzLgo

[33] Rao, C. (2020, March 14). *Was Michael Jordan Really Cut From His High School Basketball Team?* Retrieved from www.sportscasting.com: https://www.sportscasting.com/was-michael-jordan-really-cut-from-his-high-school-basketball-team/

[34] Schwartz, L. (2021, March 22). *Michael Jordan transcends hoops*. Retrieved from www.espn.com: https://www.espn.com/sportscentury/features/00016048.html

[35] Rao, C. (2020, March 14). *Was Michael Jordan Really Cut From His High School Basketball Team?* Retrieved from www.sportscasting.com: https://www.sportscasting.com/was-michael-jordan-really-cut-from-his-high-school-basketball-team/

[36] Matange, Y. (2021, July 21). *NBA Finals: Who has won the most Bill Russell NBA Finals MVP Awards?* Retrieved from ca.nba.com: https://ca.nba.com/news/nba-finals-who-has-won-the-most-bill-russell-nba-finals-mvp-awards/33ae4e5nhwxa1rmu1kc1r696w#:~:text=Michael%20Jordan%20holds%20the%20record,all%20with%20the%20Chicago%20Bulls.

[37] GQ Sports. (2019, Septemeber 24). *Mike Tyson Goes Undercover on Reddit, YouTube and Twitter | GQ Sports*. Retrieved from www.youtube.com: https://www.youtube.com/watch?v=nYRefC7E9gU

[38] Kaufman, S. B. (2011, November 08). *Why Inspiration Matters*. Retrieved from Harvard Business Review : https://hbr.org/2011/11/why-inspiration-matters

[39] Kaufman, S. B. (2011, November 08). *Why Inspiration Matters*. Retrieved from Harvard Business Review : https://hbr.org/2011/11/why-inspiration-matters

[40] Kaufman, S. B. (2011, November 08). *Why Inspiration Matters*. Retrieved from Harvard Business Review : https://hbr.org/2011/11/why-inspiration-matters

[41] Kaufman, S. B. (2011, November 08). *Why Inspiration Matters*. Retrieved from Harvard Business Review : https://hbr.org/2011/11/why-inspiration-matters

Chapter 5

Step # 3: Summarize Your Comparative Advantage

[42] HESMotivation. (2019, June 28). *Steve Harvey - IDENTIFY YOUR GOD'S GIVEN GIFT (Steve Harvey Motivation)*. Retrieved from www.youtube.com: https://www.youtube.com/watch?v=w-w_zGO6hCs

[43] Luke 2:41-52. (2021). *The Holy Bible New International Version (NIV)*. Retrieved from www.biblegateway.com: https://www.biblegateway.com/passage/?search=Luke%202%3A41-52&version=NIV

[44] Luke 2:19. (2021). *The Holy Bible New International Version (NIV)*. Retrieved from www.biblegateway.com:
https://www.biblegateway.com/passage/?search=Luke%202%3A19&version=NIV

[45] Chin, C. (2019, November 06). *The Difference Between Experience and Expertise*. Retrieved from Commonplace: https://commoncog.com/blog/the-difference-between-experience-and-expertise/

[46] IV, B. G. (2020, March 22). Why LeBron James Didn't Play High School Football in His Senior Year. Retrieved from www.sportscasting.com: https://www.sportscasting.com/why-lebron-james-didnt-play-high-school-football-in-his-senior-year/

[47] Stuart. (2020, June 27). *These are Lebron James' high school stats at St. Vincent-St. Mary High School*. Retrieved from www.interbasket.net:

[48] Stuart. (2020, June 27). *These are Lebron James' high school stats at St. Vincent-St. Mary High School*. Retrieved from www.interbasket.net:

[49] Stuart. (2020, June 27). *These are Lebron James' high school stats at St. Vincent-St. Mary High School*. Retrieved from www.interbasket.net:

Develop Section

Chapter 6

Step # 4: Specialize In Offering What Is Helpful To Others But Unique To You

[50] Munroe, M. (1991). *Understanding Your Potential, Discovering the Hidden You.* Shippensburg: Destiny Image. Publishers, Inc.

[51] Munroe, M. (1991). *Understanding Your Potential, Discovering the Hidden You.* Shippensburg: Destiny Image. Publishers, Inc.

[52] Thomas Nelson Inc. (1982). *New King James Version.* Wheaton, IL 60189: Tyndale House Publishing.

[53] Precept Austin. (2021, July 08). *Ezekiel 5:1-12 Commentary*. Retrieved from www.preceptaustin.org: https://www.preceptaustin.org/ezekiel_51-12

[54] Isaiah 6:7. (2021). *The Holy Bible New International Version (NIV)*. Retrieved from biblehub.com: https://biblehub.com/isaiah/6-7.htm

[55] Jeremiah 18:1-12. (2021). *The Holy Bible New International Version (NIV)*. Retrieved from At the Potter's House:
https://www.biblegateway.com/passage/?search=Jeremiah%2018%3A1-12&version=NIV

[56] Schwartz, T. (2012, March 12). *https://hbr.org*. Retrieved from The Magic of Doing One Thing at a Time: https://hbr.org/2012/03/the-magic-of-doing-one-thing-a.html

[57] Etienne-Gray, T. (2020, September 16). *Higgins, Pattillo*. Retrieved from Handbook of Texas Online: https://www.tshaonline.org/handbook/entries/higgins-pattillo

[58] Etienne-Gray, T. (2020, September 16). *Higgins, Pattillo*. Retrieved from Handbook of Texas Online: https://www.tshaonline.org/handbook/entries/higgins-pattillo

[59] Paembonan, A. Y., Arjwech, R., Davydycheva, S., Smirnov, M., & Strack, K. M. (2017, January 07). *Sample records for salt dome reservoirs*. Retrieved from

359

https://www.science.gov:
https://www.science.gov/topicpages/s/salt+dome+reservoirs

[60] Tracé Etienne-Gray. (2020, September 16). *Higgins, Pattillo (1863–1955)*. Retrieved from Texas State Historical Association:
https://www.tshaonline.org/handbook/entries/higgins-pattillo

[61] Langdana, F., & Murphy, P. T. (2014). *International and Global Macropolicy*. New York: Springer.

[62] Langdana, F., & Murphy, P. T. (2014). *International and Global Macropolicy*. New York: Springer.

[63] Agarwal, A. (2016, August). *The Paradox of Value*. Retrieved from YouTube.com:
https://www.ted.com/talks/akshita_agarwal_the_paradox_of_value?language=en

[64] The Editors of Encyclopaedia Britannica. (2021, April 25). *Marginal Utility*. Retrieved from www.britannica.com: https://www.britannica.com/topic/marginal-utility

[65] The Editors of Encyclopaedia Britannica. (2021, April 25). *Marginal Utility*. Retrieved from www.britannica.com: https://www.britannica.com/topic/marginal-utility

[66] OpenStax College; PhET Interactive Simulations. (2021, May 04). *Dispersion: The Rainbow and Prisms*. Retrieved from https://courses.lumenlearning.com:
https://courses.lumenlearning.com/physics/chapter/25-5-dispersion-the-rainbow-and-prisms/

[67] Lund, E. (2017, July 27). *What Small Business Owners Can Learn from Apple's Current and Former Mission Statements*. Retrieved from Businessingmag.com:
https://businessingmag.com/5252/strategy/learn-from-apples-mission-statement/

[68] Wells, S. (2016, June 01). *The Science of Rainbows*. Retrieved from ssec.si.edu:
https://ssec.si.edu/stemvisions-blog/science-rainbows

[69] It's Okay To Be Smart. (2016, March 28). *How Do Bees Make Honey?* Retrieved from Youtube.com: https://www.youtube.com/watch?v=nZlEjDLJCmg

[70] Republic of Slovenia Government of the Republic of Slovenia. (2021, May 24). *The Importance of Bees*. Retrieved from www.worldbeeday.org:
https://www.worldbeeday.org/en/about/the-importance-of-bees.html#:~:text=Food%20security&text=The%20greatest%20contribution%20of%20bees,of%20food%20depends%20on%20pollination.

[71] The Nobel Prize. (2021, May 22). *Karl von Frisch Facts*. Retrieved from www.nobelprize.org: https://www.nobelprize.org/prizes/medicine/1973/frisch/facts/

[72] The Nobel Prize. (2021, May 22). *Karl von Frisch Facts*. Retrieved from www.nobelprize.org: https://www.nobelprize.org/prizes/medicine/1973/frisch/facts/

[73] The BeeGroup @ VT. (2017, October 16). *Honey bee Waggle Dancing*. Retrieved from YouTube.com: https://youtu.be/1MX2WN-7Xzc

Chapter 7

Step # 5: Neutralize Barriers Blocking You From Fulfilling Your Dream

[74] Christian Answers. (2018, December 26). *Ephes-dammim*. Retrieved from christiananswers.net: https://christiananswers.net/dictionary/ephes-dammim.html

[75] Mark Koonz of Emmanuel Lutheran Church. (2019, August 11). *It should have been Saul versus Goliath*. Retrieved from www.union-bulletin.com: https://www.union-bulletin.com/local_columnists/pastors_columns/it-should-have-been-saul-versus-goliath/article_d6b7e042-b9f4-11e9-977a-

675b3959da68.html#:~:text=The%20oldest%20surviving%20version%20of,%2Dfoo
t%209%2Dinches%20tall.

[76] 1 Samuel 17. (2021). *The Holy Bible Message Version (MSG)*. Retrieved from www.biblegateway.com:
https://www.biblegateway.com/passage/?search=1SAM+17&version=MSG

[77] 1 Samuel 17. (2021). *The Holy Bible New International Version (NIV)*. Retrieved from www.biblegateway.com:
https://www.biblegateway.com/passage/?search=1SAM+17&version=NIV

[78] Romans 12:3. (2021). *The Holy Bible New King James Version (NKJV)*. Retrieved from www.biblegateway.com:
https://www.biblegateway.com/passage/?search=Romans+12%3A3&version=NKJV

[79] Jordan, M. (2021, June 20). *www.forbes.com*. Retrieved from Quotes Thoughts On The Business Of Life: https://www.forbes.com/quotes/11194/

[80] Stoop, P. D. (2004). *You Are What You Think*. Grad Rapid MI: Fleming H. Revell.

[81] Hendry, E. R. (2013, NOVEMBER 20). *7 Epic Fails Brought to You By the Genius Mind of Thomas Edison*. Retrieved from https://www.smithsonianmag.com:
https://www.smithsonianmag.com/innovation/7-epic-fails-brought-to-you-by-the-genius-mind-of-thomas-edison-180947786/

[82] Hendry, E. R. (2013, NOVEMBER 20). *7 Epic Fails Brought to You By the Genius Mind of Thomas Edison*. Retrieved from https://www.smithsonianmag.com:
https://www.smithsonianmag.com/innovation/7-epic-fails-brought-to-you-by-the-genius-mind-of-thomas-edison-180947786/

[83] Hendry, E. R. (2013, NOVEMBER 20). *7 Epic Fails Brought to You By the Genius Mind of Thomas Edison*. Retrieved from https://www.smithsonianmag.com:
https://www.smithsonianmag.com/innovation/7-epic-fails-brought-to-you-by-the-genius-mind-of-thomas-edison-180947786/

[84] Latson, J. (2014, October 21). *How Edison Invented the Light Bulb — And Lots of Myths About Himself*. Retrieved from www.time.com: https://time.com/3517011/thomas-edison/

[85] Rutgers School of Arts and Science. (2016, October 28). *Myth Buster: Edison's 10,000 attempts*. Retrieved from www.edison.rutgers.edu: https://edison.rutgers.edu/newsletter9.html

[86] Chesson, D. (2021, July 24th). Master Guide To Selecting The Best Book Editor. Retrieved from kindlepreneur.com: https://kindlepreneur.com/book-editors/

Deliver Section

Chapter 8

Step # 6: Organize The Delivery Of Your Niche To A Wider Audience

[87] Biography.com Editors. (2021, May 6). *Chris Rock Biography*. Retrieved from www.biography.com: https://www.biography.com/actor/chris-rock

[88] Sims, P. (2009, January 26). *Innovate Like Chris Rock*. Retrieved from www.hbr.org:
https://hbr.org/2009/01/innovate-like-chris-rock

[89] Barker, E. (2021, September 12). *How does Chris Rock create such brilliant comedy?* Retrieved from www.bakadesuyo.com: https://www.bakadesuyo.com/2012/07/how-does-chris-rock-create-such-brilliant-com/

[90] Sims, P. (2009, January 26). *Innovate Like Chris Rock*. Retrieved from www.hbr.org:
https://hbr.org/2009/01/innovate-like-chris-rock

[91] Sims, P. (2009, January 26). *Innovate Like Chris Rock*. Retrieved from www.hbr.org:
https://hbr.org/2009/01/innovate-like-chris-rock

[92] Edgers, G. (2016, February 28). *Here's how Chris Rock practiced his Oscars monologue*.
Retrieved from www.washingtonpost.com:
https://www.washingtonpost.com/news/arts-and-entertainment/wp/2016/02/28/heres-how-chris-rock-practiced-his-oscars-monologue/

[93] Edgers, G. (2016, February 28). *Here's how Chris Rock practiced his Oscars monologue*.
Retrieved from www.washingtonpost.com:
https://www.washingtonpost.com/news/arts-and-entertainment/wp/2016/02/28/heres-how-chris-rock-practiced-his-oscars-monologue/

[94] Torres, L. (2020, January 21). *The 18 best Oscar hosts of all time, ranked*. Retrieved from
www.insider.com: https://www.insider.com/best-oscars-hosts-all-time-2018-1#8-johnny-carson-hosted-the-oscars-several-times-from-1979-to-1982-and-again-in-1984-11

[95] Torres, L. (2020, January 21). *The 18 best Oscar hosts of all time, ranked*. Retrieved from
www.insider.com: https://www.insider.com/best-oscars-hosts-all-time-2018-1#8-johnny-carson-hosted-the-oscars-several-times-from-1979-to-1982-and-again-in-1984-11

[96] Lang, B., & Malkin, M. (2020, January 24). *Number of Black Oscar Nominees Hits Three-Year Low in 2020*. Retrieved from https://variety.com/2020/film/news/black-oscar-nominees-2020-1203479474/: https://variety.com/2020/film/news/black-oscar-nominees-2020-1203479474/

[97] Clevver News. (2016, February 29). *Chris Rock Hilarious 2016 Oscars Monologue!
Addresses #OscarsSoWhite*. Retrieved from www.youtube.com:

[98] Pitchandi, B. (2021, January 11). *VTS's Journey towards Engineering Excellence*. Retrieved
from www.buildingvts.com: https://buildingvts.com/vtss-journey-towards-engineering-excellence-c7554cdae47e

[99] Brown, M. (2021, August 15). *Stone Soup*. Retrieved from www.powells.com:
https://www.powells.com/book/stone-soup-9780684922966

[100] Brown, M. (2021, August 15). *Stone Soup*. Retrieved from www.powells.com:
https://www.powells.com/book/stone-soup-9780684922966

[101] Brown, M. (2021, August 15). *Stone Soup*. Retrieved from www.powells.com:
https://www.powells.com/book/stone-soup-9780684922966

[102] Ong, S. Q. (2021, January 29). *Marketing Funnels for Beginners: A Comprehensive Guide*.
Retrieved from www.ahrefs.com: https://ahrefs.com/blog/marketing-funnels/

[103] Levinson, J. C., & Lautenslager, A. (2014, June 26). *Tips for Creating a Memorable
Marketing Hook*. Retrieved from www.entrepreneur.com:
https://www.entrepreneur.com/article/234202

[104] Brown, M. (2021, August 15). *Stone Soup*. Retrieved from www.powells.com:
https://www.powells.com/book/stone-soup-9780684922966

[105] Brown, M. (2021, August 15). *Stone Soup*. Retrieved from www.powells.com:
https://www.powells.com/book/stone-soup-9780684922966

[106] Grabowski, P. (2017). *Here's How Targeting Cold, Warm & Hot Traffic Builds Successful
Customer Relationships*. Retrieved from www.singlegrain.com:
https://www.singlegrain.com/marketing-funnels/how-targeting-cold-warm-hot-traffic-build-successful-customer-relationships/

[107] Brown, M. (2021, August 15). *Stone Soup*. Retrieved from www.powells.com:
https://www.powells.com/book/stone-soup-9780684922966

[108] Grabowski, P. (2017). *Here's How Targeting Cold, Warm & Hot Traffic Builds Successful Customer Relationships*. Retrieved from www.singlegrain.com: https://www.singlegrain.com/marketing-funnels/how-targeting-cold-warm-hot-traffic-build-successful-customer-relationships/

[109] Merriam-Webster. (2021, September 26). *Occam's razor*. Retrieved from www.merriam-webster.com: https://www.merriam-webster.com/dictionary/Occam%27s%20razor

[110] Soegaard, M. (2020, September 2020). *Occam's Razor: The simplest solution is always the best*. Retrieved from www.interaction-design.org: https://www.interaction-design.org/literature/article/occam-s-razor-the-simplest-solution-is-always-the-best

[111] LeCunff, A.-L. (2021, September 26). *The Occam's razor fallacy: the simplest solution is not always the correct one*. Retrieved from www.nesslabs.com: https://nesslabs.com/occams-razor

[112] Merriam-Webster. (2021, September 06). *Acrostic*. Retrieved from www.merriam-webster.com: https://www.merriam-webster.com/dictionary/acrostic

[113] Acrosticos.org. (2021, September 26). *Acrostic*. Retrieved from www.acrosticos.org: https://www.acrosticos.org/acrostics-automatic-poetry.php?acro=microsoft&rand=2432&Submit=New+acrostic++%3E%3E+&final=ing&fs=0

[114] PLB Blogger. (2021, September 06). *How are Acrostics Different from Acronyms?* Retrieved from www.k12teacherstaffdevelopment.com: https://k12teacherstaffdevelopment.com/tlb/how-are-acrostics-different-from-acronyms/

[115] Wilson, M. (2011, September 23). *Interview: Robert Kiyosaki Discusses What it Takes to be Successful*. Retrieved from www.under30ceo.com: https://www.under30ceo.com/interview-robert-kiyosaki-discusses-what-it-takes-to-be-successful/

[116] Wilson, M. (2011, September 23). *Interview: Robert Kiyosaki Discusses What it Takes to be Successful*. Retrieved from www.under30ceo.com: https://www.under30ceo.com/interview-robert-kiyosaki-discusses-what-it-takes-to-be-successful/

[117] Merriam-Webster. (2021, September 06). *Acronym*. Retrieved from www.merriam-webster.com: https://www.merriam-webster.com/dictionary/acronym

[118] Wilson, J., & Dunbar, B. (2018, April 2). *NASA History Overview*. Retrieved from www.nasa.gov: https://www.nasa.gov/content/nasa-history-[118]overview

[119] Nickinson, S. (2015, January 27). *Studer Group acquired by Huron for $325 million*. Retrieved from www.studeri.org: https://www.studeri.org/blog/studer-group-acquired-huron-325-million

[120] Nickinson, S. (2015, January 27). *Studer Group acquired by Huron for $325 million*. Retrieved from www.studeri.org: https://www.studeri.org/blog/studer-group-acquired-huron-325-million

[121] Merriam-Webster. (2021, September 26). *Analogy*. Retrieved from www.merriam-webster.com: https://www.merriam-webster.com/dictionary/analogy

[122] Patel, A. (2021, September 06). *Analogies and Business: The Fastest Way to Get Your Point Across*. Retrieved from www.startupgrind.com: https://www.startupgrind.com/blog/analogies-and-business-the-fastest-way-to-get-your-point-across/

[123] Ask Difference. (2018, July 7). *Allegory vs. Analogy*. Retrieved from www.askdifference.com: https://www.askdifference.com/allegory-vs-analogy/

[124] Denning, S. (2018, April 6). *Does Poetry Have A Place In Business? One Unsung Success Secret*. Retrieved from www.forbes.com: https://www.forbes.com/sites/stephaniedenning/2018/04/06/does-poetry-have-a-place-in-business-one-unsung-success-secret/?sh=145942ec558a

[125] Coleman, J. (2012, November 27). *The Benefits of Poetry for Professionals*. Retrieved from hbr.org: https://hbr.org/2012/11/the-benefits-of-poetry-for-pro

[126] Rubin, H. (2007, July 21). *www.nytimes.com*. Retrieved from C.E.O. Libraries Reveal Keys to Success: https://www.nytimes.com/2007/07/21/business/21libraries.html?_r=4&ex=11856816 00&en=caab541e2182a66d&ei=5070&emc=eta1&oref=slogin&oref=slogin&

[127] Merriam-Webster. (2021, September 16). *Archetype*. Retrieved from www.merriam-webster.com: https://www.merriam-webster.com/dictionary/archetype

[128] Marshall, T., & McIntosh, A. (2020, August 5). *Terry Fox*. Retrieved from www.thecanadianencyclopedia.ca: https://www.thecanadianencyclopedia.ca/en/article/terry-fox#:~:text=Terry%20Fox%20was%20very%20determined%20from%20a%20youn g,the%20corner%20an%20hour%20early%20for%20his%20ride.).

[129] The Terry Fox Foundation . (2021, September 17). *A Dream As Big As Our Country*. Retrieved from www.terryfox.org: https://terryfox.org/terrys-story/

[130] Oleynick, V. C., Thrash, T. M., LeFew, M. C., Moldovan, E. G., & Kieffaber, P. D. (2014, June 2). *https://www.ncbi.nlm.nih.gov/pmc/articles/PMC4070479/*. Retrieved from US NAtional Library of Medicine: https://www.ncbi.nlm.nih.gov/pmc/articles/PMC4070479 /

[131] Oleynick, V. C., Thrash, T. M., LeFew, M. C., Moldovan, E. G., & Kieffaber, P. D. (2014, June 2). *https://www.ncbi.nlm.nih.gov/pmc/articles/PMC4070479/*. Retrieved from US NAtional Library of Medicine: https://www.ncbi.nlm.nih.gov/pmc/articles/PMC4070479/

[132] Oleynick, V. C., Thrash, T. M., LeFew, M. C., Moldovan, E. G., & Kieffaber, P. D. (2014, June 2). *https://www.ncbi.nlm.nih.gov/pmc/articles/PMC4070479/*. Retrieved from US NAtional Library of Medicine: https://www.ncbi.nlm.nih.gov/pmc/articles/PMC4070479/

[133] Universal Technical Institute. (2020 , May 05). *4-toke Engine: What They And How Do They Work?* Retrieved from www.uti.edu: https://www.uti.edu/blog/motorcycle/how-4-stroke-engines-work

[134] Christian Brothers Automotive. (2019, May 21). *Why Are Spark Plugs So Important To Your Engine?* Retrieved from www.cbac.com: https://www.cbac.com/media-center/blog/2019/may/why-are-spark-plugs-so-important-to-your-engine-/

[135] Newton, S. D. (2014, May 27). *Wisdom Is The Principal Thing*. Retrieved from www.huffpost.com: https://www.huffpost.com/entry/wisdom-is-the-principal-t_b_5392964

[136] Newton, S. D. (2014, May 27). *Wisdom Is The Principal Thing*. Retrieved from www.huffpost.com: https://www.huffpost.com/entry/wisdom-is-the-principal-t_b_5392964

[137] Newton, S. D. (2014, May 27). *Wisdom Is The Principal Thing*. Retrieved from www.huffpost.com: https://www.huffpost.com/entry/wisdom-is-the-principal-t_b_5392964

[138] Proverbs 11:25. (2021). *The Holy Bible New Living Translation (NLT)*. Retrieved from www.biblehub.com: https://biblehub.com/nlt/proverbs/11-25.htm

[139] Owczarski, Jim. (2021, July 20). *Milwaukee Bucks star Giannis Antetokounmpo wins NBA Finals Most Valuable Player Award*. Retrieved from https://www.jsonline.com: https://www.jsonline.com/story/sports/nba/bucks/2021/07/20/gianni s-antetokounmpo-named-mvp-nba-finals/8022360002/

[140] Edgley, R. (2015, November 18). *The truth about Insanity workouts*. Retrieved from www.gq-magazine.co.uk: https://www.gq-magazine.co.uk/article/insanity-workout-home-review-sean-t

[141] Arnold, C. (2018, January 12). *Fitness Superstar Shaun T: Keys To Workout Motivation Include Fun — And Selfishness*. Retrieved from https://www.npr.org: https://www.npr.org/2018/01/12/577660928/fitness-superstar-shaun-t-keys-to-workout-motivation-include-fun-and-selfishness

[142] Edgley, R. (2015, November 18). *The truth about Insanity workouts*. Retrieved from www.gq-magazine.co.uk: https://www.gq-magazine.co.uk/article/insanity-workout-home-review-sean-t

[143] Oleynick, V. C., Thrash, T. M., LeFew, M. C., Moldovan, E. G., & Kieffaber, P. D. (2014, June 2). *https://www.ncbi.nlm.nih.gov/pmc/articles/PMC4070479/*. Retrieved from US NAtional Library of Medicine: https://www.ncbi.nlm.nih.gov/pmc/articles/PMC4070479/

Chapter 9

Step # 7: Maximize Your Abundant Factor: Do You Have More To Give?

[144] Ross, M. (2020, January 27). *Among his trophies, Kobe Bryant was especially proud of his Oscar*. Retrieved from www.mercurynews.com: https://www.mercurynews.com/2020/01/26/among-his-trophies-kobe-bryant-was-especially-proud-of-his-oscar/

[145] Variety. (2018, March 4). *Kobe Bryant - Oscars 2018 - Best Animated Short - Full Backstage Speech*. Retrieved from Youtube.com: https://www.youtube.com/watch?v=P7WRXaxu1u4

[146] Variety. (2018, March 4). *Kobe Bryant - Oscars 2018 - Best Animated Short - Full Backstage Speech*. Retrieved from Youtube.com: https://www.youtube.com/watch?v=P7WRXaxu1u4

[147] Heck, J. (2020, February 09). *Why did Kobe Bryant win an Oscar? Remembering his Academy Award for short film 'Dear Basketball'*. Retrieved from www.sportingnews.com: https://www.sportingnews.com/us/nba/news/kobe-bryant-oscar-win-film-speech-dear-basketball/19pkc271qawt91xlkz0u0bvyx4

[148] Success | Mind | Motivation. (2013, September 4). *Tyler Perry - F.O.C.U.S. | Follow ONE Course Until Successful*. Retrieved from https://www.youtube.com: https://www.youtube.com/watch?v=Wa_4GNxEwqg

[149] Jared William LaCroix. (2020, July 15). *Tyler Perry*. Retrieved from https://www.georgiaencyclopedia.org: https://www.georgiaencyclopedia.org/articles/arts-culture/tyler-perry-b-1969/

[150] Jared William LaCroix. (2020, July 15). *Tyler Perry*. Retrieved from https://www.georgiaencyclopedia.org: https://www.georgiaencyclopedia.org/articles/arts-culture/tyler-perry-b-1969/

[151] Tyler Perry Studios. (2021, December). *Tyler Perry's Story*. Retrieved from https://tylerperry.com: https://tylerperry.com/tyler/story/

[152] Penguin Random House. (2021, December). *Tyler Perry*. Retrieved from https://www.penguinrandomhouse.com: https://www.penguinrandomhouse.com/authors/246168/tyler-perry/

[153] Penguin Random House. (2021, December). *Tyler Perry*. Retrieved from https://www.penguinrandomhouse.com: https://www.penguinrandomhouse.com/authors/246168/tyler-perry/

[154] Tyler Perry Studios. (2021, December). *Tyler Perry's Story*. Retrieved from https://tylerperry.com: https://tylerperry.com/tyler/story/

[155] Wilson, M. (2011, September 23). *Interview: Robert Kiyosaki Discusses What it Takes to be Successful*. Retrieved from www.under30ceo.com: https://www.under30ceo.com/interview-robert-kiyosaki-discusses-what-it-takes-to-be-successful/

[156] Jared William LaCroix. (2020, July 15). *Tyler Perry*. Retrieved from https://www.georgiaencyclopedia.org: https://www.georgiaencyclopedia.org/articles/arts-culture/tyler-perry-b-1969/

[157] Jared William LaCroix. (2020, July 15). *Tyler Perry*. Retrieved from https://www.georgiaencyclopedia.org: https://www.georgiaencyclopedia.org/articles/arts-culture/tyler-perry-b-1969/

[158] Jared William LaCroix. (2020, July 15). *Tyler Perry*. Retrieved from https://www.georgiaencyclopedia.org: https://www.georgiaencyclopedia.org/articles/arts-culture/tyler-perry-b-1969/

[159] MotivationHub. (2021, December). *T.D. Jakes Speech Will Leave You SPEECHLESS | One of the Most Eye Opening Motivational Speeches Ever*. Retrieved from https://www.youtube.com/: https://www.youtube.com/watch?v=pPCXgrWCEqg&t=135s

[160] Bayles, D., & Orland, T. (1993). *Art & Fear*. Santa Cruz, CA: Image Continuum Press.

[161] Merriam-Webster. (2021 , December). *Failure* . Retrieved from https://www.merriam-webster.com/: https://www.merriam-webster.com/dictionary/failure#:~:text=Essential%20Meaning%20of%20failure%201%20%3A%20a%20lack,trying%20to%20rescue%20the%20business%20from%20failure.%20%5B%3Dbankruptcy%5D

[162] Merriam-Webster. (2021, December). *Flawed*. Retrieved from https://www.merriam-webster.com: https://www.merriam-webster.com/dictionary/flawed

[163] Urquhart Orthopedic Associates, NJ. (2021, December). *Erica Rowe Urquhart, M.D., Ph.D.* Retrieved from https://www.urquhartortho.com: https://www.urquhartortho.com/erica-rowe-urquhart-md-orthopedic-surgeon-bayonne-new-jersey.html

[164] Andonovska, A. (2016 , October 14). *Alfred Nobel created the Nobel Prize as a false obituary declared him "The Merchant of Death"*. Retrieved from www.thevintagenews.com: https://www.thevintagenews.com/2016/10/14/alfred-nobel-created-the-nobel-prize-as-a-false-obituary-declared-him-the-merchant-of-death/

[165] Andrews, E. (2016, December 9). *Did a Premature Obituary Inspire the Nobel Prize?* Retrieved from www.history.com: https://www.history.com/news/did-a-premature-obituary-inspire-the-nobel-prize

[166] Andrews, E. (2016, December 9). *Did a Premature Obituary Inspire the Nobel Prize?* Retrieved from www.history.com: https://www.history.com/news/did-a-premature-obituary-inspire-the-nobel-prize

[167] Andrews, E. (2016, December 9). *Did a Premature Obituary Inspire the Nobel Prize?* Retrieved from www.history.com: https://www.history.com/news/did-a-premature-obituary-inspire-the-nobel-prize

[168] Andrews, E. (2016, December 9). *Did a Premature Obituary Inspire the Nobel Prize?* Retrieved from www.history.com: https://www.history.com/news/did-a-premature-obituary-inspire-the-nobel-prize

[169] The Nobel Institute and Library. (2021, December). *Alfred Nobel's fortune.* Retrieved from https://www.nobelpeaceprize.org: https://www.nobelpeaceprize.org/nobel-peace-prize/history/alfred-nobel-s-fortune

[170] Allen Snyder. (2021, December). *What was the net worth of Alfred Nobel? How is it possible to still give money as Nobel Prizes?* Retrieved from https://www.quora.com/: https://www.quora.com/What-was-the-net-worth-of-Alfred-Nobel-How-is-it-possible-to-still-give-money-as-Nobel-Prizes

[171] Nobel Prize Organisation. (2021, December). *The Ma Behind The Prize – Alfred Nobel.* Retrieved from https://www.nobelprize.org: https://www.nobelprize.org/alfred-nobel/#:~:text=Alfred%20Nobel%20died%20on%202010,in%20his%20home%20country%2C%20Sweden.

[172] Nobel Prize Organisation. (2021, December). *The Ma Behind The Prize – Alfred Nobel.* Retrieved from https://www.nobelprize.org: https://www.nobelprize.org/alfred-nobel/#:~:text=Alfred%20Nobel%20died%20on%202010,in%20his%20home%20country%2C%20Sweden.

[173] New World Encyclopedia . (2021, December). *Bertil Ohlin.* Retrieved from https://www.newworldencyclopedia.org: https://www.newworldencyclopedia.org/entry/Bertil_Ohlin

[174] The Nobel Prize. (2021, May 22). *Karl von Frisch Facts.* Retrieved from www.nobelprize.org: https://www.nobelprize.org/prizes/medicine/1973/frisch/facts/

[175] Teague, C. (2021, May 12). *What Happens When You Put Regular Gas In a Premium Car?* Retrieved from https://www.thedrive.com/: https://www.thedrive.com/cars-101/36538/what-happens-when-you-put-regular-gas-in-a-premium-car

[176] Guy, E. T. (2020, December). *Octane Ratings Explained - EricTheCarGuy.* Retrieved from https://www.youtube.com/: https://www.youtube.com/watch?v=8VWEwEveGTQ&list=PLfzNr9oOZnNZvHpKLf3moAC6j_3ux0F_7&index=13&t=218s

[177] Covey, S. R. (2004). *The 7 Habits of Highly Effective People.* New York: Simon & Schuster.

[178] Bureau of Engraving and Printing, U.S. Department of the Treasury. (2018). *How to Submit a Mutilated Currency Claim.* Retrieved from bep.gov/submitaclaim.html: http://bep.gov/submitaclaim.html

[179] Jeremiah 29:11. (2021). *The Holy Bible New International Version (NIV).* Retrieved from https://www.biblegateway.com: https://www.biblegateway.com/passage/?search=Jeremiah%2029%3A11&version=NIV

[180] Strong Mind Strong Life. (2021, December). *Don't Let Other People LIMIT YOU! - T.D. Jakes Motivational Speech.* Retrieved from https://www.youtube.com/: https://www.youtube.com/watch?v=LJyONcZoz7k&t=345s

[181] Strong Mind Strong Life. (2021, December). *Don't Let Other People LIMIT YOU! - T.D. Jakes Motivational Speech*. Retrieved from https://www.youtube.com/: https://www.youtube.com/watch?v=LJyONcZoz7k&t=345s

[182] Strong Mind Strong Life. (2021, December). *Don't Let Other People LIMIT YOU! - T.D. Jakes Motivational Speech*. Retrieved from https://www.youtube.com/: https://www.youtube.com/watch?v=LJyONcZoz7k&t=345s